ALGERIA, 1830–2000

Algeria *1830–2000*

A Short History

BENJAMIN STORA

Translated by Jane Marie Todd

Foreword by WILLIAM B. QUANDT

Cornell University Press

Ithaca and London

This translation was prepared with the generous assistance of the
French Ministry of Culture—Centre National du Livre.

This book contains translations, revised and updated by the author,
of three books by Benjamin Stora originally published in the
French language: *Histoire de l'Algérie coloniale, 1830–1954;
Histoire de la guerre d'Algérie, 1954–1962;* and *Histoire
de l'Algérie depuis l'indépendance.* The original volumes were
published in the series Repères by Editions La Découverte of Paris.
© Editions La Découverte, 1991, 1993, 1994, 1995

First published 2001 by Cornell University Press

Printed in the United States of America

LIBRARY OF CONGRESS CATALOGING-IN-PUBLICATION DATA

Stora, Benjamin, b. 1950
  [Selections. English. 2001]
  Algeria, 1830–2000 : a short history / Benjamin Stora ; translated
by Jane Marie Todd ; foreword by William B. Quandt.
    p. cm.
  Translation of: Histoire de l'Algerie coloniale, 1830–1954 ;
Histoire de la guerre d'Algerie, 1954–1962 ; Histoire de l'Algerie
depuis l'independance.
  Includes bibliographical references and index.
  ISBN 0-8014-3715-6
  1. Algeria—History—Revolution, 1954–1962. 2. Algeria—History—1830–1962.
3. Algeria—History—1962–1990. 4. Algeria—History—1990- . I. Title.
  DT295 .S74213 2001
  965'.046—dc21   00-012144

Cornell University Press strives to use environmentally responsible
suppliers and materials to the fullest extent possible in the publishing
of its books. Such materials include vegetable-based, low-VOC inks,
and acid-free papers that are recycled, totally chlorine-free, or partly
composed of nonwood fibers. Books that bear the logo of the FSC
(Forest Stewardship Council) use paper taken from forests that have
been inspected and certified as meeting the highest standards for
environmental and social responsibility. For further information, visit
our website at www.cornellpress.cornell.edu.

Cloth printing   10 9 8 7 6 5 4 3 2 1

FSC FSC Trademark © 1996 Forest Stewardship Council A.C.
SW-COC-098

Contents

Foreword

William B. Quandt

f Americans have any image at all of Algeria, it is that of a land of seemingly unending violence. During the 1990s, almost the only news about Algeria involved reports of massacres. No one seemed quite sure whether to blame the government or radical Islamists or criminal elements for the killing, but the toll was staggering in any event—some 100,000 dead in the course of the decade.

Those of an earlier generation will also recall Algeria's bloody civil war in which hundreds of thousands were killed, mostly by the French colonial forces, but also in internecine rivalries. When these two moments of Algeria's past are seen side by side, one might conclude that there is something in the culture, in the temperament of the people, that is conducive to violence. But such cultural explanations can be very misleading.

My own experience of Algeria dates back to the mid-1960s, a period of relative stability and domestic calm. Algerians were then establishing the early patterns that shaped their identity as an independent people. The wounds from the recent seven-year war for independence were still apparent. Algerians had paid a huge price for their freedom and yearned for an end to bloodshed and the chance to live normal lives with a government of their own choosing. Their leaders, however, seemed fearful that the hard-won independence might be lost as a result of internal quarrels that had been bottled up during the revolution and had broken into the open immediately after the departure of the French.

The solution to Algeria's perceived fractiousness and its internecine struggles was, in the minds of its first two presidents, Ahmed Ben Bella and

Houari Boumédienne, to assert the unity of the people and the dominance of a single party, the Front de Libération Nationale (FLN), to lodge power in the hands of military security, and to claim legitimacy based on the revolution. All of this was fairly typical of newly independent countries at the time. The result was nearly three decades of relative peace—but at the price of a highly authoritarian political order that actually allowed little voice to "the people" in whose name power was held.

Benjamin Stora, the author of the first full-length history of Algeria in recent years, knows Algeria, its people, and its languages in a way that few Westerners do. He grew up in the Constantine region and has returned there often, including during the crises of the 1990s. As a French professor of history, he brings a knowledge of Algeria's past to bear on its troubled present. And he is acutely aware of the close and complex bonds that link Algeria and France.

Stora reminds us that the period of single-party rule was based on a fundamental distortion of Algerian social reality. Algeria has always been pluralistic, with strong regional ties, a vigorous Berber minority, and, in modern times, several distinct political movements—Islamist, radical nationalist, liberal, and even communist. Looking at Algerian politics in the 1930s, one would have seen much more competition and diversity than anything that existed from 1962 to 1988.

But then the underlying diversity of Algerian society made itself felt. In 1989, the political system opened up, dozens of new political and civic movements found their voices, newspapers became worth reading as real issues were debated in public, and Algerians seemed on the verge of a democratic breakthrough. It is no exaggeration to say that for a moment it seemed that Algeria might become the Arab world's first democracy.

This brief moment of hope ended in January 1992 when the military intervened to end an election that would have been won by opposition Islamists of the Front Islamique du Salut (FIS). Democratic theorists have agonized ever since over the question of whether democracy would have been better served by letting the manifestly nondemocratic FIS assume power, or whether that would have spelled the end of Algeria's chances to become more democratic. The debate continues among Algerians and among those who have followed events there.

Soon after the cancellation of the election, a vicious cycle of violence began, pitting Islamist radicals against government security forces, with many innocent civilians caught in between. Stora reminds us that much of the violence of the 1990s had roots in the period of the war for independence. Blood feuds dating from that era came into the open a generation later. All who had suffered at the hands of the FLN in the 1950s—and there were many—could turn to the FIS to get revenge. This made of the FIS an unwieldy movement, as was the FLN in its heyday.

One reads Benjamin Stora's comprehensive history of modern Algeria with two strong sentiments. First, forging a national identity and building a state are challenges of a daunting nature. To be successful, the emerging political order cannot deny the past, as both the FLN and the FIS tried to do. Ultimately, Algerians must come to terms with what their country has been in order to be at peace with one another. This includes recognizing that the Algerian war for independence was not only a war against France but also a war among Algerians.

Second, a complex society such as Algeria changes slowly, despite what politicians may promise when they speak of revolution. Algerian society, despite everything, has remained relatively autonomous from the state and will in time make its weight felt. Algeria's coming to terms with its past, which Stora believes is under way, and the continued vitality of Algerian society give some reasons for hope despite the bleak political landscape of contemporary Algeria.

With this volume, English-speaking readers now have a comprehensive survey of Algerian history from the time of the French conquest up to the present. From this account, Algeria emerges as much more than a country of violence. At the same time, we learn a great deal about the origins of the violence, those elements that are distinctly Algerian, and those that are common to newly independent countries seeking to forge their identity in opposition to a strong colonial power. After reading this book, one can see Algeria in an understandable context. The violence is still a tragic part of the picture, but it is no longer the sum total of what we see and appreciate about this remarkable, and sad, country.

Preface

The Painful Formation of a Nation

At the dawn of the twenty-first century, Algeria is a country ravaged by two conflicts: a war waged with France between 1954 and 1962 whose purpose was emancipation from colonial domination and a civil war that began in 1992 as Algerian Islamists rebelled against the state. The nation of today is the result of this tragic contemporary reality. After the French conquest of 1830–1847, and then of 1871, every sort of ordeal and transformation endured by Algeria contributed to its identity. Yet a political will also had to emerge. In the nineteenth century the country did not conceive of itself as a space unified socially, economically, or even culturally. It would come into existence primarily through the desire of certain Algerians to believe in Algeria as a nation.

Pro-independence nationalism, advanced by the Etoile Nord-Africaine or ENA (North African Star) from 1926 onward, also created the Algerian nation. That nationalism made "independence" the founding and supreme value—a value that could transform an indigenous people into a citizenry. Such a restoration of the political is so significant that we run the risk of not grasping a second factor. People have a hunger for legends and desire a past of their own that extends back to the remotest times. From such desire stems the appeal to the values of Arab Islamism, to a legitimate breaking away from France, a tendency obvious during the war of independence between 1954 and 1962. How could Algeria, in contrasting itself to a conquering Europe with a weighty past, have made the break without invoking the long tradition of Islam? To embolden a people to construct a future, it was necessary to promote the ambiguity of a national ancestral mythology, even if that meant letting go of Berber specificity. The creation of a nation forms a consensus without concerning itself with the ambiguities of real history.

Those who would later be called *pieds noirs*, the descendants of European *colons*, or settlers, born in Algeria, with roots in France or the Mediterranean periphery, had no Algerian history to embrace. They rejected the notion of the melting pot. Citizenship, once established, would belong to them, not to Muslim Algerians, and by denying citizenship to others, they forged an extreme and acute version of nationalism. After independence came to the Maghreb, this false model of the Republic, having once been set in place within Algeria, would carry great weight in people's memories, both among the French and in the immigrant community from the former colonies.

Forty years after Algeria achieved its independence in 1962, the country is again confronted with the idea of the nation. The question that first arose in the colonial era is raised this time by a cruel civil war that has pitted the state against the Islamists. Colorful local differences (the Berber example is still there), the resurgence of religious feeling with a populist base (Islamism), and the vestiges of an unshared memory of the French undermine central authority. The regenerated and harmonious society promised by the "revolutionary liberties" of pro-independence nationalism clashes with the persistent force of ancient sympathies and practices. The need to progress toward a state of law remains stronger than ever, and the work of forming the nation goes on as Algeria makes the transition to the twenty-first century.

Acronyms

AFP	Agence France Presse
AG	Assemblée Générale
AIG	Armed Islamic Groups
ALN	Armée de Libération Nationale
AML	Amis du Manifeste et de la Liberté
ANP	Armée Nationale Populaire
AOA	Association des Oulémas Algériens
APC	assemblées populaires communales
APN	Assemblée Populaire Nationale
APS	Algérie-Presse-Service
APW	assemblée populaire de wilaya
BCM	Berber Cultural Movement
BNA	Banque Nationale d'Algérie
BTU	British Thermal Unit
CCE	Comité de Coordination et d'Exécution
CFLN	Comité Français de Libération Nationale
CFP	Compagnie Française des Pétroles
CFTC	Confédération Française des Travailleurs Chrétiens
CLDR	Comité de Liaison et de Défense de la Révolution
CNRA	Conseil National de la Révolution Algérienne
CPA	Crédit Populaire d'Algérie
CRP	Comité du Rassemblement Populaire
CRS	Compagnie Républicaine de Sécurité
CRUA	Comité Révolutionnaire pour l'Unité et l'Action

DOP	détachement opérationnel de protection
DP	Division Parachutiste
EEC	European Economic Community
ENA	Etoile Nord-Africaine
FAF	Front de l'Algérie Française
FAR	Forces Armées Royales
FEN	Fédération de l'Education Nationale
FFS	Front des Forces Socialistes
FO	Force Ouvrière
FP	Front Populaire
GDP	Gross Domestic Product
GMPR	groupes mobiles de protection rurale
GONS	General Office of National Security
GPRA	Gouvernement Provisoire de la République Algérienne
GSE	Gestion Socialiste des Entreprises
HSC	High Security Council
ICFTU	International Confederation of Free Trade Unions
IFOP	Institut Français d'Opinion Publique
IMA	Islamic Movement of Algeria
IMF	International Monetary Fund
ISA	Islamic Salvation Army
ISF	Islamic Salvation Front
MDA	Mouvement pour la Démocratie en Algérie
MNA	Mouvement National Algérien
MRP	Mouvement Républicain Populaire
MTLD	Mouvement pour le Triomphe des Libertés Démocratiques
NCHS	National Center for Historical Studies
NDU	National Democratic Union
NOCCI	National Office for Cinematographical Commerce and Industry
NOS	National Office of Statistics
NPDC	National Publishing and Distribution Company
OAS	Organisation Armée Secrète
OAU	Organization of African Unity
ONACO	Office National du Commerce
ONM	Organisation Nationale des Moudjahidin
OPEC	Organization of Petroleum Exporting Countries
ORP	Organisation de la Résistance Populaire
OS	Organisation Spéciale
OUP	Office of University Publications

PAGS	Parti d'Avant-Garde Socialiste
PAR	Party of Algerian Renewal
PCA	Parti Communiste Algérien
PCF	Parti Communiste Français
PPA	Parti du Peuple Algérien
PRS	Parti de la Révolution Socialiste
PS	Parti Socialiste
PSF	Parti Social-Français
PSU	Parti Socialiste Unifié
RAF	Rassemblement pour l'Algérie Française
RNAS	Rassemblement National d'Action Sociale
RPC	Régiment de Parachutistes Coloniaux
RPIMA	Régiment Parachutiste d'Infanterie de Marine
RTF	Radiodiffusion Télévision Française
SADR	Sahrawi Arab Democratic Republic
SAS	Sections Administratives Spéciales
SFIO	Section Française de l'Internationale Ouvrière
SHC	State High Commission
Sonatrach	Société Nationale de la Recherche, le Transport, la Transformation, et la Commercialisation des Hydrocarbures
UCD	Union for Culture and Democracy
UDCA	Union de Défense des Commerçants et Artisans
UDMA	Union Démocratique du Manifeste Algérien
UGEMA	Union Générale des Etudiants Musulmans Algériens
UGTA	Union Générale des Travailleurs Algériens
UGTT	Union Générale Tunisienne du Travail
UN	United Nations
UNCTAD	United Nations Conference on Trade and Development
UNEF	Union Nationale des Etudiants de France
UNFA	Union Nationale des Femmes Algériennes
UNJA	Union Nationale de la Jeunesse Algérienne
UNPA	Union Nationale des Paysans Algériens
UNR	Union pour la Nouvelle République
USTA	Union des Syndicats des Travailleurs Algériens
ZAA	Zone Autonome d'Alger

ALGERIA, 1830–2000

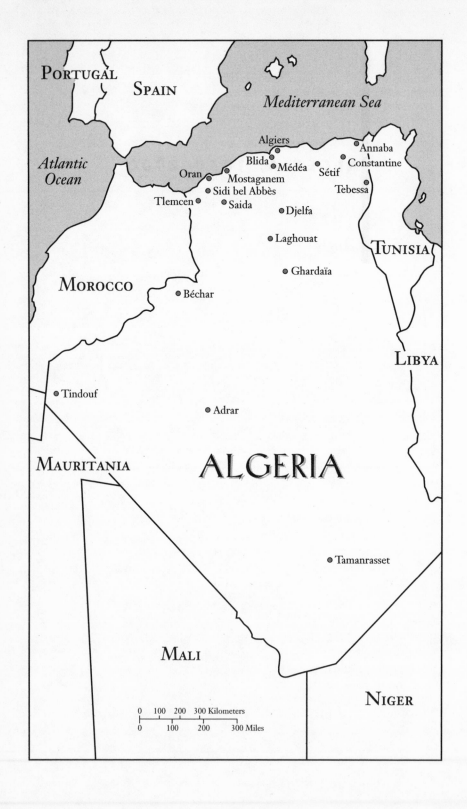

Introduction

Before the Present-Day Wars: Algeria in the Long Term

Algeria before French Colonization

The "usable" part of the Maghreb is a vast rectangle parallel to the equator. It is wedged between two neighboring regions, circumscribed to the north and on either side by the sea, and to the south by an ocean of sand and rock. In describing that land, the historian Ibn Khaldun (1332–1406) used the expression, "the island of the Maghreb." Algeria stretches about a thousand kilometers between Morocco and Tunisia. In area, it is the second largest country in Africa, 2,381,740 square kilometers.

First and foremost, Algeria is the sea. The country presents a beautiful façade to the Mediterranean, though one with very few "windows." The mountains drop off precipitously. Where there are openings along that closed coast, they are very vulnerable to squalls from the north. Corniche roads had to be built to connect the human settlements and ports. The central highlands of the Atlas Mountains, with an average altitude of over four hundred meters, are a recently formed chain. In the Aurès and Djurdjura mountains, the summits are over two thousand meters high. But the mountain formations are not uniform. As one moves eastward, the relief smooths out, becoming flat near the Tunisian Sahel.

Between two chains of mountains, the Tell Atlas to the north and the Saharan Atlas to the south, is a mass of steppes, the High Plateaux, traditionally a region for raising livestock. The low plains are crowded close to the shore, and access to these plains is facilitated by transverse valleys that cut through the mountains.

1

To the south, Algeria is the Sahara. This vast expanse belongs to a different geological world. It is not, as it was long believed to be, a seabed but a very old level shelf from which blunt massifs and volcanic peaks arise—up to three thousand meters in the Ahaggar Mountains. The Sahara is dotted with islets of greenery and life, the oases, where dates are the major cash crop.

A place of great physical contrasts, Algeria's landscape combines the characteristics of the mountainous Mediterranean with those of the steppes and semi-desert. In the past, it was a land of passages, a place of contacts between civilizations from the East and from Europe.

Let us consider its history and populations. In the beginning, there was one word: "Berber." This Latin word designated the *barbarus*, the person who did not belong to the Roman world. The Berbers called themselves *Amazighen* (sing., *Amazigh*), that is, "free men." The history of the Berbers can be traced back to a time before 4000 B.C.E., a time when Egyptian history recorded battles between "Libyans" and Egyptians. Barbary was a land that attracted Western and Eastern peoples. A land of legend, it inspired the great Greco-Roman tragedies of Athena, Atlas, the Hesperides, Odysseus, and Calypso.

Algeria was a hub uniting Europe, Africa, the Middle East, and Asia; its privileged situation and its resources would provoke six major invasions before the French arrived: the Phoenician-Carthaginian invasion, from 1100 to 147 B.C.E.; the Roman, from 146 B.C.E. to 432 C.E.; the Vandal, from 432 to 533; the Byzantine, from 533 to 633; the Arab, from 755 to 1516; and the Turkish, from 1516 to 1830. The Romans, present in force on the coasts, in Tunisia, and in Constantinois, barely ventured into the bastions of Barbary: the Atlas Mountains, the Rif, the Ouarsenis Massif, and the Kabylias. Resistance to Rome was symbolized by Jugurtha, who occupied a privileged place in the Berber pantheon. Christianity was introduced in the late second century—and one need mention only Saint Augustine and Tertullian to demonstrate that the Christian faith became firmly implanted, at least in the cities. The Vandal and Byzantine periods, a century each, were characterized by constant Berber revolts, often violently repressed. Other invaders were already on the horizon.

The first Arab conqueror was Oqba Ibn Nafi, who according to legend drove his horse into the waves of the Atlantic, chagrined that he could go no further. The first armed resistance by the Berbers was led by Koseila, the Christian chief of the Aouraba. The Arabs were repelled, and Oqba was killed in the Aurès Mountains in about 682. The second invasion, in the Aurès, was headed off by a woman, the legendary Kahina.

Even though the Arabs did not conquer the Berbers militarily, they converted their leaders to Islam. These leaders brought the message of the

Koran back to their tribes. Once Islamized, the Berbers again rebelled against the central Arab power, and it would take the Arabs more than a century to conquer North Africa. Islam managed to bring about a melding in the population between the autochthonous Berber culture and the new Koranic ethic. Islam prevailed over pagan beliefs and fostered social justice and equality among believers. To some extent, the Muslim faith gave the Berbers the cohesion their communities had lacked.

But struggles perpetually flared up. The conquests, followed by reprisals, and the chronic unrest favored the arrival of the Ottomans in the sixteenth century. The Turkish presence in Algeria lasted from 1555 to 1830. The Turkish military oligarchy, which had acquired its political power from its maritime strength, looked to the sea: it drew a large portion of its resources from privateering, and it controlled Algiers from close range even as it controlled the hinterland from a distance. Organized communities formed in the provinces, and Turkish officials left local chiefs a fair amount of autonomy. The only requirement of all subjects was an acknowledgment, which took the material form of the payment of tribute. Within this framework, the figure of the sultan gave a minimal cohesiveness to all social differences and various social groups. Indeed, the underlying history of Algeria, beyond the skirmishes among tribes, lies in the decisive effect of Islam. The gradual Arabization of the Berbers, undertaken by the sects and by an aristocracy of religious figures, gave Algeria an indisputably Eastern personality.

Gradually, the sense of belonging to the *'umma* (the Islamic community of believers) became identified with the last great theocratic empire of Islam. That sense would continue to grow even as the Ottoman empire declined and then disintegrated. When a "center" of reference was lost, the result was nostalgia; everyone forgot the undisciplined acts of Ottoman troops in Algeria. During the period of French colonial rule, everything was readied for a belated homage to be paid to the Turks.

The Establishment of French Algeria (1830–1914)

On May 16, 1830, a fleet of five hundred French ships headed from Toulon to Algiers. De Bourmont's army landed on June 14, only a few hundred meters from the peninsula of Sidi-Ferruch. The fort protecting Algiers finally fell, but not before the dey had mined it. On July 5, 1830, the dey of Algiers signed the act of surrender. The French colonial conquest had begun.

How are we to understand the deterioration of French-Algerian relations? The "fly-whisk attack" on the French consul by the dey of Algiers, in 1827, was the official pretext. Napoleon, Louis XVIII, and Charles X had never intended to honor an earlier debt to the dey, who "became agitated." But the French government waited three years before "wiping away the insult." In fact, the ultraroyalist government of the Prince de Polignac hoped to forge a connection to Napoleonic times by means of a military campaign. By consolidating the influence of France in the western Mediterranean basin, the government would open markets and create outlets for trade and nascent industry. The search for a brilliant victory abroad, but also the suppression of internal opposition in order to reestablish the absolute monarchy that was Charles X's dream, were the deep-rooted causes of the confrontation.

After the surrender of the Algiers authorities, the French military held effective power, but was divided on what course to follow. Should there be limited or total occupation? The response to that question determined the military's attitude toward the "natives." The proponents of limited occupation were Berthézène (February–December 1831), Voirol (April 1833–July 1834), Desmichels (1834), Trézel (1835), and Damrémont (November 1936–October 1837). That attitude clashed with the view, expressed with increasing vehemence, of the proponents of "total occupation," the absolute system of domination invented by Clauzel, the commander of the Algerian expedition from August 1830 to February 1831, and governor-general from July 1835 to February 1837. On his side were Commander-in-Chief Rovigo (December 1831–April 1833), Governor Vallée (October 1837–December 1840), and, above all, General Bugeaud.

The French army faced strong resistance. Within the country, religious sects called for a holy war. Although the French took possession of a few sites along the coast (Bône, occupied in 1831; Arzew and Mostaganem, in 1833), the rest of the country slipped from their grasp. Indigenous leaders, such as the dey Ahmed in the east, and the old Marabout of the Qadriyah Mahi Eddin sect in the west, mounted strong opposition. The latter, who by virtue of his Sharifian background and his religious title had real prestige among Muslim Algerians, persuaded the tribes of the Mascara region to accept his son, Abd-al-Kader, as emir. At barely twenty-four years old, Abd-al-Kader presented himself as the "Commander of the Faithful," and preached jihad. He managed to create a regular army. He engaged in continuous harassment, employing his troops in swift attacks and making life impossible for the adversary. In December 1840, Bugeaud was named governor-general of Algeria, and the army's strength went from 60,000 in 1840 to 107,000 in 1847. Uninterrupted campaigns, forced marches, mobile columns, and fortified posts were the instruments of the new war that Bugeaud would wage. The adversary had to be hunted, tracked down, and destroyed.

Beginning in 1841, columns leaving Mostaganem, Médéa, and Oran took the principal centers from the emir Abd-al-Kader: his capital, Mascara, and his fortresses, Saïda, Sebdou, and Tlemcen. The fighting continued with unprecedented violence in the Ouarsenis Mountains. Abd-el-Kader was left with the expanses of the High Plateaux. In May 1843, the duke of Aumale seized the *Smala*, a "floating" city that moved with the emir and that served as both his capital and his government. Abd-el-Kader managed to flee to Morocco and to continue his struggle. But, pushed back to the border by Sharifian troops and no longer able to escape to the south, he surrendered to General La Moricière on December 23, 1847. The war had seen many exactions. In 1842, Saint-Arnaud destroyed part of Blida; Cavaignac inaugurated "smoke-outs," asphyxiating rebels in caves on the west bank of the Chéliff; Canrobert razed a village in the Aurès to "terrorize the tribes"; Péllissier, colonel of Bugeaud's column, smoked out a thousand men from the Ouled Riah tribe who had sought refuge in the caves. That last incident led a member of the investigating commission, formed by the kingdom of France in 1833, to say: "We have surpassed in barbarism the barbarians we came to civilize."

Napoleon III, who took power in 1852, told advocates of all-out European colonization that he refused to inflict on the Arab population the fate of the Indians in North America, "an impossible and inhumane thing." On the contrary, he wanted to foster the prosperity of "that [Arab] race—intelligent, proud, warlike, and agrarian." "Algeria is not a colony...but an Arab kingdom....I am as much the emperor of the Arabs as of the French!" he proclaimed during a trip to Algeria, in spite of the discontent of the colons, who wanted pure and simple reattachment to the motherland. His generous and imaginative plan, which at a minimum conveyed the desire to treat the conquered Arab-Berbers and the conquering Europeans in the same manner, ought to have translated into the promotion of colonization and development (a sort of cooperation) in Algeria. But in 1870 France's defeat at the hands of Prussia took away that "Arab dream," which Lyautey would later aspire to realize in Morocco.

From the fall of the dey of Algiers in 1830 until 1871, the French colonial army conducted a policy to eliminate traditional economic and political ties. Algeria remained in the hands of the military. In 1871, however, it became the almost exclusive property of the colons who had settled in the country. That year saw matters disposed as the colons wished. The army was no longer allowed to impose its will; the rule of the saber had to end. As an instrument of conquest, it had no choice but to hand over responsibility to those who could make the colony profitable. The army had to resolve the native question once and for all and return to its barracks.

The year 1871 saw the defeat of Mokrani's insurrection in Kabylia. The uncertainties of the earlier years regarding the fate of Algeria gave way thereafter to a continuous, firmly applied policy that gave the colonial period of French Algeria its definitive shape. Algeria had to become a mere continuation of France on the other side of the Mediterranean. An Algeria made up of three French departments would forever "Gallicize" the territories of the central Maghreb. France meant to reject any possibility of a return to the past, or even the eventuality of a protectorate as in Tunisia and Morocco. Its aim was to ensure the absolute and complete subjugation of the population to the needs and interests of colonization. The colons enjoyed full rights; the colonized were "subjects" not "citizens," liable to special provisions: tallage, corvée, and detention without due process.

In 1881, a Code de l'Indigénat (Native Code) was established, regularizing these repressive measures. By that time the political and general framework was no longer that of a French province. Algeria was attached for administrative purposes to the Ministry of the Interior. The laws of 1898 and 1900 endowed the country with a civil identity and with an elected colonial assembly of delegations.

Until 1914, the economic future was based almost entirely on agriculture. "Colonization" and "agricultural colonization" became so nearly synonymous in Algeria that, for the Europeans of Algeria, the term *colon*, which usually designates the inhabitant of a colony rather than the metropolis, signified the farmer exclusively. The institution of private property was unknown in Algeria before the arrival of Europeans: there was only a complicated hierarchy of rights of use. These rights were devolving in the Ottoman period into two major categories of statutes: the rights of the dey in his capacity as sovereign, and the rights of the tribes. After the conquest, the French state, as successor to the rights of sovereignty, seized the lands of the dey, divided them, and distributed them to the French colons. The objective of the "partitioning" measures taken between 1847 and 1863 was to make the lands available for colonization. The tribes became "the owners of the territories of which they have the permanent and traditional possession," as stated in the senatus consultum of April 22, 1863. What did it matter if the best parcels had changed hands on that occasion, if the "partitioned" fellah now had little more than seven acres on average on which to survive? That act of despoliation was presented as a work of progress. However, the legal action produced a twofold effect. First, it destroyed in a single stroke the pyramid of rights that had assured the subsistence of the small farmer, by preventing the land from becoming a freely circulating commodity. Second, it threw all Muslim lands onto the free market, allowing the French colons to buy or seize them. The French seized the lands of religious institutions (*habbous*) as well. These seizures also violated a complicated set of rights of use.

The land decisions set out by the senatus consultum of 1863 were interrupted in 1870, and did not really resume until 1873, continuing until 1927. The laws of July 26, 1873 (the Warnier Act), and April 22, 1887, allowed Europeans to acquire or augment their properties up to one million acres. Between 1871 and 1919, 215 million acres were handed over to the colons. Colons in the department of Algiers managed to quadruple their holdings during that period (from 250,000 to 1 million acres). By 1919, the Muslims had lost 18.5 million acres, which the state, individuals, and major companies had divided up among themselves.

The "modern" agricultural sector was concentrated in the most favorable region, the Tell, where 98 percent of lands were expropriated. The application of French law regarding private ownership was accompanied by a program breaking up the major tribes. The destruction of these tribal units and of their leaders' power had several consequences. In times of famine, leaders could no longer carry out the free distribution of grain reserves accumulated from the gifts and taxes of their tribal subjects. The 1863 law also put an end to charitable distributions by the local religious "lodges" *(zaouïas)*, which drew their resources from the *habbous*. These properties, once privatized, were put on the market. Thus, a whole set of vital economic safety nets disappeared, leaving the rural population totally dependent on moneylenders and credit merchants during times of scarcity.

The "territories of the south" (in fact, the Sahara) were not conquered by the French until very late. In the last years of the nineteenth century, in fact, the populations of the eastern Sahara were under the influence of the Senusi sect, which viewed the English and French colonial conquests as an opportunity to awaken the Muslim faith. In the early part of 1873, General Galliffet crossed the six hundred kilometers that separated Biskra from El-Golea. The idea of a trans-Saharan railroad, first put forward in 1875 by the engineer Duponchet, was well received. The rail reached Aïn Sefra in 1887 and Biskra in 1888, but the plan was never completed. After numerous battles, particularly against the formidable Touareg warriors in the Ahaggar Mountains, France gradually extended its control in the south. A decree of December 24, 1902, created a new administrative unit, the territories of the south, with four districts: Aïn Sefra, Laghouat, Ouragla, and Oasis. Lyautey's occupation of the southern part of Oran made possible the occupation of Colomb-Béchar in 1903; at the same time, Commandant Laperrine completed the conquest of the great Saharan desert between 1901 and 1910. But interest in the vast Sahara would be awakened only with the discovery of oil. In the early 1950s, there was talk of enormous coal beds, deposits of iron ore, uranium. In the end, it was oil that gushed forth. The adventure began in 1952 with the first drilling. In 1954, on the eve of the

Algerian insurrection, natural gas erupted; soon, the first signs of "oil" were discovered in Hassi-Messaoud, eighty kilometers south of Ouargla.

French Minorities and the Muslim Population

Pieds noirs (literally, "blackfeet"): how are we to determine the exact origin of this term? Some say it may have been invented by the Arabs, surprised to see soldiers landing in 1830 with black boots on their feet. Others suggest it was the color of the feet of wine growers in Algeria, tramping grapes to make wine. Whatever the explanation, the French of Algeria did not encounter that characterization until they arrived in the metropolis—in 1962.

Between the end of World War I and the first gunshots in 1954, the sense of belonging to a country, Algeria, took root among them. The European population, in fact, grew from 833,000 in 1926 (657,000 French, including those who had been naturalized, and 176,000 foreigners) to 984,000 in 1954. At that time, approximately 79 percent had been born on Algerian soil. Whatever their origins, they considered themselves part of an "Algerian France"; the "French of France" were perceived as compatriots of a different sort.

Although Algeria was integrated directly into France at the institutional level in 1881, the law of December 29, 1900, conferred a civil identity and a special budget. But who were these new "Algerian French"?

After the French landing of 1830 in Sidi-Ferruch, emigrants from the metropolis followed the army. Workers came to replace soldiers. Dissidents strengthened the colony: at first, deported republicans opposed to Louis-Philippe, then those opposed to Napoleon III. So France sent a portion of its "dangerous" elements to the other side of the Mediterranean. These first French of Algeria, a combination of peasants uprooted by the industrial revolution in France and exiled "forty-eighters," then Communards, gradually acquired the views of small landowners. An old republican tradition, an amalgam of peasant individualism and the attachment to freedom, would remain robust among the European populations of Algeria.

After the defeat of the Second Empire, France undertook a policy of official colonization. The Frankfurt Treaty, which removed Alsace and a part of Lorraine from France, led several thousand faithful Alsatians to seek new lands to farm. Official colonization was directed by preference to the peasants of the south of France. In 1896, Corsicans in particular constituted the largest regional contingent, followed by those from the Pyrénées-Orientales, the Hautes-Alpes, Drôme, and Gard. These French southerners, excluded from the industrial revolution, met up with other émigrés from the Mediterranean basin: Spaniards, Italians, Maltese.

Impelled by even greater poverty, a wave of emigrants from the Mediterranean shores appeared at the end of the nineteenth century. The Spaniards came first, because history had woven age-old bonds between the "Barbary States" and the kingdom of Spain. There were nearly 35,000 in Algeria when the French began to arrive in 1849. There was also a long history of ties between Italy and Algeria; in 1886, 35,000 Italians were concentrated primarily in Constantine and Bône. In French Algeria, these emigrants resumed their usual activities. Spanish truck farmers and day laborers settled in Oranie; Italian masons worked in the east; the Maltese became goatherds and shopkeepers. Difficulty of access to the land drove most of them to the cities, where they settled and threatened to outnumber the French colony. Therefore, the law of June 26, 1889, imposed French citizenship, and "automatically naturalized every foreigner born in Algeria if, upon reaching adulthood, he did not claim the nationality of his father." In 1886, there were 219,000 French and 211,000 foreigners; in 1896, 318,000 French (including 50,000 who had been naturalized), and 212,000 foreigners. By 1896, the number of Europeans born in Algeria was greater than that of immigrants. That turning point represented the birth of an original people on Algerian land, a sort of Mediterranean mix.

We need to remember another factor in order to analyze the "*pied noir* community": the religious importance of Christianity. To dull the shock of leaving their native lands, people relied on the perpetuation of religious observance: respect for the Sabbath day of rest and religious holidays; the celebration, with particular solemnity, of baptisms, weddings, and funerals; participation in processions. The Church gradually asserted itself as an instrument for preserving the identity of the French of Algeria.

Jews constituted a minority between the Europeans and the Muslim Algerians. They had been on Algerian land for millennia, since the time when Phoenicians and Hebrews, engaged in maritime commerce, founded Annaba, Tipasa, Caesarea, and Algiers. Other Jews arrived later from Palestine, fleeing first the Egyptians, then Titus. They blended with the Berbers and formed tribes. The Jews of Spain fled the Inquisition in the sixteenth century, taking with them their culture (in which Maimonides played a major role), their expertise, and the rabbinical elite, who would standardize customs and the laws of marriage.

When the first French landed in the bay of Sidi-Ferruch, the Jews of Algeria were already organized into a "nation." In 1830, the Jewish community of Algeria was 25,000 strong, and most of them were very poor. Their destitute condition struck contemporary observers. The Jews' reaction to colonial development varied greatly, depending on the region. In Constantinois, the nomadic Jewish tribes "walked at the pace of their camels," whereas the Jews in the Algiers region, then in Oran, rushed to embrace progress. Unlike the "native" Muslims, who retreated into silence or withdrew into the interior so as to avoid contact with the occupier, the Jews of Algiers very quickly attempted to mingle with the French soldiers so they could trade with them.

The neutrality adopted by the Jews during the conquest, the example of the assimilation of European Jews during the French Revolution, and the idea that their coreligionists in France could have a "felicitous" influence on them, led the government of Louis-Philippe to pay a great deal of attention to the Jewish minority in Algeria. On November 9, 1845, the royal order of Saint-Cloud made Algerian Judaism fit the French mold. It created a central consistory in Algiers, a provincial consistory in Oran, and another in Constantine. Each consistory adopted as its spiritual leader a chief rabbi, chosen from among graduates of French schools, and as its leader a president, preferably of metropolitan origin, along with two other indigenous members. Louis-Philippe's France chose the path of assimilation. On October 24, 1870, Adolphe Crémieux, the minister of justice, submitted nine decrees to the council of the government, which ratified them. The most important were those that established the civil regime and the one that naturalized all Algerian Jews. The Crémieux decree provoked keen criticism, especially from army leaders. The collective naturalization of the Jews of Algeria in 1870 turned the latter's universe upside down, and set them apart from the Muslim community. Now listed on the official registers, they learned to read and write, discovered hygiene and modernity, and left their traditional small trades to enter other professions.

The Jewish entry into French society, which brought about a tremendous social leap forward, was not without obstacles. Twenty years after the promulgation of the Crémieux decree, Algeria suffered an extremely violent wave of anti-Semitism. The "anti-Jewish crisis" began in Oran, culminating in riots in that city in May 1897, and were accompanied by persecutions of various kinds in daily and official life. In Algiers, the rioters demanded the abrogation of the Crémieux decree "in the name of the outraged people." Jews were accused of being "capitalists" who oppressed the people, even though the vast majority were very poor (in the late nineteenth century, there were 53,000 Jews in Algeria, about 44,000 living in poverty). When World War I erupted, 2,000 of them would die on the battlefield. What we can discern in the anti-Jewish campaigns is denunciation of the "native" who had been elevated to the status of French national. Behind anti-Semitism we can glimpse fear of the "Arab peril."

Estimated at about 3 million, the Muslim population remained stagnant between 1830 and 1860 (the result of the war of conquest and the dismantling of the agricultural system), reaching 3.5 million in 1891 and nearly 5 million in 1921. In the Algerian campaigns, Mokrani's 1871 revolt in Kabylia was the only major armed resistance in about eighty years. Hostility toward the French presence was perpetuated in a veiled, latent form. More than 70 percent of the population of the country belonged to the rural world in the early twentieth century. It remained subject to the restrictive system set in place by the French administrative authorities. It survived an indigenous aristocracy that had made common cause with the French, and certain members of which had become administrators of the rural population in the name of the French state. These individuals, deprived of the tribal structure to which they had owed their power, nevertheless exercised in the name of the conquerors political functions, sufficiently extensive to mediate between the Muslim Algerians and France. How large was the ruling class? At the time of the 1954 insurrection, six hundred Muslim property owners possessed more than 1,250 acres each.

After the French conquest, Islam, which had been solidly rooted in Algeria since the seventh century, remained the only ideological "nation" of reference for the majority of Muslim Algerians. For a long time, a whole series of religious sects, which had organized society before the arrival of the French, provided a counterweight to colonial power. The peasantry's participation in the new urban world came about through the intermediation of religious associations, new forms of organization within the traditional religion. Despite colonial domination, Algeria remained linked to the rest of the Arab Islamic world, thanks to an uninterrupted stream of newspapers, books, and journals that reached it, and also the pilgrimage to Mecca, another way of keeping in contact with the wider Arab world. In 1908, a legislative bill extending obligatory conscription to Algerian Muslims caused a great stir. Two hundred notables, fearing the consequences of the planned measures for themselves and their children, emigrated in 1911 to Muslim countries: Turkey, of course, but also Tripolitania and especially Syria. The same year, Italy directly attacked the Ottoman Empire by invading Tripolitania. The Algerian population prayed repeatedly for a Turkish victory. The Italian-Turkish war produced a fervent wave of popular solidarity, which was expressed in sermons and prophesies announcing the rebirth of Islam (the *nahda*) and the imminent deliverance of Algeria. This nascent Algerian patriotism, which expressed itself in popular militant poetry wherein the desire one day to rid oneself of the foreign master was prominent also found its place within traditional Mahdism, the anticipation of a messenger of God, the Mahdi ("the rightly guided"), and the *moual es-sa'a* ("master of the hour"). Religion offered the Algerian population a means to combat the foreign colonial presence.

World War I and Social Upheaval

For the *pied noirs* in Algeria, who were connected to one another solely by national solidarity in a distant land, 1914 was a true turning point, a determining event. On French soil, they encountered other *pieds noirs* whom they had not known in Algeria. Residents of Oran, Constantine, Tlemcen, and Mostaganem discovered they had a common destiny, and set aside their local particularities. By virtue of the blood they had spilled, French nationals, indigenous Jews, Spaniards, Italians, and Maltese underscored their place within the French nation. Twenty-two thousand *pieds noirs* died on the battlefield during World War I. Recruitment among the indigenous people furnished 173,000 soldiers, including 87,500 volunteers; 25,000 Muslim soldiers perished in the war. At the same time, 119,000 Muslim Algerians were requisitioned to replace French labor in the metropolis. The war produced a loss of "innocence" among Muslim Algerians, a debunking of the myth of the benefits of Western civilization.

In 1918, a combination of new factors considerably changed the population's state of mind. Many Algerians, who were mobilized or requisitioned to replace French workers, discovered the factory and hence the protests of the French working class. News of external events arrived in Algeria: Turkish and German propaganda, Woodrow Wilson's proclamation on January 22, 1917, of peoples' right to self-determination, the October Revolution in Russia. Thanks to the impact of these elements, politics also became the work of poor peasants, the little people in the cities, and Algerian soldiers in France. After the war, the final disintegration of the Ottoman Empire brought about the bankruptcy of a certain image and vision of the "Arab nation" in many Arab countries. This led to the birth and development of a consciousness of national independence, then of solidarity among Arabs against a common enemy: the foreign powers that dominated them.

After World War I the organization of French Algeria became more pronounced. The colons obtained large loans to finance major public works projects, with irrigation of settled areas and modernization of the railroads receiving the lion's share. The consequence of colonial policy was to concentrate the lands in the hands of a small stratum of colons. The mechanization of agriculture left the smaller colons indebted to the banks; artisans were ruined, and massive unemployment ensued among Algerians, who were forced to seek exile in France. European agricultural production was sustained by credit, a vast irrigation program, and new infrastructure. Several large dams were built. In 1940, the Algerian railroads, with their 4,917 kilometers of lines, constituted a network whose major artery, running from the Moroccan border to the Tunisian border, was itself nearly a third of the line (1,300 kilometers).

The period that followed World War I saw the triumph of large-scale colonization. In 1930 there were only 26,000 European landowners remaining. At the time, 20 percent of them possessed 74 percent of the agricultural land belonging to the French (the European agricultural population, which was dropping constantly, fell to 125,300 in 1948 and to 93,000 in 1954). Techniques for cultivating grain, grapes, and tree crops made considerable progress. Mechanization increased, particularly the use of tractors. Between 1929 and 1935 the area devoted to vineyards increased from 560,000 to 1,000,000 acres. Average production almost doubled. In the interwar period, vineyards became the largest source of Algerian revenue, the base of the colonial economy, at the expense of food crops and livestock. As a result, viniculture drove out sheep, the forest, and the dwarf palm. The world crisis in 1930 shook Algeria profoundly and expanded the impact of capitalism in agriculture and society as a whole. Protected by the government, large-scale colonization grew and became stronger until 1940, all at the expense of the Muslims. Colonization led to the displacement of millions of peasants to the High Plateaux, where inferior land was very vulnerable to erosion. As Muslims were pushed into more arid lands, the production of food crops dropped; grain harvests decreased by 20 percent between 1880 and 1950, even as the population doubled.

In the modern sector of the coastal plains (the plains of Oranie, the Mitidja, and Constantinois), a true rural proletariat existed, made up of permanent and seasonal workers, whose principal source of income was wages, whether in currency or in kind. Concentrated near villages, these workers earned their subsistence in livestock (especially goats and fowl) and through the intermittent sale of their labor power (gathering legumes, doing domestic work). Some moved from the village to the regional city or to the large cities along the coast, filling the slums. A vast body of literature has described the condition of these destitute people living by their wits: the disintegration of village traditions and traditional morality, the prostitution of women, and so on. But that mass of people was not stable.

Often, in fact, some got out of the slums when they found jobs in the city or emigrated.

Between the early part of the century and 1954, the population doubled. A "rural overflow" appeared that could not be absorbed by small industrial centers. In addition, the mechanization of agriculture led to a constant reduction of employment. What became of that ever-increasing mass of people? Some remained where they were, others settled around the cities, and still others took the path of emigration to France.

In World War I, Marseilles, Paris, and the north emerged as the first settlement centers for Algerians. The state became all at once recruiter, importer, placement agent, and supervisor of colonial labor. A total of 132,321 North Africans—78,566 Algerians, 35,506 Moroccans, and 18,249 Tunisians—entered France between 1915 and 1918. Most were employed in public or private defense plants fabricating war material and munitions, in transportation, mines, gas factories, roads departments in the cities, and particularly in works projects that involved moving earth, especially digging trenches on or behind the front lines.

After the war, the needs of French industry and the works projects for devastated regions required a large labor force. The first great flood of labor arrived between 1920 and 1924, but departures were offset by a large number of returns. During the same period, between 1919 and 1925, the Algerian economy continued to suffer the consequences of the war, aggravated by a series of bad harvests. The Native Code, which constrained freedoms in Algeria itself, weighed heavily on young Algerians, especially the "colonial soldiers," who had gone to France in 1914–1918. When they returned, they found that colonial conditions had not changed. Dissatisfaction was the very logical result of the gap between the possibilities they had glimpsed in France and the wretchedness of what was now their daily fate.

The growing influx to France did not fail to cause great worry among entrepreneurs and colons in Algeria, who were concerned to see their labor force departing. Their complaints led the government of Algeria to take restrictive measures. When we study the first introduction of Algerian workers into France, we see that it usually involved recruits from dismantled tribes. This fact serves to raise serious questions about certain justifications given for the French presence in Algeria, particularly those that emphasize contributions in education and civilization. In fact, the process of migration was directly linked to the land dispossession in Algeria: the history of emigration is indistinguishable from the history of rural society and its dismantling. The women and children were left at home, and it was men alone, displaced peasants, who arrived in France, living there only to return one day to the city, *douar*, or region of origin. (The problems posed by the migration of families and their incorporation into the social fabric would be raised after 1945.)

Political Life in the Interwar Period

In 1930, the first doubts—raised by the expansion of Communism in Europe, which put colonization on trial, and the fears arising from the Rif insurrection against the French presence in Morocco—were dispelled in the celebration of the centennial of the invasion of Algiers. People preferred to celebrate a sanitized past rather than consider the future and masked the real issues in speeches and celebrations. It was the apogee of colonial Algeria. Grandiose celebrations were feverishly planned: the centennial of the conquest of Africa, and the 1931 colonial exposition at the Bois de Vincennes in Paris.

The Parisian political parties opened branch offices in French Algeria. Generally speaking, the *pieds noirs* voted with their counterparts in the metropolis. The colonial problem did not represent a fundamental dividing line between the traditional right and the traditional left. The Radicals, who represented the memory of the Republic, were very active in, and in step with, the many Freemason lodges. They were attached to the empire. During the interwar period, large farming and flour mill operations and credit institutions became interested in Algerian agriculture; most, whether overtly capitalist or vaguely cooperative in nature, were in the hands of men currently or formerly belonging to the Radical Party.

For their part, the Socialists remained ardent supporters of the principle of assimilation: "There can be only one formula to represent and characterize the Socialist colonial policy, and that is assimilation!" exclaimed J. Lagrosillière in the name of the Fédération de la Martinique at the congress of the Section Française de l'Internationale Ouvrière or SFIO (French Branch of the Workers' Internationale) in 1926. In the 1930s, the Socialists confined themselves to demanding the application of democratic freedoms to Muslims, the improvement of the status of European workers, and the readjustment of colonial structures.

On the colonial question, and particularly on the Algerian question, the Parti Communiste Français, or PCF (French Communist Party) became actively involved in the creation of the Etoile Nord-Africaine. But the relations between the two organizations became strained in 1928 and reached open hostility in 1930–1931. During the electoral campaign that led to the victory of the Front Populaire, or FP (Popular Front), the watchword "national independence" was dropped; then, on December 23, 1937, Maurice Thorez proclaimed, this time explicitly, that independence was no longer on the agenda: "The right to divorce does not mean the obligation to divorce." On February 11, 1939, he characterized Algeria as "a nation in formation in the melting pot of twenty races." For the PCF, "barring the road to Fascism" came before the "violent struggle against French democracy on the pretext of independence."

City-dwelling *pieds noirs*, whose parents, ruined by speculative farming, had moved back to the towns, were socially and politically divided. They gave their votes to the SFIO, and 25 percent to the workers' and peasants' (i.e., Communist) bloc in Algiers in 1924, electing the Socialist candidate Dubois to the Oran city hall. The large leftist electorate sent four Front Populaire deputies to the Chamber out of the ten to which Algeria was entitled in 1936. On February 12, 1934, ten thousand people, half of them Muslims, demonstrated against Fascism in front of the central post office in Algiers. The same year, fifteen thousand came out to protest the visit of Colonel de La Rocque, head of the Croix-de-Feu, to the Algerian capital. Far-right ideologies, born in Europe, later won over important sectors of public opinion in Algeria. On the nationalist right, Colonel de La Rocque set in motion the first Croix-de-Feu branches in Algeria in 1931. After the Front Populaire dissolved his movement on June 18, 1936, the colonel founded the Parti Social-français, or PSF (French Social Party), which, with 26,000 members, became the largest European party in Algeria. The creation of the PSF in Algeria came about at a time when organizations and parties on the right had united in the Rassemblement National d'Action Sociale, or RNAS (National Union of Social Action), founded by the abbé Lambert.

Beginning with the interwar period, Algerian national aspirations were expressed in multiple and often antagonistic organizations. Very schematically, four outlooks took shape: those championed, respectively, by the ulama (doctors of law), by the Jeune Algérien (Young Algerian) movement, by the Communists, and by the radical nationalist movement embodied by Etoile Nord-Africaine.

The reform movement recognized the authority of the reformist theologians, ulama, and opposed any segmentary or local forms of Islam centered around local sanctuaries and saints. These ulama represented the "*nationalitaire*" orientation, defending cultural identity in a motto that has remained famous: "Arabic is my language, Algeria is my country, Islam is my religion." The basis of their political doctrine can be summed up by the following categories: *umma* (nation), *cha'ab* (people), *watan* (homeland), and *quawmiyya* (nationality). The Association des Ouléma d'Algérie (Association of Algerian Ulama) was created in Algiers in 1931, and its president was Sheikh Abdelhamid Ben Badis (1889–1940), who came from an important

Muslim family in Constantine. It saw its struggle as essentially cultural. *Islah*, the Reformation, had to preserve the original purity of Islam, combatting the superstitions of the religious sects and Marabouts. Cultural clubs, *medersas* (colleges that relied on religious authority), and charitable organizations spread the words of the ulama. This movement, which began in the ancient cities of the interior (Tlemcen, Constantine, Nedroma), blanketed the countryside with ulama organizations, in particular, the Boy Scouts. The egalitarian message of the ulama reflected the ideal of the simple fellah; and the "dream" of agrarian reform, which would give everyone an equal share, corresponded to the first phase of nationalism in the countryside. The ulama supported the Front Populaire in 1936; Sheikh A. Ben Badis declared himself satisfied with the promised reforms, in anticipation of truly universal suffrage, which would make possible "the pure and simple integration of the Muslim collectivity into the great French family." The failure of this plan led to a radicalization of the ulama in a pro-independence direction.

During the interwar period, the first Algerian intellectuals and elements of a nascent liberal bourgeoisie found themselves represented by the Jeune Algérien movement, embodied by Ferhat Abbas. Abbas, born in 1899 in Constantinois, the son of a kaid and himself a doctor of pharmacy, actively participated in the movement that, until 1936, demanded equal rights within the framework of French sovereignty. By not equating the colonial system with France itself, he expressed a longing for the true France, which exemplified the principles of 1789. France, the country that had invented democratic culture via the Great Revolution, could impose, on the Europeans of Algeria, respect for the indigenous person deprived of rights. He therefore championed rights equal to those enjoyed by what would later be called *pieds noirs*, but remained attached to Algeria's religious personality: for him, a person could be simultaneously and fully French and Muslim. He imputed all the injustices of colonialism to the European colony. For him, there were two Frances and two policies: one a country of colonization and oppression, the other the beacon of civilization and of moral prestige. He hoped that France would choose the right path.

The main nationalist current was born in 1926 in Paris within the immigrant communities. At that time, Etoile Nord-Africaine (ENA), headed by Messali Hadj, was the only movement to openly demand independence for Algeria. Messali Hadj was born in Tlemcen in 1898. He came from a family of artisans and farmers, and did his military service in Bordeaux in 1918. The discovery of French society impelled him to emigrate after he was demobilized. He went to Paris in 1923, and worked at all sorts of jobs to survive. It was during the Rif war and the uprising of Abd el-Krim in Morocco that Messali Hadj began a truly political career in connection with the PCF—that is, in the immigrant community, like other Algerian workers. In Paris in June 1926, the ENA officially came into being with the active support of the PCF. It asserted that "its fundamental goal is the struggle for the total independence of each of the three countries— Tunisia, Algeria, and Morocco—and the unity of North Africa." Etoile Nord-Africaine was accused of subversive propaganda against France and dissolved in November 1929 by the French government. At the time, it had 3,600 militants. As the grandiose centennial celebrations were being held during 1930 in Algeria, the nationalist Algerian movement was anemic, torn apart by struggles between the nationalists and the Communists who wanted to control them. In June 1933, the ENA reconstituted itself. Its new statutes adopted a ban on concurrent membership in the PCF. Algerian immigrants, who had followed a path mapped out by others, now decided to build their own road. The organization's plan always foresaw North African independence. Etoile Nord-Africaine, which had officially been part of the Comité du Rassemblement Populaire, or CRP (Committee of Popular Unity, later the Front Populaire), nevertheless would be disappointed by the attitude of the Front Populaire representatives regarding the colonial problem.

In France and Algeria, the electoral victory of the Front Populaire in May 1936 was followed by a wave of strikes. But in Algeria what dominated the political scene was the Blum-Viollette plan, put forward in December 1936. Prior to this plan, the indigenous Muslim had been a second-class citizen. He served for twenty-four months in the military, whereas European conscripts served only ten. If he was a noncommissioned officer, he received a lower salary than his French counterpart. If he was a government employee, he did not receive the *quart colonial*, the salary bonus given to all other government employees in Algeria. And, above all, he did not vote and was not represented in the Chamber of Deputies.

Was everything going to change with the victory of the Front Populaire? Maurice Viollette was given responsibility for Algerian affairs. The Blum-Viollette plan would grant political equality to a small proportion of the Algerian population, gradually extending it to the majority. Without abandoning its Muslim status, a minority would have thus obtained the same political rights as French citizens. Hence, through Viollette the old incompatibility between fidelity to Islam and membership in the French political community would have been eliminated. The first echelon of "promoted" Muslim Algerians was to serve as an example to others. About 21,000 people who held certain academic degrees or certain military ranks or distinctions would have received French citizenship (in a personal and nontransmissible capacity). The legislation was meaningless unless complemented by measures favoring social, economic, and cultural promotion. The Blum-Viollette plan, an initiative cautious and reformist in its approach, did not raise the question of independence.

Among Algerian nationalists, the advent of the Front Populaire had elicited great hopes. But, between the infectious heat of the spring victory and the laborious discussions of the Blum-Viollette plan (announced on December 30, 1936), an attitude of distrust, then of hostility, developed between pro-independence and nationalist Algerians—embodied by Etoile Nord-Africaine—and the Front Populaire government. On January 29, 1937, Governor-General Lebeau obtained without difficulty a decree from the Front Populaire government dissolving Etoile Nord-Africaine. On August 27, 1937, Messali Hadj was arrested, along with five leaders of the Parti du Peuple Algérien, or PPA (Algerian People's Party). The dissolution of Etoile Nord-Africaine, which had nearly five thousand militants in 1937, primarily divided among the Paris, Lyons, and Bouches-du-Rhône regions (a few large groups were also beginning to exist in the east)—marked the end of one era and opened another. In fact, even though it was in France (in Nanterre) that, on March 11, 1937, Messali Hadj announced, before two thousand Algerian immigrant workers, that he and Abdallah Filali had just registered a new party (the PPA), the center of gravity of the political struggle had actually shifted. The transfer of the headquarters of the new organization to Algiers indicated a great deal more than a merely geographical move. Henceforth, priority was given to political action on Algerian soil itself, and militant immigrants inside France were gradually relegated to the rank of auxiliary forces.

When war erupted in 1939, the newspaper of the PPA, *El Ouma*, was banned, and the leaders of the PPA arrested. The Algerian nationalists, in rising up to protest, an action that seemed audacious for the period, indicated that it was no longer possible to live as before, to think as before, that in effect knowledge, work, cultural production, moral ideas, and political conceptions had changed. They rejected assimilation and the fact that only French culture was accorded any value. Their objective was partly a history that already existed and partly a history that had yet to be created. In short, all the ingredients of "modern" Algerian nationalism were already present.

World War II

Algeria was stunned by the incredible military disaster of May 1940. The European population anxiously awaited the conditions of the armistice. On June 25, they discovered with relief that the integrity of the colonial empire was to be maintained, and, for the most part, they seemed to rally behind

Marshall Pétain's government. They found the tone of the "National Revolution" appealing, a return of sorts to the early era of the conquest of Algeria. Vichy abrogated the social and unionist legislation that favored Muslim Algerians. On October 7, 1940, after the Statute on Jews had legalized Vichy anti-Semitism, Minister of Interior Peyrouton—former secretary general of the general government in Algiers—abolished the Crémieux decree that had given Algerian Jews their right to be naturalized.

Vichy appealed to the Algerian nationalist leader Messali Hadj, asking him to collaborate. He refused and, on March 17, 1941, was sentenced "to sixteen years of forced labor, twenty years of banishment, a downgrading of civil status, and the confiscation of his present and future possessions, for an attack on French sovereignty and state security."

On November 8, 1942, an American fleet landed a large expeditionary force in Algiers, Casablanca, and Oran. A handful of *pied noir* Resistance fighters had paved the way for that landing. It was the first major defeat of the French colonial army in Algeria since 1830. The defeats of November 1942, coming after those of June 1940 and defeats in Syria (1941) and Indochina, set off the crisis of the French empire. A provisional accord was signed in Algiers between US General Clark and Admiral Darlan. General Giraud became commander-in-chief of the troops; then, after Darlan's murder on December 24, he received the civilian and military command. The Anfa accords of January 24, 1943, among Roosevelt, Churchill, and Giraud, made explicit the relations between France and the Allies. Reactionary measures taken by Vichy were rescinded, and in particular the Crémieux decree was reinstated on October 26, 1943, after three years of official anti-Semitism. The European population changed sides once again, celebrating around the American "liberators" who had brought along food, clothing—and jazz music.

In 1942, the million French of North Africa supplied the armies with twenty-seven age cohorts between nineteen and forty-five years old, plus volunteers, that is, 16.35 percent of individuals of French stock; similarly, 15.8 percent of the Muslims were enlisted, most of whom did not have citizenship. On August 15, 1944, ships flying the U.S. flag carried divisions of the *pied noir* army and Muslim Algerians to the landings in Provence: many of them had never been to France.

At the same time, beginning in 1943, the political battle raged in Algiers. General de Gaulle arrived there on May 30 of that year; in November of the same year, he formed the Comité Français de Libération Nationale, or CFLN (French Committee of National Liberation)—a true provisional government of unoccupied France—and an appointed, consultative Assembly which would return to Paris after the French capital was liberated in August 1944. De Gaulle's first concern upon settling in Algiers (after a host of intrigues, haggling, and plots of all sorts between local governors and military leaders) was to consolidate "French prestige everywhere in the world where the tricolor waves." A commission for Muslim reforms was created and it prepared reforms, which General de Gaulle announced in his Constantine speech on December 12, 1943.

The president of the CFLN announced that French citizenship was being granted to several tens of thousands of Muslims, who would keep their personal status. Disregarding some colon opposition to his "policy of abandonment," De Gaulle signed an order on March 7, 1944, giving Muslims access to all civilian and military positions; it increased their representation in the local assemblies from one-third to two-fifths, and abolished the measures of exclusion. But was it not already too late?

At the initiative of Ferhat Abbas ("disappointed" by Pétain's regime, to which he had appealed), on May 26, 1943, Algerian notables set forth a manifesto demanding a new status for Algeria. Messali Hadj, while being transferred to Sétif from the Lambessa convict settlement in the south, met with Ferhat Abbas and proposed an addendum, which would be adopted on June 10, 1943: "At the end of hostilities, Algeria will be set up as an Algerian state endowed with its own constitution, which will be elaborated by an Algerian constituent assembly, elected by universal suffrage by all the inhabitants of Algeria." On March 1, 1944, the organization Amis du Manifeste et de la Liberté, or AML (Friends of the Manifesto and of Freedom) was born. The PPA decided to support the association. On April 2, 1945, during the general conference of the AML, the PPA faction easily prevailed. The general resolution no longer spoke of "an autonomous Republic federated with the French Republic," but rather of an "Algerian Parliament and government." By a huge majority, the AML congress pronounced itself against independence "under the aegis of France and within the framework of French federalism." The association grew at lightning speed on Algerian soil: 257 local branches and nearly 100,000 members or sympathizers. On April 23, 1945, the colonial authorities decided to deport Messali Hadj to Brazzaville.

It was within this context of political radicalization that a grave economic crisis, aggravated by a bad harvest, hit Algeria and caused famine in the countryside. Thousands of hungry peasants streamed toward the cities; for lack of work and means, they congregated around the soup kitchens. On May 8, 1945, the day the armistice was signed, Muslim Algerians paraded in most of the cities of Algeria, with banners bearing the slogan "Down with fascism and colonialism." In Sétif, the police fired on Algerian demonstrators, who countered by attacking police officers and Europeans. It was the beginning of a spontaneous uprising, supported by the PPA militants of

Constantinois. In the rural areas, peasants revolted in La Fayette, Chevreuil, Kherrata, and Oued Marsa. Among the Europeans, 103 were listed as killed and 110 wounded. On May 10, the authorities organized a true "war of reprisals"—to borrow the Algerian historian Mahfoud Kaddache's expression—which turned into a massacre. Shootings and summary executions among the civilian population continued for several days under the direction of General Duval. Villages were bombed by the air force, and the navy fired on the coast. The French general Tubert spoke of 15,000 killed among the Muslim population. Algerian nationalists put forward the figure of 45,000 dead.

In Algeria, nothing could ever be as it had been before May 8, 1945. The rift had widened between the majority of Muslim Algerians and the European minority. Plebeians from the cities (the underclass, the unemployed), the proletariat, and the Algerian peasantry had experienced the power of collective action; a new generation was making its entrance, one that would make armed struggle an absolute principle. Nine years later, the Algerian War would begin.

On the Eve of War, Algeria in 1954

Contrary to tenacious legends, which imagine *pieds noirs* in the rural areas carefully overseeing their large land holdings, on the eve of the Algerian War most of the French of Algeria lived in cities and large towns. A few figures give some idea of the scope of this phenomenon. In 1872, 60 percent of Europeans were (already) city dwellers; that proportion reached 63.6 percent in 1886, 65.4 percent in 1906, and 71.4 percent in 1926. After World War II, Algiers and Oran with their suburbs, along with Constantine and Bône, in themselves contained more than half the European population. These cities benefited greatly from the influx of French, Spaniards, and Italians, who arrived as workers, artisans, small tradespeople, and fishermen.

An entire working world mixed together in the cities and formed the greater part of the million Europeans present in Algeria in 1954. Most of the labor power of the urban European community was composed of government employees, men of law, merchants, tradespeople, entrepreneurs, and artisans. Of 355,000 people in the labor force, there were 190,000 lower-echelon wage earners, including 90,000 industrial workers and 92,000 government employees. There were also 56,000 middle and upper managers, and 60,000 merchants, artisans, or members of the liberal professions. Clearly, Algerian society did not in any way constitute a microcosm of French society. But was it therefore a privileged society? Barely 3 percent of

Algerian French had a standard of living above the average for the metropolis; 25 percent were more or less equal; and 72 percent had an income that was 15 to 20 percent lower, even though the cost of living in Algeria was not lower than that in France. The reason for that disparity in income lay in the economic relations between France and its principal colony. Within the framework of the "colonial pact," Algeria was a source of raw materials and a mere outlet for the manufactured products of the metropolis. It would be wrong to consider the *pieds noirs* a homogeneous "people." Very often, because of their social situation, they clashed with a ruling class made up of large property owners or big capitalists. But, despite this opposition, they were unanimous in defending their privileges, which made the most insignificant French government employee superior to any Arab. Their unity was due to a shared fear of the Muslim majority.

On the eve of the 1954 insurrection, the proportion of workers in the cities was clearly lower than it was in France. Processing industries suffered from the absence of a skilled work force and, above all, from competition from the European market, which was too close and too well equipped. Algeria had only industries linked to agriculture and to domestic needs: chemical products (sulfur and phosphates); the construction of machinery; agribusiness (flour mills, pasta factories, distilleries, tobacco factories, canneries); and building industries, favored by the growth of the cities. The indigenous industries of wood, metal, and pottery, which suffered from European competition, were declining. The "industrialization plan" of October 15, 1946, was followed by measures providing for the introduction of new industries. The slight improvement in comparison to the prewar period, however, could not conceal the real situation of Algerian industry: the weakness of basic and processing industries (barely 10 percent of national revenue) and a production rate lower than the country's real capabilities. Urban growth was not part of industrialization but, for the most part, originated from the destruction of the peasant world. In cities the mechanisms of exclusion played a greater role than those of integration, in effect creating a "caste society."

The absence of industrialization and the setting in place of a "caste society" had two consequences, which would shape the nationalist movement in the urban setting: the deterioration of the Muslim city and the creation of slums. According to Jacques Chevallier, the mayor of Algiers at the time, "in 1938, the Muslim population living in the slums of the Algiers urban area was no more than 4,800 persons; in 1953–1954, it was 125,000....In the city of Algiers alone, excluding its outskirts, 120 slums, like a cancer growing on all available land, had some 80,000 Muslims crowded together in unbelievable living conditions, whereas the Casbah, also overpopulated, crammed 70,000 residents into its 50 acres, breaking world records in human density." Living in these "subcities" were transplanted rural people, as well as city dwellers pushed out of the urban center by the establishment of a European society.

The city became a permanent stage for latent violence, justified by social exploitation, combined with national oppression, and which manifested itself from time to time in sudden outbreaks of open conflict. The expropriated Muslim Algerians poured into the cities and slums, and competed with European wage earners, who had higher salaries and rights that the Muslims did not have. Competition with European workers and the vast numbers of Algerians whose land had been expropriated aggravated the conflict between the two communities. The more bitter the competition, the greater became that antagonism. Hence, in 1954, there were 65,120 European office employees and tradesmen, versus 15,190 Algerians; 51,650 European professional workers, versus 49,830 Algerians; 7,200 European manual laborers, versus 141,130 Algerians; 33,890 European domestics and service personnel, versus 47,400 Algerians. There were 200,000 unemployed counted, not including the "underemployed" in the slums.

Schooling or training was the foundation of social life. During the French period, Algeria was an educational district, administered by a rector and conceived on the model of educational districts in the metropolis; except that the rector had broader powers, especially where primary education was concerned. The teaching of Algerian "natives" dated to the beginnings of the French presence, but developed only very slowly. For a long time, some representatives of the colons maintained that "the instruction of natives presents a real peril to Algeria." In 1894, they suggested that the goal of education ought to be "to procure skilled farmhands, masons, and shoemakers for the colons." At the National Assembly, de Boisserie, the representative of Algeria, worried that "the native schools are training insurgents and social upstarts." In 1954, of 1,250,000 Muslim Algerian children of school age, more than 100,000 received a primary education in 699 schools. Among Europeans, 2,000,000 children went to 1,400 schools. According to the rector of the time, one Algerian child in ten went to class (in fact, one boy in five, one girl in sixteen). But in rural areas, the proportion was only one in fifty, and sometimes one in seventy. According to Germaine Tillon, the proportion of Algerian Muslims who could not read or write in French stood at 94 percent among men, and 98 percent among women. In higher education, there were 133 students at the University of Algiers in 1879, when the schools of higher learning were founded; 751 in 1910, after the schools were transformed into Faculties; 937 in 1914; 1,592 in 1925; and 4,000 in 1945, with only 150 Muslim Algerians.

On health matters, there were 1,033 doctors in Algeria in 1939, and 1,855 in 1954. Hence, in the latter year, there was one doctor for every 5,137 inhabitants (versus one doctor per 1,091 inhabitants in France). Similarly, there was one dentist for 19,434 inhabitants in Algeria (one for 3,199 in France); one pharmacist for 14,553 inhabitants in Algeria (one for 2,454 in France). Also in 1954, more than 50 percent of the total population of Algeria benefited from free medical help. With improving health conditions, infant mortality dropped: it fell from 1,050 per 10,000 births in 1906 to 130 per 10,000 births in 1954 (120 in France). Particularly in the rural areas, the distrust of doctors, who had arrived in the wake of colonization, subsided. In 1954, doctors were no longer perceived as mere auxiliaries of colonization. Thanks to these men, fully committed to their humanitarian mission, the mortality rate fell from 20 per thousand to 11 per thousand, and the Algerian population doubled in fifty years.

According to the census of 1950–1951, in the agricultural sector 160,000 permanent farm workers (Muslim Algerians) worked 250 days per year per person, with an annual salary of 75,000 francs. A total of 400,000 temporary workers worked on average 90 days per year, with annual earnings of 20,000 to 25,000 francs. In 1954, the annual average individual income of the Muslim Algerian farmer was estimated at 22,000 francs, versus 780,000 francs for the European farmer. Before 1939, farm products represented nearly 82 percent of Algerian exports. The average cereal crop was 1.8 billion kilograms. The yield was very low: 200 kilograms per acre for hard wheat, 400 at the most for soft wheat. Before 1939, vineyards, an innovation of the colons, covered nearly 1,000,000 acres; that year, they produced nearly 21.5 million hectoliters. Modern agriculture took advantage of costly irrigation projects; for the most part, its products were destined for export, usually to continental France.

On the political level, General Duval, who was responsible for the terrible repression of 1945 in Constantinois, had warned: "I have given you peace for ten years. But make no mistake. Everything must change in Algeria." The tragedy is that nothing did change, or almost nothing. At the end of World War II, Algeria looked like a set of "juxtaposed departments" whose unification resulted from central organizations, foremost among them the general government. The 1946 constitution, under the name "French union," determined the different territories on which France had exercised its jurisdiction in the post.

Because of its timidity, the new status given Algeria on September 20, 1947, did not open great possibilities for change. Muslim Algerians obtained the separation of the Muslim religion from the state, and not insignificant financial powers for their representatives. But this status safeguarded most European interests through the existence of two separate bodies in the newly created "Algerian assembly." That assembly was to have "parity of representation": sixty delegates in the first college, sixty in the second. The first college represented 464,000 citizens with French civil status (men and women) and 58,000 Muslims; the second represented about 1,500,000 officially canvassed Muslim voters aged 21 or older. Remember that the Algerian population at the time consisted of 922,000 Europeans and 7,860,000 Muslims.

The municipal elections of October 1947 were a triumph for the nationalist candidates supporting Messali Hadj and Ferhat Abbas's Union Algérienne. Governor-General Y. Chataigneau, judged too liberal, was replaced, and elections for the Algerian assembly put off. That gave E. Naegelen, the new governor-general, time to fix the elections. In 1948, of sixty seats in the second college, forty-one were awarded to "administrative" candidates, most of them unknown; nine were conceded to the Mouvement pour le Triomphe des Libertés Démocratiques, or MTLD (Movement for the Victory of Democratic Freedoms); and eight to the party of the increasingly embittered Ferhat Abbas. At the same time, these "good elections" drove many moderate nationalists to despair or rebellion.

After the war, the principal nationalist organization (the PPA) reconstituted itself as the MTLD. The events in Constantinois in 1945, which led to a decisive rift with the European community of Algeria, affected all social strata and impelled Algerian intellectuals to reformulate their political positions. In 1948–1949, most of the leaders of the Fédération de France adopted positions defending Berber identity, and criticized the direction— judged too "Arab and Islamic"—taken by the party's main faction. As a result, the Fédération de France once more found itself in the forefront of the MTLD leaders' concerns; these leaders decided to send someone to reestablish, to "normalize," the situation. Several dozen cadres of the Algerian immigration movement in France were excluded from the nationalist organization. The MTLD may have feared French society's influence—its secularism, the position of young intellectuals in France who had left behind their family customs and traditions, and the desire of some in Algeria to abandon a nationalism judged too narrow in focus to be integrated into the larger social struggles in France. With that first crisis quelled, another of greater scope was to emerge. In December 1952, Messali Hadj, under house arrest in Niort, challenged the majority of the members of the central committee (called "centralist" at the time), by making the Fédération de France his base of support. The accusation of reformism was made against the central committee. He accused it of not controlling the underground militants in the OS (Organisation Spéciale), a paramilitary branch created in 1947.

Most of them had been arrested in 1950. A battle began between two factions, the "Messalists" and the "centralists," and deteriorated at the Hornu Congress held in Belgium by the Messalists on July 13, 1954. This dry summary can hardly suggest the violence of the resolutions and the clashes that prefigured the particularly deadly battles waged between the Messalist militants and the FLN during the Algerian War.

The crisis of the largest Algerian nationalist organization continued to develop, while international events put independence of the colonies on the agenda. In Paris on February 2, 1951, a pact was drafted among nationalist organizations for the independence of the Maghreb. In Egypt on July 23, 1952, a military coup d'état announced the advent of Gamal Abdel Nasser. Late that same year, between December 7 and 13, popular riots erupted in Casablanca following the assassination of Ferhat Hached, leader of the Union Générale Tunisienne du Travail, or UGTT (Tunisian General Labor Union) in Tunisia. In neighboring countries, the test of strength with France was under way. On August 20, 1953, Mohammed V was deposed. That initiative of the French colonial authorities precipitated a situation that would culminate, on March 2, 1956, with the independence of Morocco, and, on March 20, 1956, with that of Tunisia. But, above all, May 7, 1954, saw the fall of Dien Bien Phu in Indochina, a defeat that sounded the death knell of an entire era. So began the disintegration of the French colonial empire.

While the battle raged between Messalists and centralists, a new faction was created in March 1954 to impel immediate action. It was the Comité Révolutionnaire pour l'Unité et l'Action, or CRUA (Revolutionary Committee for Unity and Action), which would give birth to the FLN (Front de Libération Nationale). The latter would launch the insurrection of November 1, which inaugurated the war of Algerian independence and marked the end of colonial Algeria. That war would last more than seven years and would lead to independence in 1962.

Part I

The Algerian Civil War, 1954–1962: Why Such a Bitter Conflict?

At noon on March 19, 1962, the cease-fire, which had been agreed upon the previous day at the signing of the Evian accords, went into effect. It put an end "to the military operations and armed struggle throughout Algerian territory." So ended a ninety-two month war which had taken a very heavy toll on both sides.

In Algeria the conflict resulted in hundreds of thousands of dead, the displacement of millions of peasants, and the dismantling of the economy. In addition, it brought the FLN (Front de Libération Nationale) to power, a group that presented itself as the sole heir to Algerian nationalism. Benefiting from extraordinary popularity among the Algerian masses in 1962, it subsequently took root as the only party and, for nearly thirty years, negated any political or cultural pluralism.

In France, although there were far fewer casualties, the trauma was no less intense. Do we need to recall that nearly 2 million French soldiers crossed the Mediterranean between 1955 and 1962, that is, most young people born between 1932 and 1943 who were eligible to be called up? An entire generation thus found itself embarked upon a war whose stakes it did not understand. Politically, the conflict led to the fall of six prime ministers and the collapse of one Republic.

The war of Algerian independence, then, was one of the two cruelest wars of French decolonization in this century; the other was the war in

Indochina (1946–1954). How are we to understand the bitterness of the Algerian conflict?

When the insurrection of November 1, 1954, erupted, the motto of François Mitterrand, then minister of the interior in the cabinet of Pierre Mendès France, was: "Algeria is France." Algeria constituted three French departments. Thus it was much more than a distant colony like Senegal or a mere protectorate like Tunisia.

After the very deadly conquest begun in 1830, which translated into a dispossession of the Muslim Algerians' land, a large settlement colony took root (Stora 1991a). By 1954, nearly 1 million Europeans, who would later be called *pieds noirs*, had worked and lived there for generations. Not all of them were "big colons" overseeing their land holdings. Most had a lower standard of living than residents of the metropolis. That colony of proletarianized settlements was represented by the traditional major parties of the French Hexagon (on the left and the right), whose operations and conceptions were based on the model of Jacobin centralization.

In the late nineteenth century, Algeria was not administrated by the Ministry of Colonies, but rather belonged to the Ministry of the Interior. Therefore, it seemed out of the question to abandon a territory attached to France for the past one hundred and thirty years, even longer than Savoy (1860). In the course of the war itself, the discovery of oil and the decision to use the vast Sahara for the first nuclear or space experiments came to be added to these rationales.

France thus sent its soldiers to fight in a "southern" French territory that was demanding its right to secede. Nine million Muslim Algerians were sham citizens of a Republic that saw itself as assimilationist: since 1947, they had voted in a college separate from that of Europeans. The principle of equality, "one man, one vote," was not respected. The idea of independence, shared by a growing proportion of Algerians, seemed to be the only way to undo that contradiction.

When the war ended, people on either side of the Mediterranean labored to efface its real and bloody traces. In France, there was no commemoration to perpetuate the memory of the soldiers on all sides, and the succession of amnesties led people to forget a shameful conflict. In Algeria, a commemorative frenzy founded the legitimacy of the military state, dissimulating the pluralism and clashes that had existed between the pro-independence movements and within the FLN itself.

For a long time, however, the memories of seven years of war resisted effacement. The pain and rage of the drama's protagonists permeated the field of writing about that history. Nearly forty years later the war in Algeria has begun to be an object of historical study.[1] New paths of reflection and knowledge are opening up regarding the war mentality, the deadly propaganda, the social practices, the confusion of civilians, the attitudes held in the regions of France and Algeria, and the shaky involvements and retreats of individuals and groups.

1. On the beginnings of historical work in France, see *Les chemins de la décolonisation de l'Empire français*, edited by C. R. Ageron, proceedings of a colloquium of the Centre National de la Recherche Scientifique in 1984 (Paris: CNRS, 1987); *La guerre d'Algérie et les Français*, edited by J.-P. Rioux, proceedings of a colloquium of the IHTP in 1988 (Paris: Fayard, 1990). On the Algerian side, see the works of Slimane Chikh (1981), Mohammed Harbi (1980), Ramdane Redjala (1988), and Mohammed Teguia (1984).

1

The "Phony War"
(November 1954–July 1955)

October, Eve of a War

In October 1954, France was living at the slow pace of the Fourth Republic, which had borrowed a great deal from the Third. Politics always took place in sealed offices; elected officials in the provinces rushed from banquets to inaugurations and from hollow speeches to obscure disputes. René Coty was in the Elysée Palace, and Pierre Mendès-France was premier in the Hôtel Matignon. For nine years, Charles de Gaulle, having withdrawn from public affairs, had been biding his time in Colombey-les-Deux-Eglises. Guy Mollet, his spectacles at the tip of his nose, watched the omnipotent SFIO, one of the ancestors of the present-day Parti Socialiste, from the corner of his eye. The Communists were still shaken up over the death of Stalin, which had occurred twenty months earlier. Nasser was the strongman in Cairo, and his revolution of Arab nationalism was continuing.

Eisenhower was in the White House. He had just named a black man to be general of the U.S. Army's Air Force. He was the first. In London, Admiral Mountbatten was named First Sea Lord. In Stockholm, the Nobel Prize committee gave its award to a war writer, Ernest Hemingway. The decision was poorly received. Italian troops had just reentered Trieste, which the Yugoslavs had returned to them. Scenes of jubilation. In Paris, the Franco-German accords on the Saar were signed. People everywhere wanted to settle the accounts of World War II.

But how many dark spots were on the planet! In the USSR, the gulag did not die with Stalin; in Africa, decolonization was yet to come; whole stretches of Asia wallowed in poverty and underdevelopment. In China, the Communists had taken power five years earlier. The term "Third World" appeared and circulated to designate these impoverished zones. Franco still held Spain under his sway. And, in the United States, McCarthyism was raging. Batista was elected in Cuba; he would very quickly become a fierce dictator.

Officially, France was at peace. On the other side of the Mediterranean, in Carthage in July 1954, Pierre Mendès-France had promised an evolution toward autonomy for Tunisia and Morocco, which had been on the brink of a general rebellion for three years. The true war, the war in Indochina, was over. Bigeard and many emaciated, defeated paratrooper officers left the Viet Minh prison camps. They were reflecting on the causes of the military defeat of Dien Bien Phu on May 7, 1954, a terrible lesson they were not ready to forget.

The weekend of late October 1954 was deadly: thirty-four perished. The highways were beginning to kill in great numbers. France was confronting the problems of a nation at peace that was beginning to grow richer. Its victims, and its defeats, were now in sports stadiums. In the Parc des Princes, Puig Aubert had just led the XIII of France [a soccer team] to a victory over New Zealand. The stabilization of prices, achieved under the premiership of Antoine Pinay in 1952, was a major event. The old specter of price inflation that had so profoundly marked the postwar period was vanishing. This fact reduced "the diplomatic and colonial catastrophes to the rank of political mishaps, and thus comforted the French, who intended to take advantage of the fruits of the expansion once they had got on their feet by consolidating their purchasing power"(Rioux 1990).

Cultural news remained plentiful in 1954, however. People were reading the latest Prix Goncourt, *Les Mandarins* by Simone de Beauvoir, which was a fresco of a social milieu she knew by heart. That year, Françoise Sagan, a young new writer from a good family, published her first novel, whose title was borrowed from Paul Eluard: *Bonjour tristesse*. Jean Giono, who published *Voyage en Italie*, was received into the Académie Goncourt. Nor was Albert Camus absent from that landscape. A collection of his texts contributed to the debate of ideas of the moment (*Actuelles II*), and a long prose text, haunted by flashes of insight and by worry, also appeared (*L'Eté*). In October 1954, in darkened theaters film lovers could see *Touchez pas au grisbi*, by the great Jacques Becker, who was in a certain sense the heir to Jean Renoir; *Tant qu'il y aura des hommes*, by Fred Zinnemann; *Roman Holiday*, by William Wyler, with Audrey Hepburn; *On the Waterfront*, by Elia Kazan; and *Dial M for Murder*, by Alfred Hitchcock.

On October 31 the deputies packed their bags, preparing to return to Paris, where the parliamentary session was set to reopen in two days. Pierre

Mendès-France, the man who had made peace in Indochina, was preparing to leave for the United States. He was dreaming of reshuffling his cabinet. The previous week he had offered five Socialists a place in his government. The French stock market immediately dropped, then rose again, reassured. Edgar Faure would remain at Finances until the budget vote.

All Saint's Day 1954 began with a symbol. Very far away, in Pondicherry, the sun rose on a new flag. It was green, orange, and white. At sunset on the previous day, the French flag, still waving on the largest of the four trading posts, had been removed. The empire of French India no longer existed. Everything had gone well in Pondicherry.

The Outburst

Between midnight and two o'clock a.m. on November 1, 1954, Algeria was awakened by explosions. From Constantinois to Oranie, fires and commando attacks revealed the existence of a concerted, coordinated movement. In Algiers, Boufarik, Bouïra, Batna, Khenchela, and on and on, thirty almost simultaneous attacks on military or police targets were perpetrated.

Very quickly, François Mitterrand, minister of the interior, placed three companies of state security police (CRS), that is, six hundred men, at the disposal of the Algerian general government; they flew from Paris in the early afternoon. A first battalion of paratroopers moved in under the command of Colonel Ducourneau. Three others followed the next day. In fact, the war secretary was already in place in Algiers for a different reason: he was also a deputy and mayor of the city. This was Jacques Chevallier. The SFIO daily, *Le Populaire*, was upset: "The attacks came precisely at a time when France has a government whose comprehensive policy in North Africa is likely to bring calm everywhere there has been tension." The fact is, on that day, it was a hard fall for Paris. Hadn't François Mitterrand come back from his trip to Algeria some weeks earlier with the feeling that things were going better there?

The insurrection caused the death of seven people. The murder of the teacher Guy Monnerot in the Aurès and of the pro-French kaid from M'Chounèche, Hadj Sadok, elicited strong emotion. But the attacks against the police stations, barracks, and industrial plants did not have the scope that the initiators of the November 1 attacks had hoped. In Algiers the network set in place was broken up by the police in less than two weeks. Only the Aurès in Constantinois posed a real military problem: there, the "rebels" secured the cooperation of "bandits of honor" (in particular, the famous Grine Belkacem), who had been in the underground for years. There was also Great Kabylia, where several hundred men, trained in clandestine operations under the leadership of Amar Ouamrane and Krim Belkacem, were ready for prolonged action.

On November 1 no one seriously thought that France had just entered a new war. The "events" made two columns in *Le Monde*. A single column in *L'Express*, dated November 6, violently denounced the "subversive schemes" of the Arab League and the old leader of the radical pro-independence current, Messali Hadj. Yet he was not the one behind the November 1 outburst; rather, it was other young leaders, in revolt against the French colonial presence and the conservatism of their own party, which was torn apart by internal struggles.

The Men of November

On November 1, 1954, an organization, heretofore unknown, claimed responsibility for all the military operations: the Front de Libération Nationale (FLN). That "rebellion" was conducted internally by six men: Larbi Ben M'Hidi, Didouche Mourad, Rabah Bitat, Krim Belkacem, Mohamed Boudiaf, and Mostefa Ben Boulaïd. The acts outside Algeria, in Cairo, were spearheaded by Hocine Aït Ahmed, Ahmed Ben Bella, and Mohammed Khider. All were from a single organization, the Parti du Peuple Algérien/Mouvement pour le Triomphe des Libertés Démocratiques (PPA-MTLD), which had nearly twenty thousand militants in its ranks. For several years, all had been involved in the political struggle championed by the party.

It was on the basis of a claim for the autonomy of a "culture, heir to a long and glorious past," and for an entitlement transmitted by history, that this movement worked to legitimate the demand for independence. In that sense, Arab Islamism appeared as a return to the source of ancestral ethics. A centralizing movement, it tended to struggle against particularism, especially linguistic particularism. This was clear in 1949 when the advocates of Berber culture, denounced as "Berber materialists," were discharged from their leadership posts. The PPA-MTLD championed a strategy of scission with the French presence. Its young activists, advocates of armed struggle, laid the foundations for the FLN, and clashed violently with the old head of the PPA-MTLD, Messali Hadj, who founded the Mouvement National Algérien, or MNA (National Algerian Movement) in December 1954.

Within the leadership of this "activist" current, the youngest person (Omar Belouizdad) was twenty-six in 1954, the oldest (Mostefa Ben Boulaïd) was thirty-seven. Only one of these leaders, Mohammed Khider (age forty-two in 1954), who joined the group on the eve of November 1, was familiar with Etoile Nord-Africaine, the first pro-independence organization in 1936; he had been involved in the political holdup of the Oran post office, organized in 1949 by the OS (the branch of the PPA-MTLD charged with paving the way for a military insurrection, which was broken up by the French police in 1950–1951). This fact is not without importance. What united these men was that all of them, without exception and whatever their age, had been part of the OS, and had had to flee and hide to avoid repression. The orientation they gave to transmitting the legacy bequeathed by the pioneers of nationalism can be summed up in their recourse to *direct action*. Many activist cadres in the PPA who were called upon to play a "historic" role in the subsequent conduct of the Algerian revolution came from important families, themselves affected by the general downward mobility at work in Algerian society.

Hocine Aït Ahmed, born on August 20, 1926, in Aïn-el-Hammam (formerly Michelet) came from a very important line of Marabouts from Kabylia. Larbi Ben M'Hidi, born in 1923, in the douar of El Kouahi in Constantinois, near Aïn M'Lila, came from a family of Marabout notables from the high plains of Constantinois. Mohamed Boudiaf, born on June 23, 1919, in M'Sila in Hodna, was from a well-off family that had lost its status as a result of decolonization. Krim Belkacem, born on December 14, 1922, in the douar of Aït Yahia near Dra-El-Mizan in Kabylia, was the son of a village policeman, Hocine Krim, who was eventually named a minor kaid. Extremely well known, these four leaders joined the PPA during World War II and rapidly obtained significant responsibilities. They had all gone to school: Aït Ahmed passed the first part of the *baccalauréat* (high school degree); Boudiaf went to the secondary school of Bou Saada; Larbi Ben M'Hidi studied the dramatic arts; and Krim Belkacem earned his *certificat d'études* (primary school diploma). These studies ended when the men entered politics and went underground.

Although the sons of important rural families were affected by pro-independence propaganda, there were also nationalists who belonged to the category of notables, beginning with the interwar period. These are particularly unusual examples, but they deserve to be pointed out as well, since they indicate the shift in the rural areas from a situation of resistance to foreigners to modern national feeling. A very well-known leader, Mostefa Ben Boulaïd, is a telling example of the presence of that social category within the leadership of the pro-independence current. Born in 1917, he was the son of small landowners. He succeeded his father and became a miller by profession. Mobilized in 1939, he fought in the French army, was discharged after being wounded in 1942, then remobilized in 1943–1944 in

Khenchela. As a chief warrant officer returned to civilian life, he became president of the guild of fabric merchants in the Aurès, and established a small flour mill in Lambessa. At that time, he obtained a license to operate a line of buses between Arris and Batna. The results of his life journey are well known: a member of the central committee of the MTLD and founding member, in April 1954, of the CRUA (Comité Révolutionnaire pour l'Unité et l'Action), which would give rise to the FLN, he died in combat in 1956.

The new political activists, living in the midst of varied activities, suspecting they might be able to escape their social conditions through the studies they had undertaken or the positions they occupied, discovered different ways of life, different possibilities for political action. They were more "critical," more "rational" than the veterans of the 1930s nationalist struggle; the search for a political shortcut predominated in their analyses. Slow, patient collective work seemed outdated to them. For them, the turning point of 1945, marked by the Sétif massacre, served more as an accelerator than as a revelation, and precipitated the eclipse of the group built up around Messali Hadj in the interwar period. Hadj, who had been the impetus behind the first pro-independence organizations, was still the true charismatic leader of the national Algerian movement (Stora 1986). He was blind to the emergence of people no longer believing in classic political action (strikes, petitions, demonstrations). The "activists" in his party recommended recourse to armed struggle to escape the colonial impasse.

Reforms and Repression

"Algeria has been French for a long time. Therefore, secession is inconceivable." So asserted Premier Pierre Mendès-France on November 13 before the National Assembly. Minister of the Interior François Mitterrand added: "My policy will be defined by these three words: will, steadfastness, presence." As for the political bureau of the PCF, it declared on November 9 "that it could not approve of the recourse to individual acts likely to play into the hands of the colonialists, if, in fact, they were not fomented by them." Nevertheless, Communist militants, particularly in the Aurès, joined the underground forces of November. Trotskyists and anarchist militants, very much in the minority, were the only ones in France to pronounce themselves resolutely in favor of Algerian independence.

How was it possible to believe, in that autumn of 1954, that this was a mere flare-up of violent crime, of isolated individual acts? The governor of Algeria, Roger Léonard in Algiers, and Jean Vaujour, the director of Sûreté (the criminal investigation bureau), had warned the government of the imminence of an insurrection. On November 20, 1954, Tunisia had its right to internal autonomy recognized. Contacts had already been made to return the sultan of Morocco to his throne. The Arab world was under the influence of the Nasserian revolution. The decisiveness of the official declarations concealed only poorly the tremors that were shaking the colonial empire. *But, as far as Algeria was concerned, no one as yet in the French political class imagined any possibility of independence.* The French government proved to be very steadfast in its repressive will. On November 5, 1954, the main pro-independence organization, the MTLD, was dissolved, its leaders arrested, and hundreds of militants forced to go underground. Most went on to swell the ranks of the first guerrilla groups. Military reinforcements were sent to Algeria. On February 2, 1955, in the Chamber, François Mitterrand declared:

> Before the government was formed, that is, before mid-June 1954, there were 49,000 men in Algeria, including three companies of state security police (CRS). Before November 1, that is, in the first phase when, under the premier's authority, I was responsible for the Algerian affair, 75,000 men were sent as reinforcements. After November 1, 26,000 were sent to Algeria, not including the goums trained on site. The figure today is 83,400 men. It is therefore 60 percent higher than what the government found in Algeria when it came to power.

On January 15, 1955, the main leader of the FLN in Constantinois, Didouche Mourad, was killed during a skirmish with the French army. A month later, on February 11, the FLN leader in the Aurès, Mostefa Ben Boulaïd, was arrested. But the sending of reinforcements and the military operations were accompanied by deep reforms. In January 1955, the government elaborated a program for Algeria:

> —the creation in Algiers of a school of administration to give Muslim Algerians access to posts of responsibility in the public sector: of two thousand employees in the general government of Algeria, eight were Muslims; only 15 percent of Muslim children attended school; there was one European student for every 227 European residents of Algeria and one Muslim student for every 15,342 Muslim residents;
> —a reduction of the gap between Algerian and European salaries: the gross income of the European in Algeria was twenty-eight times that of the Muslim;
> —the initiation of major public works projects: entire zones had no roads, city hall offices, or post offices;

—the recognition of the state of economic poverty of many regions of Algeria and the difficulties caused by very strong demographic pressure: there were 850,000 under- or unemployed for an active population of 2,300,000 potential wage earners.

This program was little discussed, and for good reason. On February 5, 1955, the government of Pierre Mendès-France was overthrown. At five o'clock in the morning, at the end of a debate on North Africa, the result of the vote came in. By a margin of 319 to 273, the deputies delivered a no-confidence vote to the government. The right, the centrists, and the Communists applauded. The Catholics in the Mouvement Républicain Populaire, or MRP (Popular Republican Movement, a centrist party) participated in that downfall, an attitude that the weekly *Témoignage Chrétien* did not understand, judging that "we have concluded seven months marked by unquestionable innovation" (February 4, 1955).

Jacques Soustelle went to Algiers the day after the fall of the Mendès cabinet, which was replaced by that of Edgar Faure on February 11. The new governor of Algeria, an ethnologist and a Gaullist, had a justified reputation as an open, liberal man. He had the courage to include in his cabinet Major Vincent Monteil, a great Arabist, and the ethnologist Germaine Tillion, a specialist on the Aurès. Jacques Soustelle was poorly received by those in charge in Algiers. This Cévennes native of Protestant origin was baptized "Ben Soussan" [the implication was that he was Jewish—trans.] Was everything still possible in Algeria, even though the FLN had officially been recognized at the Bandung Conference of nonaligned nations in April? Jacques Soustelle met with the leaders of the ulama (religious reformists) and with Ferhat Abbas, who had his movement (founded in 1946), the Union Démocratique du Manifeste Algérien or UDMA (Democratic Union of the Algerian Manifesto), participate in the district elections of April 1955.

Until mid-1955, Soustelle labored to understand the discontent of the Muslim population. His trips to the Aurès and Kabylia revealed to him the under-administration of the regions agitated by Algerian nationalism, especially the Aurès, and the futility of the military deployments, which encircled nothing more than a vacuum. In March 1955, he asked the government for the right to adapt legislation to the conditions of that war, which still did not dare speak its name. On March 31, 1955, the National Assembly voted in a state of emergency that strengthened the powers of the army in the limited zone of the Aurès, and authorized the displacement of "contaminated" populations to "settlement camps." A first camp opened in Khenchela, where one hundred and sixty people were confined. On May 19, the government recalled several annual contingents of soldiers. The army launched major sweeping operations in the second half of 1955. But these measures did not weaken the "rebellion." The authority of the FLN was demonstrated by the district elections in April: the abstention order it issued was followed by 60 percent of the voting population in Constantinois.

Jacques Soustelle promised "integration" and reforms. It was too late: everything fell apart on August 20, 1955, the anniversary of the deposing of the sultan of Morocco. The "phony war" ended, and the Algerian War began in earnest.

2

The Open War
(August 1955–December 1956)

The Uprising of August 20, 1955

On August 20, 1955, thousands of Algerian peasants revolted and rushed to attack cities in North Constantinois within the quadrilateral formed by Collo, Philippeville, Constantine, and Guelma. The initiative behind that large-scale action fell to Zighoud Youcef, Didouche Mourad's successor at the head of the FLN's North Constantinois zone, and on his assistant, Lakhdar Ben Tobbal. On that day, the FLN leaders intended to mark the second anniversary of the deposing of Sidi Mohammed Ben Youcef, sultan of Morocco, by the French. The war assumed its true face in Constantinois, where the coexistence of communities had always been tenser than in the rest of Algeria. Ten years after the "events" of Sétif and Guelma in May 1945, an identical outburst of violence recurred, followed by an excessive and indiscriminate repression. At about noon several thousand *fellahs* (peasants, agricultural workers) moved into about thirty cities and villages. They were weakly organized by a few uniformed soldiers of the Armée de Libération Nationale, or ALN (National Liberation Army, the armed branch of the FLN), and they attacked police stations, the gendarmerie, and various public buildings. These peasants were agitated: a rumor of an Egyptian landing in Collo circulated. Many French people, but also Muslims, were murdered with axes, billhooks, picks, or knives. Political figures were attacked, including Saïd Chérif, UDMA delegate to the Algerian assembly, and Abbas Alaoua, Ferhat Abbas's nephew, who was murdered in his pharmacy in Constantine. The death toll of the riots came to 123, including 71 in the European population.

The repression was terrible. The army set to work and, as in May 1945, private militias were formed. The official death toll was fixed at 1,273. After an investigation, the FLN put forward the figure of 12,000 victims, which has never been disproved. On August 20, 1955, the myth of "peacekeeping operations" in Algeria came to an end. France was going to war, and it recalled sixty thousand reservists. Jacques Soustelle, governor-general of Algeria, overwhelmed by the spectacle of mutilated European cadavers in Philippeville, now gave the army carte blanche. The time for reforms was past. On September 30, 1955, the "Algerian question" was on the UN's agenda. The pro-independence Algerians, via the August 20 uprising, succeeded in attracting worldwide attention to Algeria. The conflict entered its phase of internationalization.

In face of the developing nationalist insurrection in Algeria, the French government hastened to settle matters for the two French protectorates of Tunisia and Morocco. It negotiated with the nationalist leaders Habib Bourguiba and Mohamed V, whom its predecessors had exiled and imprisoned; it granted internal sovereignty to Tunisia (independence would become effective in March 1956) and outright independence to Morocco in November 1955.

The Soldiers' Movement

After August 20, 1955, the repression in Algeria openly took on the look and dimensions of a true war. The battalions of security police, gendarmes, legionnaires, and paratroopers who were already in Algeria were supplemented by more conscripts. On August 24, 1955, 60,000 young soldiers who had recently been liberated were "recalled" to service, and on August 30 the government decreed that 180,000 "dischargeable" soldiers would remain in the military.

Very quickly, those who were called back tried to oppose these measures, sometimes with the support of their families and the general population. On September 1, at the Gare de l'Est in Paris, two thousand young people refused to board the trains, shouting "Civilian life!" "No war in Algeria!" and "Morocco for the Moroccans!" On September 2, six hundred of the "recalled" in the air force demonstrated at the Gare de Lyons. Similar events were repeated in Brives, Perpignan, and Bordeaux. The contingent demonstrated to shouts of "The civilians are on our side!" But, in fact, that soldiers' movement, which did not find support among the masses of "civilians," quickly ran out of steam because of individual lassitude and also a lack of political prospects. The organizations and major parties proved to be more preoccupied with the tumult of political life within France. On November 29, by a margin of 318 to 218, the Assembly passed a vote of no-confidence directed at Edgar Faure's government, thus setting in motion its dissolution. Legislative elections were set for January 2, 1956.

The Election and "The Day of Tomatoes"

Despite the dissolution of the Chamber, Jacques Soustelle continued the state of emergency. The government decided to postpone the elections in Algeria. The elected officials in Ferhat Abbas's Union Démocratique du Manifeste Algérien decided to resign from the Algerian assembly,[1] in the footsteps of the sixty-one Muslim elected officials who, on September 26, 1955, had opposed the integration policy championed by Soustelle. On December 20, 1955, *L'Express* reproduced photographs taken in August depicting the execution of an Algerian "rebel" by an auxiliary gendarme. The electoral campaign proceeded against the background of the Algerian tragedy, and the left called for "peace in Algeria." The Socialists and Radicals formed a Front Républicain, which won the election on January 2, 1956. The major event of these legislative elections was the making of inroads by Pierre Poujade's movement, which won 52 of the 623 seats, including one for Jean-Marie Le Pen. Pierre Poujade's movement, the Union de Défense des Commerçants et Artisans, or UDCA (Defense Union of Tradespeople and Artisans), campaigned against the "crooks" in the government and against the tax system. The Communists won 50 seats.

On February 1, the National Assembly invested the new government. Guy Mollet became premier, and General Georges Catroux, minister resident in Algeria. Jacques Soustelle, who had received such a poor welcome upon his arrival in Algiers, left a city in frenzy on February 2, 1956. More than 100,000 people, most of them Europeans, noisily demonstrated their affection, and stood in the path of the armored car that was trying to make its way to the port: "Don't go! Mendès in the Aurès! Catroux in the sea!" Old general Catroux, a liberal, would never reach the Summer Palace in Algiers. On February 6, a demonstration of "ultras," proponents of French Algeria, shouted down the government's policy; various projectiles hit Guy Mollet. This event would become known to

---

1. The statute on Algeria, passed by the National Assembly on September 20, 1947, created an Algerian assembly of 120 members (60 in each electoral college, one for Europeans, one for Muslim Algerians). That assembly passed the budget of Algeria, and could also modify metropolitan legislation, subject to the ratification of the government. Municipal and general councillors in the second (Muslim) college had the right to only two-fifths of the seats (Ageron 1979).

posterity under the name of "the day of tomatoes." The premier, still neutral, abandoned his policy, seeking peace in Algeria: the Republic had capitulated in the face of a few projectiles thrown onto this Glières plateau of Algiers, which had become the cauldron of Algerian rage. Pierre Mendès-France resigned his post as state minister. The Socialist government was about to plunge into war.

The "Special Powers"

The extremist *pieds noirs* and the army demanded an increase in the number of soldiers, already 190,000 strong in February 1956, and the addition of helicopters to support the partitioning of the "bled." Robert Lacoste, former Resistance fighter and member of the SFIO, named minister resident in Algeria by Guy Mollet on February 9, 1956, introduced a legislative bill in the National Assembly, "authorizing the government to set in place a program of economic expansion, social progress, and administrative reform in Algeria, and enabling it to take all exceptional measures in view of reestablishing order, protecting persons and property, and safeguarding the territory."

Via the decrees of March and April 1956, which would allow increased military action and the recall of reservists, Algeria was divided into three zones (a zone of operation, a pacification zone, and a forbidden zone), in which three specific army corps would move. In the zone of operation, the objective would be to "crush the rebels." In the pacification zones, the "protection" of European and Muslim populations was foreseen, with the army struggling against the deficiencies of the administration. The forbidden zones were to be evacuated, and the population assembled in "settlement camps" and placed under the control of the army.

On March 12, the Parliament (by a margin of 455 to 76) overwhelmingly passed that law on special powers which, among other things, suspended most of the guarantees of individual liberties in Algeria. The PCF voted for the law. The "special powers" constituted the real turning point in a war that France had decided to wage totally.

On April 11, the recall of the reservists was decreed. Tens of thousands of soldiers crossed the Mediterranean. Prior to that application of the law, the directors of the journal *Les Temps Modernes* realized where it would lead and said so. "The left, for once unanimous, has voted for 'special powers,' powers perfectly useless for negotiation but indispensable for the continuation and escalation of the war. This vote is scandalous and runs the risk of being irreparable." It would in fact be so.

1956, Total War

On March 16, 1956, four days after the vote on special powers, the first FLN attacks struck Algiers. Robert Lacoste imposed a curfew on the city, continuously crisscrossed by his patrols. In France, a few final spontaneous demonstrations took shape around train stations and barracks, against "the departure of the recalled reservists." Public opinion balked at the extension of military service to twenty-eight months. In Algeria, "the bled" continued to "rot," and terrorism took root nearly everywhere. Oran was hit by FLN strikes in February, Algiers by similar strikes in May. The dissemination of the French troops and their mediocre training made them vulnerable to ambushes: in Palestro, on May 19, twenty young recalled reservists from Paris fell during an attack by members of the "Ali Khodja" ALN commando, assisted by the general population. Five days later the sole survivor was rescued by paratroopers.

In July and September of 1956, discreet negotiations opened between the delegates of the FLN (M'Hamed Yazid and Abderrahmane Kiouane) and of the SFIO (Pierre Commun) in Belgrade and Rome. The SFIO urged Guy Mollet to obtain a pause in the fighting through the intervention of the sultan of Morocco and of Habib Bourguiba, president of Tunisia, which had won its independence on March 20, 1956. Hocine Aït Ahmed, Mohamed Boudiaf, Ahmed Ben Bella, and Mohammed Khider discussed these prospects in Rabat on October 21, and flew off to Tunis the next day. But the Moroccan DC-3 carrying them was intercepted by the French air force and forced to land in Algiers. Robert Lacoste and the military, who did not miss that opportunity to "root out the rebellion," made it impossible for Guy Mollet to pursue the beginnings of a negotiation. The European population of Algiers, which had endured the nightmare of explosions in bars frequented by its young people, noisily demonstrated its confidence in Robert Lacoste, who was congratulated for his energy. But, in Algeria and the metropolis, attention was soon diverted from the fate of Ben Bella and his companions (they would remain incarcerated until the end of the war) by the Suez expedition on November 5 and 6, 1956.

Guy Mollet, haunted by the memory of the capitulation of Munich in 1938, and comparing Nasser to a "new Hitler," launched the foolhardy military expedition of Port Said. The Franco-British operation aimed to wrest the Suez Canal from the control of Egypt, which had nationalized the company in July. In the minds of the French general staff, the operation would serve to take down Nasser, who was considered the most active supporter of the Algerian insurrection. But the tactical success, acquired with the cooperation of the Israelis, who had attacked to the east, was transformed into a political rout: the Americans and the Russians made the troops depart again on November 15, and the UN put the Algerian question on its agenda.

The FLN took advantage of these events to make its presence known in the countryside and in the cities. In the late part of 1956, the Algerian War took a nasty turn. The army had increased in size from 54,000 to 350,000 men within two years. Several classes had to be recalled, and the length of military service was extended to nearly thirty months. The repression pushed thousands of young Algerians toward the guerrilla forces (students in particular, who organized a strike in March 1956). The French sector forces combed the territory with little zeal. The paratroopers and the Legion, constantly on call, suffered heavy losses. In late 1956, the ALN had tens of thousands of *djounouds* (warriors) in its ranks. Things were deteriorating everywhere. Certain regions represented real sanctuaries for the FLN. Most of the Muslim elected officials, including Ferhat Abbas, joined the camp of Algerian nationalism.

Since autumn, Robert Lacoste had been calling for a new commander in chief. On November 15, 1956, Guy Mollet installed General Raoul Salan in place of General Henri Lorillot, who had been unable to respond to the guerrilla war, despite the reinforcements landing each month in Algeria. The arrival of Raoul Salan, a veteran of Indochina and a "strategist" of subversive war, opened a new chapter in the Algerian War, especially since the FLN had decided to change its field of operation: in January 1957, it took the war to the heart of Algiers, making repeated attacks and issuing the order for a general strike.

3

The Cruel War (1957)

The "Battle of Algiers"

On December 27, 1956, Amédée Froger, president of the federation of mayors of Algeria and a virulent spokesman for the minor colons, was murdered in Algiers. The next day his funeral occasioned truly brutal *ratonnades* (Arab-bashings), which caused several Muslim casualties. Tension was extreme between the Europeans and the Muslim Algerians. Robert Lacoste's general government decided to react. On the basis of the "special powers" passed in March 1956, he entrusted the "pacification" of Algiers to General Jacques Massu, commander of the Tenth Paratroopers' Division.

On January 7, 1957, eight thousand paratroopers moved into the city, charged with a policing mission. The "battle of Algiers" had begun. On January 9 and 10, two explosions caused panic in two stadiums in Algiers. But the horror reached its peak on January 26. Within a few minutes of each other, two charges exploded, the first in the bar L'Otomatic, the second in the café Le Coq Hardi, in the very center of Algiers. Two Muslim Algerians were lynched by an agitated European mob. On January 28, to coincide with the United Nations debates, the FLN launched an order for an eight-day general strike. The army broke the strike. At every moment and at every location, helicopters landed on the terraces of the Casbah. The city was divided into sectors, and the Muslim neighborhoods were isolated behind barbed wire, under searchlights. General Massu, endowed with policing powers over the city, had the responsibility of restoring order, and broke apart the FLN's "autonomous zone of Algiers" (ZAA) which was located primarily in the Casbah and headed by Yacef Saadi. The FLN set up a true organization estimated at five thousand militants. Terrorism served to justify recourse to every means possible. Massu's men made massive arrests, systematically took down names, and, in the "transit and sorting centers" located on the periphery of the city, practiced torture. The leader of the FLN, Larbi Ben M'Hidi, was arrested on February 17, and subsequently was said to have "committed suicide." The "very exhaustive" interrogations produced results.

It was truly "blood and shit," as Colonel Marcel Bigeard said, a horrendous battle, during which bombs blew dozens of European victims to pieces, while paratroopers dismantled the networks by uncovering their hierarchy, discovered caches, and flushed out the FLN leaders installed in the city. Their means? Electrodes (known as *gégène*, a slang term for generator), dunkings in bathtubs, beatings. Some of the torturers were sadists, to be sure. But many officers, noncommissioned officers, and soldiers would live with that nightmare for the rest of their lives. The number of attacks perpetrated fell from 112 in January to 39 in February, then to 29 in March. The FLN's command center, run by Abbane Ramdane, was forced to leave the capital. Massu had a first victory.

On March 28, 1957, General Paris de Bollardière asked to be relieved of his duties. He could not allow the use of torture, which he had experienced and fought against during the German Occupation. The chaplain of the Tenth Paratroopers' Division responded by declaring: "One cannot fight against revolutionary war except with methods of clandestine action." General Paris de Bollardière was sentenced to sixty days in prison on April 15, 1957.

In early June the attacks resumed. On June 3, a bomb went off near a bus stop; on June 9, the dance hall of a casino was targeted, causing 8 deaths and 92 injuries. The repression began again, aided this time by a network of "reformed" militants (called the "overalls"), who, under the leadership of Captain Léger, infiltrated the FLN and brought down many leaders. Yacef Saadi was arrested on September 24, 1957. His assistant, Ali La Pointe, finding himself surrounded, committed suicide in a cache to avoid arrest. The "battle of Algiers" was over. The European population rediscovered the pleasures of the beach and the restaurants, and worshiped its paratroopers. That idyll would continue on May 13, 1958.

The FLN networks had been destroyed, thousands of Algerians had been arrested or "disappeared." But that military victory was accompanied by a grave moral crisis. On September 12, 1957, Paul Teitgen, secretary general of the Algiers police, resigned in protest against the practices of General Massu and the paratroopers. He put forward the figure of 3,024 disappeared. The "question" of torture was about to divide France.

The Question of Torture

Torture, employed as an ordinary procedure of "pacification" during the "battle of Algiers," was certainly the great scandal of these Algerian years (Vidal-Naquet 1975).

As early as January 15, 1955, the writer François Mauriac had published an article in *L'Express* entitled "The Question." At the same time, the journalist Claude Bourdet also denounced what he called "Your Algerian Gestapo" in *France-Observateur*. On March 2, 1955, Roger Willaume, an inspector general in the administration, remitted a report to Jacques Soustelle, governor-general of Algeria, which made it very clear that torture was commonly practiced on "suspects." On December 13, 1955, Premier Edgar Faure received a report prepared by Jean Mairey, director of Sûreté Nationale, that reached the same conclusion. Torture was being used by the *détachement opérationnnel de protection*, or DOP (protective operation detail), special units of the army charged with "exhaustive" interrogations.

Beginning in mid-February 1957, the weekly *Témoignage Chrétien* published the "Jean Müller dossier," by a recalled reservist in Algeria: "We are far removed from the pacification for which we were supposedly called; we are desperate to see how low human nature can stoop, and to see the French use procedures stemming from Nazi barbarism." In March 1957, a few recalled reservists put out a brochure, *Des rappelés témoignent* (Recalled reservists bear witness) under the aegis of the Comité de Résistance Spirituelle (Committee of Spiritual Resistance). In it, there are accounts such as this: "I was thinking of the kid, who I imagined terrorized at the bottom of the jeep trailer, where he had been shut up at night. Yet it was the kid they were torturing." In April, the journal *Esprit* published the wrenching account by Robert Bonnaud, "The Peace of the Nementchas": "If France's honor can go along with these acts of torture, then France is a country without honor."

In September 1957, Paul Teitgen resigned his post as secretary general of the police in Algiers. He wrote: "In visiting the settlement centers, I recognized on certain detainees the deep marks of abuse or torture that I personally endured fourteen years ago in the basement of the Gestapo in Nancy." In November 1957, at the initiative of the mathematician Laurent Schwartz and the historian Pierre Vidal-Naquet, the Comité Maurice-Audin was formed, named after a young mathematician who disappeared after being abducted by paratroopers and tortured. In January 1958, Henri Alleg's *La question* appeared, which troubled consciences and publicly revealed the torture. So began the "affair" that deeply divided public opinion, the Church, families, and the parties: Why did the French army practice large-scale torture? Many thought that torture could become an institution, first of the police, and then of the military.

The publication in newspapers and journals (*L'Humanité, Les Temps Modernes, Esprit, Vérité Pour*) of works such as the Catholic writer Pierre-Henri Simon's *Contre la torture* (Against torture) got intellectuals involved; they soon formed into networks that fought against disinformation and human rights violations. Communist militants, writers, the Catholic intellectuals François Mauriac, André Mandouze, Pierre-Henri Simon, and André Frossard, and priests proved particularly active in the circulation of the war "secrets." Some belonged to the Mission de France, set up in Pontigny, Yonne, in August 1954, under the supervision of Cardinal Liénart.

Despite the censorship and the shroud of secrecy covering Algeria, the French public gradually discovered the true nature of a conflict that, to be sure, no longer had anything to do with a mere "peacekeeping mission."

Censorship, Prisons, Camps

The Algerian war brought about major restrictions on the freedom of the press, of publication, and of visual images. Censorship was set in place on a large scale. The law of April 3, 1955, declaring "the state of emergency," allowed administrative authorities, the minister of the interior, the general government, and the prefects to "take all measures to ensure control of the press and of publications of all kinds, as well as radio transmissions, showings of films, and theatrical performances" (article 11 of the law of April 3, 1955, declared applicable by that law). The decree of March 17, 1956, within the framework of the "special powers," repeated a similar formula, extended to "every means of expression." Printed texts could be seized by the administration and the courts, or subject to police measures or additional penalties, as an attack on state security.

The many newspapers and books seized by the prefects came about by virtue of article 10 of the criminal investigation code, which became article 30 of the penal procedures code. That article allowed the prefect to temporarily seize books or periodicals that contained a press violation, as stipulated by the law of July 29, 1881, if it also constituted "an attack on state security." In its section on crimes and misdemeanors committed via the press, the law of July 28, 1881, restricted freedom of opinion by repressing incitement to crimes and misdemeanors against the body politic. Article 25 of that law, used many times during the Algerian War, "represses the incitement of military personnel to disobedience, even when it remains without effect." A decision of April 27, 1961, defined the grounds that could justify a ban: support of an act of subversion directed against the authorities or laws of the Republic, or the dissemination of secret information, military or administrative.

Under the Fourth Republic, certain newspapers, such as *L'Express, France-Observateur, L'Humanité, Le Canard Enchaîné, La Vérité des Travailleurs,* and *Le Libertaire* were particularly targeted. Nearly thirty works from the publishers Jérôme Lindon and François Maspero would be seized under the Fifth Republic, between 1958 and 1962.

As of 1955, the police and the army championed house arrest for Algerian nationalist militants. Detention camps were established in Algeria by virtue of the law of March 16, 1956. Tens of thousands of Algerians were put into camps without due process, in Bossuet, Saint-Leu, and Lambessa.

The law of July 26, 1957, extended to France the provisions set out in the so-called special powers law. It stipulated the possibility of restricting to a detention center, in places located within the metropolis, any person convicted in application of the "laws on battle squads or private militias." Only one mode of application was envisioned for the detention thus set in place: internment in a guarded residence center. Between 1956 and 1959, then, four detention centers under guard were gradually established: Mourmelon-Vadenay (Marne), Saint-Maurice-l'Ardoise (Gard), Thol (Ain), and Larzac (Aveyron). The militants brought to these centers, after their sentences had been served, were those considered by the police to be "most active in the rebellion, whose return to freedom, that is, to separatist plots, poses a serious danger." The optimal use of these legislative provisions made it possible to obtain, within two years, the signing of 6,707 detention orders, of which 1,860 were executed.

The Fourth Republic was also a time of massive trials and death sentences. Ahmed Zabana, judged by the armed forces tribunal in Algiers, was the first to be sentenced to death; he was executed in the Barberousse Prison on June 19, 1956.

The Battles of the French Army

The bazooka attack committed on January 16, 1957, against Salan's office seems to have been separate from the "battle of Algiers": supposedly, the goal of the plot was to eliminate a general who was suspected of liberalism. In fact, Salan managed to straighten out the military situation. As it happened, in the bled, the combat methods of Colonel Jeanpierre's legionnaires, Bigeard's paratroopers, and others, paid off. The "rebels" bringing armaments from Tunisia and Morocco were intercepted and pursued into the interior of the sectors patrolled by conventional regiments. Helicopters and intelligence became the instruments of the troops, who were freed from policing Algiers in early summer 1957.

Despite a noticeable increase in its losses, the ALN was strengthened, thanks to the weapons and reinforcements that, in spite of everything, it received from Morocco and especially Tunisia, where it sent its recruits to be trained and armed. To isolate Algeria from these countries, Minister of Defense André Morice (a member of the Bourgès-Maunoury government from June to September 1957) decided to build, behind the border lines, networks of electrified and mined barbed wire (called the *barrages* or the "Morice Line"). In the desert zones, these were supplemented by batteries of cannons that would fire automatically when set off by radar. These obstacles could be breached, but as soon as they were, the break in the electrical current would send a signal to the military forces that someone had gone through.

In late May 1957, a very bitter skirmish occurred in *wilaya* IV between Bigeard's paratroopers and five hundred "fellaghas" (the name given the peasant insurrection movement in Tunisia) led by Azzedine, who escaped; ninety-six "rebels" were killed. At the same time, Salan undertook "social" pacification and dispatched SAS (special administrative section) officers to the bled: these men were paid to promote literacy and provide medical assistance, which also served as counterpropaganda and intelligence. In the rural areas, the relocation of the evacuated populations from the "forbidden zones" and the SAS actions had a negative effect on the FLN-ALN's recruitment, supply operations, and intercommunications. The recruitment of *harkis* and other auxiliaries from the peasantry resistant to the authority of the insurgent leaders, and from former "rebels," facilitated the actions of the military forces (in 1962, a report sent to the UN estimated the number of Muslims who fought in the auxiliary units or in self-defense groups at 263,000).

In early 1958, the French command judged that the war was virtually won. Minister Resident Robert Lacoste kept repeating victory would come to the one who held out for "the last quarter hour." That entailed "forgetting" the profound political and moral crisis permeating the Fourth Republic in 1957. In addition, the FLN leadership, installed outside the country, still hoped to win by combining an offensive of its troops from Tunisia and Morocco with diplomatic pressure on the UN, as a way to internationalize the conflict with an Algerian "Dien Bien Phu."

Crises in the Republic

In 1957, the conflict intensified throughout Algeria, outside the large cities. Soldiers of the contingent were now engaged in war, while in the metropolis more and more people were speaking out against torture. The UN demanded that France apply a "peaceful, democratic, and fair" solution to the Algerian problem. The American senator John F. Kennedy publicly declared himself in favor of this approach on July 2, 1957. In Paris, the Guy Mollet government, whose budget was reeling under the weight of heavy expenses incurred by the "peacekeeping operation" in Algeria, was overthrown on May 28, 1957. The cabinet of Maurice Bourgès-Maunoury succeeded it. It decided to focus on the Sahara, where oil had been discovered, and asked Robert Lacoste, who was kept in his post, to prepare an outline law that would bring a "new Algeria" into being. The international repercussions of the Algerian affair were obsessing the parties in the Front Républicain and, by September 1957, the gap had widened between the politicians and the military, between the metropolis and the *pieds noirs*, and within the left itself. A large proportion of "democrats" and "leftists" in the Fédération de l'Education Nationale, or FEN (National Education Federation), the Force Ouvrière, or FO (Workers' Power), and the Ligue des Droits des Hommes (Human Rights League), spoke of "the indigenous populations" and of "the territories," not of peoples and nations. Individual oppression was recognized, not national oppression. The republican left (which had come into existence during the Dreyfus affair) with its passion for universalism and the principles of 1789, opposed nationalism (French or Algerian) and religious circles. Logically, it rejected the proclamations of the Algerian nationalists, which were "marked by Islamic religiosity." At the same time, it could not understand why the republican principle of equality had never really been applied to Algeria and the colonies.

The Algerian affair, in fact, legitimated a republican reading of the FLN as a "symbol of justice"; but a different reading saw the organization as the conveyor of an "archaic nationalism to be transcended." The PCF also proved incapable of deciding between these two readings. That failure led to the involvement of a significant faction of young people in a radical Third World movement against "National Molletism" and the PCF, considered obstinately faithful to Moscow. The largest aid network to the FLN was run by Francis Jeanson, a philosopher and managing editor of the journal *Les Temps Modernes*, who, with his wife, Colette, had published *L'Algérie hors-la-loi* (Outlaw Algeria) in 1955. Jeanson had long hoped for a burst of energy on the part of the French left, which the "people" had brought to power in 1956 under the Front Républicain label; he was weary of meetings, placards, and the pious motions of a left that "continued to put the brakes to a movement that it prided itself on promoting." Observing that "none of the people who spoke of putting an end to the war, which they themselves declared absurd, conceded that one might help French young people refuse to become mired in it," and that "they were denouncing colonialism, but considered criminal any sort of practical solidarity with the colonized," he came to the logical conclusion: provide direct aid to the FLN.[1]

During this time, the Socialist Robert Lacoste was attempting to escape the political impasse. He prepared an outline law that included a "single college," which would get rid of the voting inequality in the two colleges (one European vote was worth seven Algerian votes, according to the statute drafted in 1947). On September 13, this proposal for an outline law was adopted in the Council of Ministers. But it was in turn shouted down by the majority of Europeans. It did not even manage to convince the National Assembly: on September 30, 1957, Bourgès-Maunoury was overthrown. It was not until the following November 6 that the assembly awarded its confidence to the new government of the Radical Félix Gaillard. The outline law on Algeria, greatly watered down to reduce the influence of Muslim elected officials, was finally passed on November 29, and its application postponed until the end of the war. Funds were allocated to build the electrified barriers on the borders of Morocco and Tunisia, the "Morice Line" (named after the short-lived minister of defense). Robert Lacoste remained resident minister in Algeria, but his authority was gone. General Salan now exercised vast prerogatives, and intended to win the war with his spirited colonels.

1. F. Jeanson, interview for the televised series *Les années algériennes*.

4

The War of the Algerians
(1954–1958)

November 1, 1954, the official date of the outbreak of the Algerian War, did not coincide with the imposition of a single leadership (the emergent FLN, for example) or with the collapse of all earlier political currents. As it turned out, the FLN was to structure and consolidate itself over two years, culminating in the Soummam Congress on August 20, 1956. In these two years, cadres were recruited and selected, the population trained, the idea of independence developed, channels established, and guerrilla warfare reinvented. But, above all, it took two long years to have the envied title of "authorized representative" recognized through the integration of all other currents into the FLN, with the exception of the proponents of the old nationalist leader Messali Hadj, who in December 1954 founded the Mouvement National Algérien (Stora 1985).

Differences among Nationalists

The dissolution of the MTLD by the Council of Ministers on November 4, 1954, led to the arrest of several hundred Algerian nationalist leaders and militants. Those who were not arrested had no choice: they had to go underground or join the guerrilla forces. The FLN took full advantage of the dissolution of the MTLD. It set structures in place to intercept the majority of disoriented Messalists and welcome them into the underground forces; they took possession of the stocks of weapons inherited from the

OS, the paramilitary organization of the MTLD; and they initiated contact with the Tunisians and the Moroccans. A large number of immigrants joining the guerrilla forces were taken in hand by the FLN. But, in the first phase of the insurrection, it also suffered very cruel blows. On January 15, 1955, Didouche Mourad, leader of Constantinois, died in battle; on February 11, Mostefa Ben Boulaïd, leader of the Aurès, was arrested; on March 16, Rabah Bitat, who had organized the urban guerrilla war in Algiers, was also arrested.

Under these conditions of very active repression (between November 1954 and April 1955), efforts at reconciliation took place between "activists" (the members of the MTLD who had perpetrated the events of November 1, 1954), "centralists" (the majority of the former members of the central committee of the MTLD), and "Messalists" (the followers of Messali Hadj). During this period, the FLN was still seeking its identity, assessing its strength. In Algiers, in Cairo, and among the guerrilla forces, contacts and efforts at reconciliation took place between "Messalists" and "Frontists" (supporters of the FLN). That did not fail to promote confusion within the immigrant community in France, and in Algeria. To be sure, the grass-roots nationalist militants had to expend a great deal of effort disentangling the maze of triangular relationships among all the parties involved (Messalists, CRUA, centralists) and understanding the disputes, which were Byzantine in their view, in the period preceding and immediately following the insurrection of November 1, 1954.

Confusion was also at its height among the guerrilla forces. All currents, though not acting in concert, accepted the designation "ALN" as the sole military structure. A large portion of Messalist militants decided on their own to resort to weapons as soon as the November 1 operations became known. In certain regions of Algeria, particularly the Aurès and Kabylia, armed groups formed independent of the existing leadership. They were "taken in hand" after the fact. Animated simply by patriotic desire, some were familiar with the FLN, while others embraced Messali. On November 1, 1954, the pamphlets clearly distinguished between the FLN, the movement's political organization, and the ALN, a military organization. But in the Aurès, for example, the entire political side answered to the authority of Chihani Bachir, Ben Boulaïd's second in command. The Aurès zone leaders did not see the usefulness of the distinction. They believed it was enough to proclaim open revolution and to train militants. In Kabylia, and especially in the Bouïra region, the militants fought under the name "Armée de Libération Nationale," which tended to create ambiguity regarding the designation "ALN," shared by the FLN and the MNA. Things came to a head politically in 1955.

The FLN-MNA War

In early 1955, the "activists" of the former MTLD, who had founded the FLN, managed to pull the members of the "centralist" current along with them. Conversely, the Messalists, heirs to a long political tradition, and who did not believe exclusively in military action to achieve independence, rejected the activist aims, which they judged simplistic. For Messali Hadj, formed within the French left, the activists were the victims of an "infantile disease." The two organizations, the FLN and the MNA, were about to engage in violent confrontations.

On June 1, 1955, the murder of Saifi, an old PPA militant, whose hotel and restaurant on rue Aumaire, in the third arrondissement of Paris, harbored illegal aliens, precipitated the confrontation. In a pamphlet issued in late November 1955, Abbane Ramdane, assistant to Krim Belkacem and leader of the FLN in Algiers, called Messali Hadj "a shame-faced old man who holds the Angoulême front, at the head of an army of police officers, which assures his protection against the anger of the people." After various insults and accusations exchanged via pamphlets, weapons took the place of words. On December 10, 1955, in Algiers, Salah Bouchafa and Mustapha Fettal, FLN militants, executed Sadek Rihani, the leader of the MNA in Algiers. The test of strength had begun. For both organizations, the nature of the future independent Algerian society was not at issue. The violent rivalry took place at a different level: who ought to be, who could be, the exclusive representative of the Algerian people?

From 1955 to 1962, the "shock commandos" of the FLN and the MNA waged a long, cruel battle using every means possible: traps, betrayal, infiltration, and executions to serve as an example, all of them sowing fear. In Algeria, this internecine struggle was exemplified, in May 1957, by the FLN's bloody massacre of 374 villagers in Melouza, who were suspected of Messalist sympathies. The massacre spurred the MNA fighters, especially those of Mohammed Bellounis, to immediately join the French army.[1] On March 20, 1962, the newspaper *Le Monde* published statistics on the scope of the confrontation between nationalists in France (the FLN versus the MNA): more than twelve thousand assaults, four thousand deaths, and more than nine thousand injuries. In Algeria itself, the toll of that civil war was very heavy: six thousand dead and fourteen thousand wounded. In total, in France and in Algeria, the number of victims rose to nearly ten thousand dead and twenty-five thousand wounded in the two camps.

1. Nevertheless, Mohammed Bellounis was murdered, along with his followers, by the men of the third Régiment Parachutiste d'Infanterie de Marine, or RPIMA (Paratrooper Regiment of the Marine Light Infantry) on July 14, 1958.

The FLN would emerge victorious in this war within a war. But thousands of militants who had been trained for modern political life in the immigration movement in France, in particular, were killed in the process, and would be cruelly absent from the leadership of an Algeria at war, and then of an independent Algeria.

Converts to the FLN, the Soummam Congress

In 1955 and 1956, the FLN increased contacts and discussions with the other Algerian components. All the same, aware of the "bankruptcy" of the earlier parties, it expected them simply to dissolve and their members to join the FLN in a purely individual capacity. Following in the footsteps of the "centralists" (Ben Youssef Ben Khedda, Saad Dhalab, M'Hamed Yazid, and Hocine Lahouel), Ferhat Abbas's UDMA rallied behind the FLN in late 1955.

The FLN was to obtain this massive conversion of the "old elites," so avidly desired, from another organization, the ulama (a religious reformist movement that championed the rebirth of Islamic identity in Algeria). That religious organization, worried about its lack of control over the events, went over to the FLN camp during its conference on January 7, 1956, and glorified the "resistance to colonialism." Then there was the case of the Parti Communiste Algérien, or PCA (Algerian Communist Party). In May and June 1956, Ben Khedda and Abbane Ramdane, representing the FLN, and Bachir Hadj Ali and Sadek Hadjeres, representing the PCA, began protracted discussions. On July 1, 1956, the Algerian Communists were integrated into the ALN.

The Soummam Congress, which was held on August 20, 1956, made official "the bankruptcy of the former political organizations of the old parties," and noted that the "grass-roots militants" had rallied behind the FLN, and that the UDMA and the ulama had been dissolved. With this congress, held in the Soummam Valley in Kabylia, the "Algerian revolution" changed its aspect. The long (twenty-day) debates culminated in a well-defined program, the structuring of the FLN-ALN, and the affirmation of the primacy of political over military action and of the domestic scene over the exterior (Teguia 1984).

Initially planned for July 31 in the region of the Bibane, the congress did not open until August 20 in a forester's cottage close to the village of Igbal, on the western slope of the Soummam. Sixteen delegates participated; they very unevenly represented the different regions of Algeria. In addition to the absence of the external delegation, there was no representative of the Aurès—their leader, Mohammed Ben Boulaïd, had been killed, and his brother Omar could not come, given the constant movements of the French army. Oranais was represented only by Larbi Ben M'Hidi. Six delegates came from Zone II (North Constantinois): Youcef Zighoud, Lakhdar Ben Tobbal, Mostefa Benaouda, Brahim Mezhoudi, Ali Kafi, and Rouibah. Four came from Zone III (Kabylia): Belkacem Krim, Mohammedi Saïd, Amirouche, and Kaci. Three came from Zone IV (Algérois): Amar Ouamrane, Slimane Dehilès, Ahmed Bouguerra. And one came from Zone VI (the south): Ali Mellah. These fifteen men were representatives of the combatants. The sixteenth, the only political secretary, was Abbane Ramdane.

From the deliberations of this congress, three major concerns emerged:

• an assessment of the material forces of the revolution, judged by the delegates to be moderately satisfactory. There was criticism of the weakness of weapons supply operations, and imbalances in the introduction of political structures were pointed out (good for Kabylia, despite the existence of a few Messalist strongholds, and for Constantinois; acceptable for Algérois; clearly lagging behind for Oranais);

• the drafting of a political platform—partly put together by Amar Ouzegane, but profoundly bearing Abbane's mark—which was articulated around the principles of a collegial structure of the leadership, the primacy of the political over the military, and the domestic over the external;

• a reorganization of the structure of the ALN, now modeled on a regular army. Algerian territory was carved up into six new *wilayas*, themselves subdivided into *mintaka* (zones), *nahia* (regions), and *kasma* (sectors); Algiers was set up as an autonomous zone. A strict hierarchy of battle units and ranks was instituted, which would give birth to the army, a true linchpin of the future Algerian state.

This "counterstate" in gestation was justified by the suffocating power of the colonial state. According to that argument, the pursuit of the pluralist traditions of Algerian nationalism prior to 1954 appeared too feeble a means for breaking free of the ponderous weight of French tutelage (Slimane Chikh 1981).

Although the Soummam Congress, the only one in the FLN's history, was historic in the "legislative" work it accomplished, it also inaugurated the struggle for control in the highest echelons of the nationalist organization. On September 23, 1956, Abbane Ramdane (a native of Kabylia) sent a letter to Mohammed Khider, informing him of the congress's decisions. When Ben Bella learned of the letter and received the minutes of the congress, he decided to compose a three-point response. He insisted on the "nonrepresentative" character of the congress. "The Aurès, the external delegation, Oranie, and the eastern zones did not attend, nor did the Fédération de France." He attacked "the questioning, once again, of the Islamic character of our future political institutions" and thereby demonstrated his rejection of the secularism of the state, and his refusal to make a place for the European minority. Finally, he denounced the presence of former leaders of parties within the leading organizations. This reply repeated word for word the themes of the leadership of the PPA-MTLD against "the Berberists" of 1949 (Stora 1991a: 111). But did not Abbane also accuse Ben Bella "of distrusting them because they were Kabyles"? Part of the reason for the dispute over legitimacy can be found in a "regionalist" explanation.

The Battle of the Guerrilla Forces

The principal unit of the ALN was the *katiba*—the equivalent of a light company—which might reach the size of one hundred men, or the platoon, about thirty men. These men eked out an existence in the territory constituting their field of operation, which they knew intimately for having traversed it in every direction.

Their solidarity was that of combatants waging war for the duration of the conflict, without any thought of return, constantly facing the same dangers and the same privations, whatever their rank or duties: the officer was no less Spartan than the *djoundi* (soldier); the secretary, the medic, the radio operator if there was one, all engaged in combat. It was not military ritual that made for cohesion. The link that united the *mujahideen* (fighters) was the blood spilled, the cause served, the danger marking their existence. It was also the acquisition of a discipline that, if breached, might entail a punishment of death—for example, for indecent behavior or a weapon in poor condition. It was also the shared background of these men, almost all of whom were coarse, rural folk, trained for a hard life since birth. Each man carried his ration of semolina or couscous; as often as possible, oil, chickpeas, and onions were part of the daily menu, as were sugar and coffee. Mutton and fresh fruit appeared only rarely. The medic did not always have the medications needed for the ill and wounded. Whereas battle was an ordeal, marching was hardly so for a mountain dweller or a peasant. Once he had become a soldier, he was equipped by the ALN with lightweight laced boots, called "Pataugas," made of coarse canvas with rubber soles. His equipment was limited to the minimum. He had no change of clothes. Except for a few food rations and possibly a blanket, nothing counted more than his weapon and ammunition. The unit was moving more or less constantly. In the first place, it had to be present everywhere, at intervals close enough to keep the population aware of its strength.

Truly offensive action always required that the *katiba* (or platoon) move secretly and quickly from one point to another that was as far away as possible, since in guerrilla warfare nothing works like surprise. That meant that marches, except those in the forest, were usually done at night along ridges, in wadi beds, or at best over goat trails. The soldiers slept out in the open. Without warning, an SAS post would be assaulted with mortar; a rural bus would be attacked and burned; or an ambush, carefully set up at a bend in the trail, would patiently wait for the military convoy that informers in the neighborhood had said was likely to pass. A hand-made mine, camouflaged in the dust, would blow up a vehicle, block the convoy line, and set off machine gun fire; then came the assault. At every moment, the FLN leader's concern was to avoid the surprise of an unexpected encounter with the adversary in full strength, or the chance of having his unit spotted out in the open. In that respect, the ALN's conditions of existence varied markedly depending on the period and region considered. In some rocky, wild, or wooded massif, or one still barely penetrated by the French army, an ALN unit would have its cantonments, usually several of them, sometimes in shelters dug in the ground, sometimes in a relatively depopulated hamlet: between two changes of location or two interventions, it could rest there more or less at ease.

In that underground war, the ordinary world was closed off for the fighter, who had no means of escape except death or definitive peace. It was in the years 1956 and 1957 that the ALN (with about sixty thousand men) had its greatest successes against French army troops, thanks primarily to the weapon supplies from Morocco and Tunisia. Things would be different after the construction of the barriers at the Tunisian and Moroccan borders.

Immigration, the Second Front

The 1954 census listed 211,000 Algerians in France; the 1962 census listed 350,000. During the same period, the Ministry of the Interior put out the figure of 436,000. Apart from considerations regarding the delicate problem of nationality and citizenship (who, in effect, was Algerian in 1962, the year of the census in France and of Algerian independence?), one fact became clear: Algerian immigration to France had doubled between 1954 and 1962, the very years of the war.

Most of the immigrants were men age twenty to forty. Of all the upheavals that rural Algerian society had experienced between 1955 and 1962, those that had been caused by the relocation of the population were the most profound and the most consequential. In 1960, half the rural population, that is, a quarter of the total population, was brutally displaced.

In addition to the "displacements," let us mention that one million "men of working age" were unemployed in Algeria. One wage earner out of two worked fewer than one hundred days per year. In total, from 1954 to 1960 only 45,000 new industrial jobs were created, of which 25,000 were in construction and public works. Demographic pressure worsened the process leading to unemployment. The population of Muslim Algerians went from 4,890,000 in 1921 to 8,800,000 in 1954. The active male population increased by 385,000, which means that beginning in 1955 it would have been necessary to create 70,000 new jobs annually for the young men of working age. Since that was far from the case, immigration became the last hope.

The need to replace men of the French contingent sent to fight in Algeria and the renovation of the internal French social structure are the two essential elements allowing us to understand the paradox of the large number of Algerians who emigrated to a country that was at war with them.

In examining the geographical distribution of Algerians in the metropolis, we find that five departments continued to serve as centers of attraction: the Seine; the Nord, with the Lille-Roubaix-Tourcoing agglomeration, which had coal mining and heavy industry; the Moselle, which was experiencing an industrial boom; the Rhône, with Lyons; and the Bouches-du-Rhône, with Marseilles. There were few Algerians engaged in agriculture; most were located in the industrialized regions. Their concentration in the industrial zones only became more pronounced in the years 1948–1955.

The FLN federation in the metropolis retained roughly the same structure as the MTLD, to which a large number of its members belonged. The FLN divided the country into five regions: the Paris region and the west (Paris); the northern and eastern region (Longwy); the central region (Lyons); the southeastern region (Marseilles); and the southwestern region, still unorganized in 1956. The organization had approximately eight thousand members in June 1956, but thanks to an improvement in recruitment the number of militants registered approached fifteen thousand in 1957 (Stora 1992).

The Algerian nationalist movements, applying the principle that the success of an enterprise is a function of the financial means its organizers possess, devoted their efforts to developing and increasing their sources of revenue. The high cost of weapons for the guerrilla forces, the requirements of diplomatic action, and the support of families of militants who had been detained or killed pushed expenses ever higher. The development of the clandestine organization also required installing new cadres paid by the parties.

To take the year 1961 as an example, given the number of paying members in the FLN (150,000) and the MNA (10,000), and the increase in membership fees to 30 francs per person, we obtain the figure of 58 million new francs total (about 400 million 1993 francs) for the single year 1961. Nearly 6 billion centimes raised for the single year 1961! In the seven years of war, approximately 400 million new francs (slightly more than 3 billion 1993 francs) were collected from the Algerian immigrants in France. An altogether substantial contribution, made by the "second front" of Algerian nationalism, a contribution obtained sometimes voluntarily and sometimes by force.

The FLN's Doctrine

The radical pro-independence movement drew its strength from the fact that it was located at the intersection of two major projects: that of the Socialist movement and that of the Islamic tradition.

Of the first aspect, that of the French influence, let us say first of all that the birthplace of the pro-independence movement (Paris in 1926) influenced its subsequent ideological development. The French experience taught the first radical Algerian militants the models of organization and the rudiments of socialist ideology by which they would analyze the situation of their nation and seek to understand the mechanisms and values of an alien world; in the end, that experience put them in contact with industrial and urban models of life. But once they had returned to Algeria, they could not realize their aspirations in the leftist unions or parties, which were dominated by the Europeans.

Regarding that "French influence," let us also note that most of the nationalist cadres in the FLN were rootless, cut off from their social origins and integrated in a way that often led them to become "professional revolutionaries." The movement had few peasant leaders or intellectuals. For the most part, however, these leaders were better educated and better informed than the majority of the Algerian people. Many had gone to French schools, and had completed elementary school. It is an irony of history that the French school system, which saw itself as assimilationist, in fact appears to have opened paths of criticism and liberation.

On the benches of French schools in the Third Republic, the republican credo and the episodes in the "Great Revolution" of 1789 left a lasting impression on the minds of the Muslim Algerians who become nationalists. Their curiosity about France's history was sustained by a hope; they took an interest in it because they felt at a loss about their own freedom. An abstract

France with universal principles was contrasted to the temporal France. That conception continued to be asserted during the time of the Algerian War, as this letter from prison attests, written by Mohammed Larbi Madi, an FLN leader: "I confess to you that I am less and less able to separate the real France from the statutory France. I am seeking the France I learned of in school, and I find it only in a few French people, who, in fact, are embarrassed to be French where the Algerian War is concerned" (Pervillé 1984).

Regarding the second principal factor, that of Islam, we must first of all explain that almost all Algerians in the first half of the twentieth century remained faithful to the religious customs of their ancestors. That fidelity was composed of social relics and habits, an attachment to practices where conformity played as great a role as personal conviction. Pro-independence politics reactivated the religious factor. Islam was both a combat ideology and a social project. The reacquisition of the terms and rights fixed by time, the increasingly lost "paradise" of origins, became more and more vital through religion. The promised pro-independence revolution still had certain characteristics of revolts based on millenarian hopes, or of riots for subsistence. This type of nationalist ideology produced a *refusal to compromise* with the existing world. A central event, independence, was the long-awaited and un-hoped-for moment, the sense of a future and especially of a pure present. The Algerian militants experienced the colonial institutions in which they were destined to live not as founded in reason but as perfectly arbitrary.

The historical merit of the leaders who set off the insurrection in November 1954 was that, through weapons, they unjammed the colonial status quo. They allowed the idea of independence to take on substance for millions of Algerians. But, as the Algerian sociologist Abdelkader Djeghloul (1990) notes, "the war set in motion a process of destruction of the capital of democratic experience and modern politics, which the different political organizations had begun to accumulate before 1954."

The FLN, aware of the contradictions that permeated it, constantly bowed to the tactical emergency: draining off convictions, mobilizing the available energy in the cause of independence, while putting off until later any examination of the particulars. That conception of an undifferentiated society "guided" by a single party implied a particular vision of the nation. After independence, an undecomposable bloc, the nation, was perceived as a unified and unanimous—indissociable—figure.

The theme of the "people united" reduced the threat of external aggression (Gallicization, assimilation) and internal disintegration (regionalism, linguistic particularism). The latter had to do primarily with the "Berber question," which was disregarded in the establishment of national institutions in the postwar period. The recourse to populism increased the rift between the real society, which was socially and culturally diverse, and the one-party political system, forged primarily during the second part of the war, between 1958 and 1962. In December 1957, the murder of Abbane Ramdane (the organizer of the Soummam Congress who had advocated the supremacy of "politicos" over the "military"), ordered by other FLN leaders, opened the way for the "border army's" political domination of Algerian nationalism. After the construction of the barriers along the Tunisian and Moroccan borders, the army was camped outside Algerian territory. Led by Houari Boumédienne, its importance and its role increased as of 1958.

The International Action of the FLN

The Algerian nationalists realized the risk of finding themselves face to face with the formidable French war machine. Very quickly, they became aware of the need to broaden their audience to the international level. The armed struggle was thus combined with political and diplomatic action. The objective was to heighten public awareness throughout the world of the cause of Algerian independence, to interest foreign governments, and to mobilize such international authorities as the UN and the Red Cross. That internationalization of the conflict, desired by the FLN, would allow it to find material support (deliveries of weapons, especially from Eastern countries), and moral support (pressure on France regarding its Algerian policy).

From the beginning of the conflict in January 1955, the members of the Arab League, especially Egypt and Saudi Arabia, directed the attention of the UN's Security Council to the gravity of the situation in Algeria. The Bandung Conference of nonaligned nations in April 1955 heard the communications of the Algerian leaders. In September of the same year, the UN placed the problem of the "events of Algeria" on its agenda for the first time. In July 1956, the Union Générale des Travailleurs Algériens, or UGTA (General Union of Algerian Workers), a union organization linked to the FLN, was recognized by the ICFTU (International Confederation of Free Trade Unions) over its competitor, the Union des Syndicats des Travailleurs Algériens, or USTA (Algerian Workers' Federation of Unions), run by MNA militants. At the same time, the Union Générale des Etudiants Musulmans Algériens, or UGEMA (General Union of Muslim Algerian Students), actively participated in different worldwide cultural groups and developed an intense propaganda campaign (Pervillé 1984).

In that way, the Soummam Congress in August 1956 established the FLN's international actions: "Externally, seek out the maximum material, moral, and psychological support. Among the governments of the Bandung Congress, incite the intervention of the UN as well as diplomatic pressure ... on France." In 1956, when the UN once more put the Algerian question on the agenda (Gadant 1988), FLN delegations set off on a mission: to Eastern Europe (East Berlin, Prague), Western Europe (Bonn, Rome, London), the United States (New York), China, India, and Latin America.

The two events that accelerated and broadened the internationalization of the Algerian conflict were the hijacking of the plane of FLN leaders on October 22, 1956, and the French bombing of the Tunisian village of Sakiet-Sidi-Youssef on February 8, 1958, which had a particularly strong emotional effect on world opinion. On the eve of the Fourth Republic's fall, France found itself brought up on charges by the UN. Atlantic and European solidarity was very uncertain on the question of North Africa.

In waging war against France, the Algerian nationalists set in place "a diplomacy of guerrillas." Very early on, they constructed a diplomatic apparatus, an external presentation that would continue to function effectively after independence in 1962.

5

De Gaulle and the War (1958–1959)

Toward the Fall of the Fourth Republic

On January 11, 1958, a platoon of draftees was ambushed near the Tunisian border. Four soldiers of the contingent were taken across and held captive. Salan appealed for the right to pursue, and the government consented. For its part, the navy seized a Yugoslav freighter, *The Slovenija*, off Oran on January 18. It was transporting 148 metric tons of weapons from Czechoslovakia to the ALN training camps in Morocco.

In fact, a number of countries were now aiding the FLN, including the United Kingdom and the United States, which delivered weapons to Tunisia. On February 8, Salan authorized bombers to pursue an ALN column into Tunisian territory. The village of Sakiet-Sidi-Youssef was targeted. Sixty-nine civilians were killed, one hundred thirty wounded. After that scandal, a true disaster for France's international image, the French government found itself obliged to accept an Anglo-American "goodwill" mission. That mission would study the problem of the French presence in Tunisia, and especially the Bizerte base, which Bourguiba was demanding be evacuated.

During these three months, the ALN pursued its efforts against the Morice Line: the electrified barrier demonstrated its utility and allowed the government to consider shortening the length of military service (to twenty-four months instead of twenty-six in 1957), and to cut back on the army's expenses. That was enough to aggravate the *pieds noirs* and the army, who were united against the parties supporting the government. The *Courrier de la Colère*, run by Michel Debré, who was close to General de Gaulle, lashed out against the use of the UN. On March 13, 1958, police officers violently demonstrated against the government in front of the Palais-Bourbon. On April 15, Félix Gaillard, who appeared to be ceding to the pressures of NATO and the "missionaries" Robert Murphy and Harold Beeley,[1] was voted out by the coalition of Communists, Gaullists, and Poujadists. The government teetered on the brink (Winock 1985).

The crisis of the parliamentary government, the paralysis that set in within the administration, the fall of the franc, linked to France's loss of credit in the world market, the foreign trade deficit, and finally, the climate of powerlessness that was reaching the highest echelons of the state, which faced thorny problems raised by the Algerian War, joined together to make the the Fourth Republic succumb to impotence. In Algeria, there was an ineluctable chain of events. The "centurions" in the paratrooper units, who had sullied their hands, the officers of the bled, and the SAS leaders who dreamed of resuming Lyautey's work, pledged their honor and their word. They could no longer tolerate the constant upheaval in the government, the secret contacts with emissaries of the FLN, the pressure from abroad.

May 13, 1958

On April 26, 1958, several thousand demonstrators marched in Algiers to demand a government of public safety. The previous day General Salan had announced that the army would accept nothing less than the total defeat of the "rebels," followed by the possibility of amnesty. For a month, the Parliament had proved incapable of finding a new premier. On May 8, President René Coty was at a loss and appealed to the centrist Pierre Pflimlin (MRP), who publicly announced his intention to open negotiations with the FLN. Salan officially protested and many leaders of the Europeans of Algeria denounced this "diplomatic Dien Bien Phu." The same day, the FLN announced the execution of three prisoners of the contingent. The situation had gotten away from Robert Lacoste, who was summoned to Paris on May 10.

In Algeria the army remained the sole authority; the "defense committees of French Algeria" and the veterans called for a mass demonstration on May 13 as a tribute to the executed soldiers, and to force a change of government in France. That day had extraordinary

1. Harold Beeley was undersecretary of state at the Foreign Office, in charge of Mideastern affairs; Robert Murphy, who had been President Roosevelt's personal representative in Algiers in 1943, was diplomatic adviser to the U.S. Department of State.

consequences. The students in Algiers who formed the shock troops of the supporters of French Algeria decided to gather on the Forum in front of the offices of the general government to attract the official procession paying tribute to the memory of the executed soldiers. The operation succeeded beyond the hopes of its various protagonists. The mob did not disperse and finally threw itself against the gates of the general government, defended by the state security police (CRS), which Colonel Godard quickly replaced with the paratroopers of Colonel Trinquier's Third Colonial Paratroopers' Regiment (RPC). A GMC truck belonging to this regiment providentially served as a battering ram for the most determined of the rioters, who were swept into the building beside the paratroopers. A few moments later, the high command joined in the revelry. Stunned by the spectacle, Massu and Salan were trapped inside the building by the throng of demonstration leaders: Léon Delbecque, Lucien Neuwirth, Pouget, Pierre Lagaillarde, and Thomazo.

While the Pflimlin government, which was invested at night between May 13 and 14, asserted its will in the metropolis to defend French sovereignty by declaring a blockade on Algeria in reaction to the riot, General Salan took over the unplanned meeting of the "Committee of Public Safety," presided over by General Massu, who was head of the Tenth Paratroopers' Division. This committee, imitated by dozens of others, assigned itself the mission of facilitating General de Gaulle's accession to power. Salan proclaimed as much the next day in front of the crowd. For months, in fact, the rumor had been gaining strength. First a mere murmur, a hypothesis made by the jurist Maurice Duverger in the columns of *Le Monde*, an idea accepted by René Coty, who said he was ready to step down, the solution gradually took root everywhere: only General de Gaulle could pull France out of the Algerian quagmire. Would he be the champion of independence or of steadfastness? A skillful politician, he refused to commit himself so long as he did not have power. What he desired first was "to restore state authority," to join a new government tailor-made for him, endowed with strong presidential power.

General de Gaulle's Return to Power

After several weeks of urging by his supporters, General de Gaulle finally broke his silence by declaring on May 15 that "in the face of the ordeals once more mounting" in the country, he stood "ready to assume the powers of the Republic." The army, whose chief of staff, General Paul Ely, had resigned, no longer obeyed the government. The rumor spread that paratroopers were preparing to land in the metropolis to impose a government of public safety. On May 19, General de Gaulle, in front of the press summoned to the Palais d'Orsay, again asserted that he was at the disposition of the country. He declared that, at sixty-seven, he had no intention of "beginning a career as a dictator." Antoine Pinay, who had been premier in 1952, returned from his visit to Colombey-les-Deux-Eglises on May 22 with the assurance that General de Gaulle had refused to lead a coup d'état fomented by the regular army. But the dissidence moved to Corsica on May 24, where the prefecture was besieged by the men of May 13, Thomazo and Pascal Arrighi in the lead, with the support of the paratroopers of the Eleventh shock troops in Calvi, which disarmed the state security forces (CRS) without encountering resistance. The population of Bastia gleefully witnessed the expulsion of the vice-mayor, who had remained faithful to the government.

At that moment public opinion in the metropolis was convinced that only General de Gaulle could resolve the crisis, eliminate the prospect of civil war, and end the Algerian War. The images of the May 16 "fraternization" in Algiers [when some *pieds noirs* went into the Casbah to demonstrate their sympathy with the indigeneous people, but not their support for independence—trans.] had spread the illusion that the Muslims wanted assimilation. Reconciliation seemed possible.

On the night of May 26–27, the officers' work finally paid off: Pfimlin and de Gaulle exchanged their viewpoints in a building in the park of Saint-Cloud in Paris. The premier was persuaded to resign. The next day, a press release from General de Gaulle announced that he "was beginning the regular process necessary for the establishment of a republican government capable of ensuring the unity and independence of the country." The Europeans of Algeria put out the flags: this time, the general had "spoken," as he had been invited to do on May 11 by the former Pétainist Alain de Sérigny, in his newspaper *L'Echo d'Alger.* The army and the *pieds noirs* witnessed the series of events with joy: Pfimlin's resignation, followed on June 1 by General de Gaulle's investiture by the assembly, despite the success of the demonstration held by the left on May 28 to "defend the Republic."

Between June 4 and 7, General de Gaulle took a trip to Algeria. He gave speeches in Algiers (with the famous "I have understood you"), in Mostaganem (where he shouted "Long live French Algeria," for which he would later be sharply criticized), to Oran, Constantine, and Bône, proclaiming that there were in Algeria "only Frenchmen through and through, with the same rights and the same duties." It was the end of the Fourth Republic and the advent of the Fifth. A new constitution was put forward that gave the president of the Republic a great deal of power. He could dissolve the National Assembly (article 12), he possessed full powers in case of grave events (article 16). In that constitution, the executive power was placed beyond the reach of Parliament, whose role was considerably reduced.

On September 28, 1958, the Europeans and the Muslims (both men and women) voted overwhelmingly in favor of the constitution of the Fifth Republic. And, on October 3 in Constantine, they learned from General de Gaulle's own mouth of the future economic and social transformations that the government had committed itself to financing in Algeria: 15 billion francs in public works projects and urban development, and a gradual program for schooling young Muslims. On December 21, 1958, General de Gaulle was elected president of the French Republic and of the French Community.

General de Gaulle's Algerian Policy

In hindsight, there can be no doubt about General de Gaulle's will. The notorious "I have understood you" was a statement, not a commitment. There was also a "Long live French Algeria" in Mostaganem—but only one. Very quickly, the plan became clear. Between June and December 1958, General de Gaulle asserted his will to bring together the Muslims and the Europeans, but banished from his speeches the expressions "French Algeria" and "integration." Beginning on August 28, a sentence uttered during one of his trips to Algeria put the proponents of French Algeria on the alert: "The necessary evolution of Algeria must come about within the French framework." The *pieds noirs* began to worry. The obligatory departure of military personnel from all the committees of public safety and the notice they received that they were banned from running in the Algerian legislative elections managed to cast suspicion on General de Gaulle's intentions. At the same time, de Gaulle was decolonizing Madagascar and the rest of Africa. The press conference on October 23, 1958, shook the last souls clinging to the memory of May 13 and the Mostaganem speech: General de Gaulle offered "the peace of the brave" with no conditions other than that of leaving the "knife in the cloakroom." But the FLN, which formed the Gouvernement Provisoire de la République Algérienne, or GPRA (Provisional Government of the Algerian Republic), on September 19, 1958, rejected that call for surrender and increased its actions in the metropolis. All the same, 1958 ended with goodwill gestures: a presidential pardon for convicts in the FLN, which in response, liberated French prisoners of war.

On the evening of September 16, 1959, General de Gaulle appeared on television. He explained that eighteen months after his return to power the economy was recovering. But then came the shock:

> Given all the facts in Algeria, national and international, I consider it necessary that the recourse to self-determination be proclaimed beginning today. In the name of France and the Republic, by virtue of the power vested in me by the constitution to consult the citizenry, on the condition that God may grant me life and that the people may listen to me, I commit myself to asking, on the one hand, the Algerians in their twelve departments what they definitively want to be, and, on the other, all the French people to endorse that choice.

General de Gaulle did not set precise deadlines or a timeline for a possible negotiation. He also asserted that, in case of secession, "all arrangements would be made for the exploitation, transport, and shipping of Saharan oil, which, be assured, is the work of the army and in the interests of the West as a whole, whatever may happen."

But, after five years of a cruel war, begun on November 1, 1954, a war that still did not dare speak its name, the taboo word had been uttered: "self-determination." The illusions and ambiguities of General de Gaulle's policy were now dispelled. The head of state, rejecting integration, which he called "Gallicization," offered the Algerians the choice between partnership and secession. That speech of September 16, 1959, marked a true turning point in French political life, which had been poisoned by the Algerian question. It implied open negotiation with the FLN, and granted the Muslim population (who had a nine-tenths majority) the right to decide Algeria's fate. The proponents of French Algeria immediately cried treason and shouted that they had been duped. They pointed out that the principles proclaimed in the days of May and June 1958 were being called into question, since French Algeria was no longer a matter of fact, but was becoming a referendum question. Following that speech, it was not long before the political battle set in motion revealed divisions within the Union pour la Nouvelle République, or UNR (Union for the New Republic): nine Gaullist deputies left the organization on October 8, 1959. On September 19, Georges Bidault created the Rassemblement pour l'Algérie française, or RAF (Union for French Algeria). In it were Christian Democrats as well as "Soustellian" Gaullists and Algerian elected officials favoring integration. The only party that completely embraced General de Gaulle's position was the MRP. During the parliamentary debate of October 6, General Challe spoke of "integral pacification." That was the sign of a hardening of the army, which would not hear of "negotiation" and wanted to continue the war until victory was achieved.

On the other side, on September 28, 1959, the GPRA set out independence as the prerequisite to any negotiation. On November 20, the Algerian nationalists designated Ahmed Ben Bella and his fellow prisoners to negotiate with France, which rejected that suggestion. The Algerians' distrust can be explained in great part by the considerable scope the war had taken on under General de Gaulle's orders.

Under General de Gaulle, the War Continues

In 1959, in fact, General de Gaulle ordered the army to strike its harshest blows against the ALN, to force it to negotiate for the conditions set by France. Salan was transferred to Paris on December 19, 1958; General Challe replaced him.

In 1959, General Challe, with his 500,000 men, launched large-scale combined operations against the guerrilla forces of the ALN. His "hunt commandos" obtained conclusive results and broke up the *katibas* in the *wilayas* of Kabylia and the Aurès, which were already weakened by internal purges incited by the poison introduced by the Second Bureau (the intelligence service). On March 28, Colonels Amirouche and Si Haouès, responsible for *wilayas* III (Kabylia) and VI (Sahara), respectively, were killed in battle. On July 22, a general military action, the "Jumelles" operation, which put more than twenty thousand men on the line, was set in motion in Kabylia under General Challe's control. Nevertheless, "pacification" remained spotty in these "thousand villages" where displaced populations had been assembled by force. But, among the officers, thanks to the major operations of General Challe, the impression prevailed that they were finally gaining ground: the FLN *katibas* were tracked down, and many were destroyed. Small, hungry groups holed up in the most remote of the mountainous massifs. It was a terrible war for the Algerians: more than 2 million peasants were displaced. On April 28, 1959, Michel Rocard, then a young high official, had sent a report to the minister of justice criticizing the resettlement camps in Algeria. And, on January 5, 1960, *Le Monde* published the international commission's report on the internment camps in Algeria, which caused a great stir.

On January 18, 1960, the German newspaper *Süddeutsche Zeitung* published an interview in which General Massu declared that the army, "which has the forces" and "will call on them if the situation requires it," no longer understood General de Gaulle's Algerian policy. A denial was published, but

Massu was summoned to Paris and was replaced on January 22 by General Jean Crépin as commander of the army corps in Algiers. Rumors of insurrection circulated. In April 1959, General de Gaulle had indicated, "The old Algeria is dead, and if you don't understand that, you will die along with it." In early 1960, the Algerian War entered a new phase, that of a Franco-French confrontation in which some would want to "die for Algeria."

6

The Wars within the War (1960–1961)

Barricades Week

The *pieds noirs* knew that, since they were outnumbered nine to one, they were done for if France abandoned them. There had been too many deaths, personal assaults, acts of torture, and summary executions. The day "they" would come down from the Casbah or the mountains would be a massacre. "They" were already beginning to demonstrate in the cities, to the cries of "Long live de Gaulle," "Long live the FLN." For the residents of Bab-el-Oued, on the outskirts of Algiers, or of Oran, it was the beginning of the great panic. The time was past for *tchatche* (chitchat) that scoffed at the *patos* (metropolitans). Without their help, it was "the suitcase or the coffin."

On January 24, 1960, in Algiers, the *pied noir* activists clashed with the gendarmes. A shooting on boulevard Laferrière left twenty dead (fourteen gendarmes and six demonstrators) and one hundred and fifty wounded, before the paratroopers intervened. Pierre Lagaillarde and Joseph Ortiz[1] then set up an entrenched camp in the center of Algiers in the name of French Algeria. General Gracieux's Tenth Paratroopers' Division and the European community did not bring them the hoped-for support. On January 28, Paul Delouvrier, general delegate in Algeria, launched an appeal to the army, the Muslims, and the Europeans, asking them to trust General de Gaulle. On January 29, in a televised declaration (this was at a time when he was

1. President of the Etudiants d'Alger (elected deputy in 1958), and owner of the Forum Bar in Algiers, respectively.

appearing often on television), General de Gaulle formally condemned the rioters and, addressing himself to the army, declared: "I must be obeyed by all French soldiers."

Disheartened, the rioters in Algiers surrendered on February 1 and abandoned the barricades. Joseph Ortiz fled. Pierre Lagaillarde was transferred and incarcerated in the La Santé Prison. The next day, on February 2, the National Assembly, summoned for a special session, granted the government special powers for a year, "to keep the peace and safeguard the state." But "Barricades Week" had revealed some wavering in the command. General de Gaulle ordered changes: General Challe was transferred and replaced by Crépin on March 30. Jacques Soustelle, an ardent supporter of French Algeria, left the government on February 5. And Alain de Sérigny, managing editor of *L'Echo d'Alger*, was charged on February 8 with conspiracy to attack the internal security of the state. The Algerian affair defined the shape of a true Franco-French confrontation under way. General de Gaulle tried to be reassuring, tried to head off the danger. From March 3 to March 5, he undertook a "tour of the canteens" in Algeria, and declared that the Algerian problem would not be settled until after the victory of French arms. He knew, however, that the question was political, and that a resolute change of course was needed.

Initiatives for an End to the War

In spring 1960, the French army believed it had won the war. The "pacified" Oranie was cited as an example: civilian vehicles could now circulate without escort in the rural areas. The leaders of *wilaya* IV, that of Algérois, judged that the battle was lost, and made contact with French officers. They were secretly brought to the Elysée Palace: this would be "the Si Salah affair," named for the nationalist Algerian leader who met with General de Gaulle on June 10, 1960. His real name was Mohamed Zamoum and, unbeknownst to the FLN leaders in Tunis, he intended to undertake direct negotiations with France.

Would there finally be the peace of the brave with those who had fought so fiercely in the field? No. De Gaulle had already begun the negotiation with the FLN "politicos," who possessed the beginnings of international recognition and the notorious "border army," which had never been able to cross en masse the two electrified barriers isolating Algeria from Tunisia and Morocco (as for "Si Salah," he would be executed on June 20, 1961, by special units of the French army).

The first talks between the FLN and the French government opened in Melun on June 25, 1960. They were a failure, but the negotiation created enormous hope in France: peace and the return of the contingent seemed at hand. The Algerian leaders Ferhat Abbas and Lakhdar Ben Tobbal traveled the world to gather votes for the forthcoming UN debate. The recognition of the FLN's representativeness grew among France's African allies. On August 3, 1959, a conference of nine independent African states had invited France to recognize the Algerian people's right to self-determination. In the metropolis, the leftist organizations publicly affirmed their solidarity with the "Algerian cause." On June 2, 1960, fifty-three youth movements, taking a common position for the first time, expressed their desire to see the Algerian War end. On June 9, the Union Nationale des Etudiants de France, or UNEF (National Union of Students in France) met with one of the leaders of a dissolved organization, the Union Générale des Etudiants Musulmans Algériens (UGEMA), and demanded a cease-fire and self-determination. On June 30, the Confédération Générale du Travail, or CGT (General Confederation of Labor), the Confédération Française des Travailleurs Chrétiens, or CFTC (French Confederation of Christian Workers), the FEN, and the UNEF signed a joint declaration affirming their desire to see negotiations truly begin between the French government and the GPRA.

Just as the trial of the members of the FLN's support network, called the "Jeanson network," was getting under way (September 5), 121 major figures made public a "manifesto on the right to insubordination" (published by François Maspero) on September 6, 1960. Several indictments followed. An order published on September 29 in the *Journal Officiel* set out particular sanctions for the signers who were government employees, and a ban on radio or television appearances for all signers. On October 1, fifteen of the accused in the "Jeanson network" were sentenced to ten years in prison. In spite of that act of repression, the antiwar protest movement grew. On October 27, UNEF held an important demonstration at the Mutualité "for peace through negotiation."

In Algeria the Europeans and the high command had their minds made up. The old Algeria was truly dead, and the FLN had recovered through politics and diplomacy all the ground lost by the use of force. On November 4, 1960, General de Gaulle tried to precipitate a resolution of the affair: he used the expression "Algerian Republic" and announced a referendum on the principle of self-determination in Algeria. In December 1960, General de Gaulle's trip to Algeria was the pretext, in Algiers and Oran, for violent demonstrations by Europeans. But the important new fact was the massive uprising of the urban Algerian masses. The demonstrators shouted "Muslim Algeria!" and "Long live the FLN!" Gendarmes and state security troops (CRS) fired on them. The official death toll was 112 Muslims in Algiers.

On January 8, 1961, General de Gaulle's Algerian policy was submitted to a referendum vote. In the metropolis 72.25 percent and in Algeria 69.09 percent voted yes. The success of this referendum, even in Algeria, where only the large cities voted no, demonstrated to the diehards of French Algeria that they had to make haste. Georges Pompidou, in the name of the Debré government, led a secret diplomatic mission to Switzerland. The day after the meeting between General de Gaulle and Bourguiba in Rambouillet, on February 27, a relieved France learned that negotiations would open in Evian on April 7. It was then that General Salan, banished from Algeria, believed that the moment had come to plan a kind of counterrevolution with the help of the regular army, disheartened by the fighting, and of panic-stricken Europeans. Contacts were established in the metropolis. The Organisation Armée Secrète, or OAS (Secret Army Organization), was created. The revolt against General de Gaulle did not mobilize only fanatics dreaming of an impossible Algeria. Barricades Week in January 1960 had already shown the crisis of conscience within certain units.

The Generals' Putsch

During a press conference on April 11, the head of state confirmed his new orientation: "Decolonization is in our interest, and, as a result, it is our policy," said General de Gaulle. Thereafter, a few of the most highly placed people in the French army decided to organize a putsch against him. To hold onto French Algeria, General Challe, who arrived secretly in Algiers, launched the adventure of a coup d'état against the Republic, along with Generals Jouhaud, Zeller, and Salan.

At midnight on Friday, April 21, 1961, the Green Berets in the First Foreign Regiment of Paratroopers marched on Algiers and seized the general government, the airfield, the city hall, and the weapons depot. Within three hours the city was in the hands of the putschists and in the morning Algiers residents could hear over the airwaves this communiqué, which had fallen into the army's hands: "I am in Algiers with Generals Zeller and Jouhaud, and in contact with General Salan to keep our pledge, the army's pledge to keep Algeria."

In Paris the government confined itself to announcing that it was "taking the necessary measures" and decreed a state of emergency. Moreover, the army was not moving to rally behind the putschists. General de Gaulle already seemed persuaded of the failure of the military guerrillas. At five o'clock p.m. in the Council of Ministers, he commented: "The grave thing about this affair is that it is not serious."

But as Salan was being cheered by the mob in Algiers, Paris was in fear of a military coup d'état and a disembarkation in the capital. De Gaulle decided to apply article 16 of the constitution, which conferred nearly all powers on the president of the Republic. On Sunday evening, he spoke on television in a peremptory tone. He denounced "the attempt of a smattering of generals on the retired list," who possessed "a hasty and limited know-how" but saw the world "only through their delirium."

For the soldiers of the contingent, who made up the greater part of the troops stationed in Algeria, the effect was devastating. Heard on transistor radios that the officers had not managed to confiscate, the speech legitimated the resistance of those who opposed their "Challist" officers and led the contingent to go over to the putsch's opposition. In Paris, Prime Minister Michel Debré was nevertheless panic-stricken and appeared on television at midnight to ask everyone to walk or drive out to the airport to prevent a possible action by the putschist generals.

In Algiers on Tuesday, April 26, the generals were cheered one last time on the balcony of the general government. Then Maurice Challe surrendered, as Algiers cried treason. The putsch had failed. On April 28, a decision was made to set up a military high tribunal charged with judging the insurgents. General Marie-Michel Gouraud, then Generals Pierre-Marie Bigot and André Petit were charged and committed to La Santé Prison. On April 30, General Jean-Louis Nicot, a participant, like the others, in the "generals' putsch," was put in state prison. On May 3, the Council of Ministers decided to dissolve the Algiers Bar Association and to ban *L'Echo d'Alger* indefinitely. Former General Zeller fell into the hands of Algiers authorities on May 6. But R. Salan and E. Jouhaud fled and went underground. The OAS now took their place.

The Era of the OAS

From before the April 1961 putsch, the acronym OAS (Organisation Armée Secrète) was known to the European population of Algiers and Oran. It was a small underground movement, probably founded in early 1961, for which Pierre Lagaillarde, who had taken refuge in Madrid, always claimed paternity. All the same, its numbers barely exceeded two or three hundred militants, and it coexisted with other "activist" groups that had tried for several months to mobilize the European population of Algeria via violent action in the cause of French Algeria: the underground Front de l'Algérie Française, or FAF (Front of French Algeria), Réseau Résurrectionpatrie (Homeland Resurrection Network, the movement of the vintner Robert Martel), Etudiants Nationalistes, and so on.

In any case, it was under the acronym "OAS" that, in May 1962, General Paul Gardy, Colonels Roger Gardes and Yves Godard, Lieutenant Roger Degueldre (who had deserted on April 4), Doctor Jean-Claude Perez, and Jean-Jacques Susini chose to meet in Algiers. An "OAS leadership committee" was constituted, and contact was established with Generals Raoul Salan and Edmond Jouhaud, who were wandering in the Mitidja (the great plain of Algérois) under the protection of Martel's networks; General Salan was given the supreme command. A first organization chart, inspired by the example of the FLN and the lessons on psychological action by the military bureaux, was set up by Colonel Godard, a veteran of Vercors, and tasks were distributed. Colonel Godard was assigned intelligence; Colonel Gardes, "the organization of the masses"; Doctor Perez and Lieutenant Degueldre, direct action; Jean-Jacques Susini, propaganda and psychological action.

The objectives were simple: remain faithful to the spirit of May 13, 1958, resist the policy of Algerian "disengagement" conducted by the Gaullist government, construct a new "fraternal and French" Algeria. For the immediate future, the only plan was to prepare for popular insurrection in Algiers and perhaps in Oran. That, it was believed, would break up the negotiation process begun on May 20, 1961, in Evian, between the French government and the FLN. That in turn would construct an insurmountable obstacle to continuing the Fifth Republic's Algerian policy.

The opening of negotiations between the FLN and the French government ushered in a period marked by every sort of danger. The FLN, which wanted to undertake negotiations from a position of strength, increased the number of actions, which produced 133 deaths between May 21 and June 8. During the same period, the OAS practiced a worst-case policy and a series of terrorist actions. The organization's commandos attacked Muslim tradespeople, and government employees in the tax administration, law enforcement, and education. Its control over the European population of Algeria gained strength, and General de Gaulle, who was nicknamed *la Grande Zohra* ["Zohra" is a common woman's name in Arabic—trans.], was now shouted down and despised. The *pieds noirs* were disappointed when they learned he had escaped an assassination attempt on September 9, 1961, at Pont-sur-Seine.

For the OAS the autumn of 1961 was the season of hope. In terms of internal organization the movement had definitively discovered the conditions for its unity and cohesion. The authority of General Salan and his staff was no longer disputed. In the large cities of Algeria, nearly the entire European population, often with tumultuous enthusiasm, awarded the organization its participation or complicity. Large collective demonstrations—the day of pots and pans (September 23), the day of streamers (September 25), the day of traffic jams (September 28)—the proliferation of pirate radio broadcasts, and the "lightning operations" that struck hard at the leaders of political repression, stoked the fire of the *pied noir* common people and mobilized their ardor and their faith. On October 9, 1961, General Salan was able to announce that, before the end of the year, he would possess an army of 100,000 "armed and disciplined" men.

Algerian Determination

The Gouvernement Provisoire de la République Algérienne (GPRA) came into being on September 19, 1958. It was headed by Ferhat Abbas and replaced the Comité de Coordination et d'Exécution, or CCE (Coordination and Execution Committee), the first centralized FLN leadership. A year later, in December 1959, an ALN general staff was instituted, under the direction of Colonel Houari Boumédienne. Despite the contradictions that would emerge between them, these two structures at first planned to be complementary: the task of the GPRA was to win support on the international political scene and to undertake any eventual negotiations with France. The mission of the general staff, by contrast, was to reorganize the ALN, which had been weakened in 1958–1959 by the offensives of the French army quartered on the Moroccan and Tunisian borders.

In record time, the FLN managed to unify or neutralize all the Algerian political organizations and social categories. The hegemony it had achieved over Algerian society constituted its decisive advantage in the final negotiations with the French government. They opened in Melun in 1960, then proceeded in Evian in 1961. The FLN's monopoly on representing the Algerian people was difficult for the French government to accept. It is true that, in the major urban demonstrations, the obvious support for the GPRA in 1960 contributed toward establishing that legitimacy.

In the second part of the war (beginning in 1958, when General de Gaulle came to power in France), a heroic history was forged that presented "a single hero, the people," joined together behind the FLN alone. Isolated individuals were transformed into a collective being, the people, the sole hero for the new nation, and erected into supreme legitimacy as the sole actor of the revolution to be achieved. In *El Moudjahid* (the central newspaper of the FLN) on November 1, 1958, Krim Belkacem wrote, "Our revolution is becoming the melting pot where men of all conditions—peasants, artisans, workers, intellectuals, rich and poor—mingle in such a way that a new type of man will be born from that development." In that version, the violence of the colonizer sets in motion a dynamic of unity, of liberation, by a unanimous people. Frantz Fanon, a West Indian doctor who joined the camp of Algerian independence, theorized that approach in 1959, in his *L'an V de la révolution algérienne* (Year 5 of the Algerian Revolution). He mentions the need for colonial peoples to shake off foreign oppression by force and violence, which were to be used not only as military techniques, but also as an essential psychological precondition for the march toward independence.

All the same, as a result of the strikes of the French military operation led by General Maurice Challe, the *wilayas* of the interior collapsed in the years 1959–1960. On March 27, 1956, after the death of Mostefa Ben Boulaïd, who had escaped from the prison in Constantine a few months earlier and became the victim of a booby-trapped package, dropped by parachute by the French Second Bureau, the guerrilla forces in the Aurès could not manage to reorganize. In *wilaya* III in Kabylia, Amirouche toyed with the idea of a restructuring of the organization that would restore the primacy of the "interior" over the exterior. Si Haouès, the head of *wilaya* VI (the Sahara), shared Amirouche's concerns: he too protested the lack of weaponry and the isolation of the *wilayas* of the interior. But Amirouche and Si Haouès died in an ambush on March 28, 1959. Their deaths further demoralized the fighters in the interior and led to attempts at separate negotiations with France, conducted in particular by Si Salah in June 1960 in the name of those fighters.

All the same, France was isolated at the international political level. The FLN, which continued to fight to maintain the integrity of Algerian territory within the framework of the colonial borders, would prevail politically. On September 5, 1961, General de Gaulle recognized the Algerian character of the Sahara. On March 5, 1962, the Evian negotiations would open, now with the GPRA as the sole interlocutor of the French. In that final phase, when the one-on-one dialogue with the colonial state came to an end, the leadership of the FLN imploded. The image of unity, forged in war, could no longer stand up when the possibility of taking power became imminent.

In late 1960, the GPRA accused the general staff of abandoning the *wilayas* in the interior, and demanded it enter Algeria before March 31, 1961. That set off a crisis. The general staff refused to comply, submitted its resignation on July 15, 1961, and itself installed an interim leadership. During the meeting in Tripoli between August 6 and 27, 1961, of the Conseil National de la Révolution Algérienne or CNRA (National Council of the Algerian Revolution), Ferhat Abbas's replacement by Ben Youssef Ben Khedda aggravated the crisis. The general staff left the CNRA. Ben Khedda failed in his attempt to reorganize the army by dividing the command in two (Morocco and Tunisia). In the test of strength, "the border army" displayed its unity behind its leader, Colonel Houari Boumédienne. It received the support of three of the "historic chiefs" imprisoned in Aulnoy: Ahmed Ben Bella, Mohammed Khider, and Rabah Bitat. Who would lead the future national government, the advent of which seemed very close at hand? The general staff suspected that the GPRA, which was conducting the negotiations with France, wanted to oust it.

In spite of these divisions, the determination of the majority of Algerians to achieve independence was growing. And the repression continued in late 1961, especially for Algerians living in France. As of October 4, an eight o'clock p.m. curfew was imposed on them in Paris. On October 17, thirty thousand protested. The repression, headed by Prefect of Police Maurice Papon, was savage; the police made nearly twelve thousand arrests, and close to two hundred demonstrators were killed. The number of injured was in the thousands (Levine 1986; Einaudi 1991).

In Algeria, the ALN took advantage of the moment when negotiations were getting under way and attempted to reconstitute its forces. But the barrier of the "Morice Line," still impenetrable, precluded any possibility of a military Dien Bien Phu. The guerrilla forces in the interior were exhausted, but the French army abandoned major operations. The "hunt commando" had a period of respite while the contingent was bored to death. On October 2, 1961, General de Gaulle announced "the institution of the sovereign and independent Algerian state via self-determination," and softened his position on the Sahara and the French military bases in Algeria (Lacouture 1986). Indeed, the Saharan question had profoundly hindered negotiations. In the course of the war itself, the Sahara represented a twofold interest for France: it was the location of the first nuclear tests, and the site of major fossil fuel deposits. The Algerian nationalists thus continued to reject any possible partition of the "southern territories" envisioned by the French authorities.

7

The War and French Society (1955–1962)

French Public Opinion: Between Misunderstanding and Indifference

French public opinion became roused, thundered, and fumed. Compared to the war that had just ended in Indochina, the Algerian War seems at first sight to have been a time of intense consciousness-raising and scissions: the turbulence of a strong *pied noir* community and of the army; the antiwar involvement of intellectuals and trade unionists; the glorification of France's "civilizing mission" and the apologia for French Algeria; the vehement denunciation of colonialism and the mobilization for "peace in Algeria." Was the Algerian War a new Dreyfus affair? It would be tempting to believe so, in view of the rage and passion unleashed.

A careful examination of the reality, however, obliges us to nuance this assessment. "The events of Algeria," as they were called at the time, did not really rouse the public until 1956, the year of the "special powers" and the large-scale dispatch of the contingent. The campaigns directed against the use of torture did not truly begin until 1957, in the aftermath of the terrible battle of Algiers (thanks to the Comité Maurice-Audin in particular), that is, three years after the start of the war. The major student demonstrations for peace took place in late 1960, that is, a year and a half before Algerian independence. And the first large, impressive demonstration—more than 500,000 people—to rouse the French people against a war that had lasted for seven long years took place on February 13, 1962, on the occasion of the funeral of the victims of the Charonne metro, all Communist militants (see chapter 8), barely a month before the signing of the Evian accords that put an end to military combat. Let us add that between two hundred and three hundred rebellious or insubordinate soldiers, plus (merely) a few thousand militants, organized networks of sympathy with the Algerians; though they bear witness to the courage of a minority, they did not really constitute "French resistance" to the Algerian War (Hamon and Rotman 1979).

If we consider, among other sources, the changes in the opinion polls between 1955 and 1962, we realize above all that the majority of French people were not as attached as is sometimes believed to maintaining Algeria within the framework of a French nation. As the historian Jean-Pierre Rioux observes, that is no doubt because France had never made colonization "a collective project on a broad social, ideological, and moral plane" (Rioux 1990). Hence the "passive acquiescence" to decolonization. That point of view is shared by another historian, Charles-Robert Ageron: "The colonial impulse was the act of only a small minority.... The colonial vocation was always rare and imperial consciousness came late. Was France colonial?"

In late 1955 the Front Républicain was victorious after an electoral campaign centered on "peace in Algeria." In February 1958, according to a poll by the Institut Français d'Opinion Publique, or IFOP (French Institute of Public Opinion), the Algerian War placed sixth in the concerns of the French people. In October 1960, in an opinion poll in Paris for the newspaper *Afrique-Action*, 59 percent of individuals queried thought that "de Gaulle cannot return peace without negotiating with the FLN"; 24 percent were of the opposite view. Public opinion, eager to be done with the matter, designated the FLN as the Algerian interlocutor.

In May 1962, the filmmaker Chris Marker made *Joli Mai*, a documentary that shows the climate reigning in France on the eve of the Algerian declaration of independence. No one questioned in the film said that the essential event of May 1962 was the end of the Algerian War. And, in another opinion poll in September 1962, when *pieds noirs* and *harkis* were arriving en masse, only 13 percent of French people still maintained that "the Algerian tragedy" constituted a real concern.

In the face of such indifference, we might ask ourselves another question: might that attitude not be explained by a misunderstanding? Did the French know what was going on in the Aurès or in Kabylia? Yes, necessarily, through the mass of soldiers involved in that conflict. Nearly 2 million! Thus thousands of families were affected, accounts and stories were later told at home, in the neighborhood, at the factory, in the village. In addition, there were committees, newspapers, and books that despite the censorship managed to divulge the "secrets" of an unacknowledged war. More than sixty thousand copies of Henri Alleg's *La question*, which brutally raised the problem of torture, were sold in 1958, before being seized (the book would continue to circulate under the counter).

France engaged in a cruel war against the Algerians, but society refused to live in a state of war. The majority of the French people took refuge behind the moral certainty that their country, fresh from fighting for its own liberation in 1944, would not be in the position of oppressing and torturing. To look lucidly at the course of the Algerian War was to run the risk of revisiting the dark Vichy period. That would be reason enough not to speak of either period. One ought not to conclude, however, that the period of the Algerian War was not auspicious for political involvement of all sorts, or that it was not a very important moment for a true cultural "reconstruction."

Cultural Changes, Intellectual Involvement

The years 1956–1957 witnessed the sudden rise of the LP and the introduction of Bach, Beethoven, and Vivaldi to mass consumption. Through the transistor, which would be useful to the contingent in its refusal to follow the generals' putsch, the noise of American rock arrived: Bill Haley, Elvis Presley, the Platters. In terms of film, in 1957 Fellini made *Nights of Cabiria*; in the United States, Brigitte Bardot triumphed with *And God Created Woman*. (Roger Vadim's film earned twice the receipts of *Around the World in Eighty Days*.) However, 1959 was the real turning point for the silver screen. A fine foursome was shown at the Cannes film festival: *Hiroshima mon amour*, *Les cousins*, *Black Orpheus*, and, above all, François Truffaut's *Les quatre cents coups* (*The Four Hundred Blows*), which was awarded the Palme d'Or. The "new wave," an expression coined by the journalist Françoise Giroud for a survey in *L'Express* of eighteen- to thirty-year-olds, was launched. In 1960 the true shock came with Jean-Luc Godard's *A bout de souffle* (*Breathless*): a hero, mirroring the tragedy that France was living through, marches toward his ineluctable destiny. It is clear that everything has been determined from the first sequences, but a carefree atmosphere reigns. *A bout de souffle* tells the story of those who were going to the Aurès, and it became a mirror for youth in the contingent. In these "Algerian years," other images appeared on the small screen. And, on December 14, 1956, readers saw in *L'Express:* "Already at the present time, with the four hundred thousand officially declared sets, RTF [Radiodiffusion Télévision Française, the French television system] touches millions of French people, for whom it has replaced recreation and serious newspapers. In the hands of a government resolved to use it shamelessly in its propaganda, television may become another unsuspected weapon of power."

In 1957, with Alain Robbe-Grillet, the author of *La jalousie* (*Jealousy*) and literary editor at Editions de Minuit, a new literary school called the *"nouveau roman"* appeared. It was Roger Vaillant, however, who won the Prix Goncourt with *La loi* (*The Law*). On the intellectual scene, Jean-Paul Sartre and Albert Camus dominated. Camus, who "ached for Algeria," reasserted his solidarity with the Algerian people as a whole in the columns of *L'Express*, a newspaper with which he had become affiliated in order to be able to support Pierre Mendès-France, the only man, in his view, capable of solving the crisis while avoiding the worst outcome.

With the approach of the January 1956 elections, Camus launched an appeal for a reasonable compromise whereby the French would admit the failure of assimilation, and the Algerian nationalists would renounce their intransigence and the temptation of pan-Arabism. On January 22, 1956, that appeal was repeated in Algiers. But it was too late: already the voices of those holding liberal opinions could no longer be heard. Pacification took on the aspect of war. Camus did not approve of the radical position of the French of Algeria, but he also did not accept the idea of one day becoming an alien in his own country. He went through a period of doubt tinged with bitterness. The writer decided to be silent, once and for all. Only one sentence was needed, however, to bring about his downfall. They were simple words, almost dragged out of him by an Algerian student challenging him during a lecture given in Stockholm after Camus had received the Nobel Prize for literature in December 1957: "I believe in justice, but I will defend my mother before justice." This line, often distorted, was only the touching confession of an intellectual in the grip of the uncertainty and confusion brought on by an outcry on the left. Camus the "traitor" was said to have definitively rallied behind the camp of French Algeria. Camus returned to his solitude. He died in a car accident on January 4, 1960. In contrast to Camus stood Jean-Paul Sartre. On January 27, 1956, the Comité d'Action des Intellectuels contre la Poursuite de la Guerre en Afrique du Nord (Action Committee of Intellectuals against the Continuation of the War in North Africa) held a meeting in Salle Wagram. Jean-Paul Sartre, who was part of the committee, spoke: "The only thing we can and must attempt, but it is the essential thing today, is to struggle beside both the Algerians and the French to deliver them from colonial tyranny." In 1958, he wrote an article on Henri Alleg's *La question*, in which he tried to show that torture was not an epiphenomenon but a necessary method in the type of war France was waging, and that one had to "put an end to these vile and dreary advances." Torture and terrorism, democracy, the rights of a people, and human rights: it was not the time for consensus, but for involvement.

With Frantz Fanon's works, which were banned, "Third World" ideology was asserted: to discover new "wretched of the earth," apart from a French working class still controlled by the PCF, was to rediscover a historical force embodying the revolution. The 1959 Cuban revolution reinforced that conviction. But that swing to extreme involvement, clandestine activities, or marginality was not found exclusively on the left. The refusal to abandon French Algeria pushed many intellectuals, whether *pieds noirs* or metropolitans, toward dissidence against the state, and into the OAS. A few days after the *Manifesto of the 121* in October 1960, a countermanifesto was published, bearing three hundred signatures by political personalities on the right. Among the signers were Roland Dorgelès, André François-Poncet, Henri de Monfreid, Roger Nimier, Pierre Nord, Jules Romains, Michel de Saint-Pierre, and Jacques Laurent. They condemned both the subversive activities of the Algerians and the practice of torture. The "trial of the barricades," which opened on November 3, 1960, was the occasion for the supporters of French Algeria to publicly set forth their theses. The anti-Third World ideologies for "the defense of the West" against "Muslim fanaticism" took shape. Thanks to the Algerian War, a generation, primarily belonging to the student world, entered politics and took a position in one camp or the other. The historian Jean-François Sirinelli, however, raises the question of that "war of writing" conducted by the French intelligentsia:

> Did not the shock of the photos in *Paris-Match*, with its readership of 8 million French people, carry more weight than the words of intellectuals? And, as of January 1959, what was the impact of the televised reports of *Cinq colonnes à la une* [Five Columns on the Front Page], some of which have remained much more firmly rooted in the collective memory than one petition or another by intellectuals? This was a "war of writing," then, but also a period of change, when pictures and sounds continued their rise in power within French society. (Sirinelli 1992)

Sociological Upheaval

In the brief period before and after the Algerian War, a period combining crises, tears, and violence, France set out on the path of the most extraordinary development it had ever known. The French people, who between the change of government and the threats of civil war did not have time to be bored, did not see that upheaval. And yet, the face of the country changed more in fifteen years (1950–1965) than it had in a century.

Between 1950 and 1960 the number of motor vehicles on the road would increase from 2,150,000 to 7,885,400. The number of airline passengers increased fivefold. It was the era of the Caravelle airliner. Trans-Europ-Express began service in early 1957. Between 1950 and 1960 the total length of electric lines doubled. In 1950 there were only 92 kilometers of highways; in December 1955, the Ministry of Public Works planned the construction of 2,000 kilometers of highways, a plan that was realized within ten years. Thanks to the large electrical dams, blackouts became nothing but a bad memory for the French people. And, in 1957, the EDF began work on its first nuclear plant in Avoine, near Chinon. The natural gas processing plant in Lacq began operation in May 1957; thanks to that production, by 1960 there were only 182 coal-fired power stations remaining, of the 546 existing in 1945. The examples could be multiplied: they constitute the signs of a massive introduction into the modern era. The construction of Europe was advancing and took a decisive turn with the signing of the Treaty of Rome. On July 9, 1957, the National Assembly, by a vote of 512 to 239, authorized the ratification of the Common Market treaty.

In these decisive years, France definitively wrested itself from its rural character. But it was ill prepared for that enormous upheaval. The peasant worldview found itself radically transformed. The older and younger generations disagreed on the methods of production, but also on the very values of that society. The majority of peasants' sons who waged war in Algeria came back changed.

The war waged in a distant land awakened and reinforced the peasant's sense of belonging to his "little homeland," his village, his region. For the young peasants, the Algerian War also symbolized the end of economic competition from the colonies. The retreat to the Hexagon favored the rise of regionalism, which manifested itself in the 1970s in Brittany, the Basque region, and Corsica. Now people no longer spoke of peasants, but of farmers. These farmers were supposed to think in terms of productivity, investment, depreciation, and not simply in terms of savings. They confronted a radically different mode of production and sale. The structural transformation that was taking root would "kill" the weakest members. Traditional farming was fated to evolve or to die. "The Dominici affair," which held France enthralled at the time, was also a symbol of the putting to death of the rural world (Gaston Dominici, found guilty of a triple murder in Lurs, was sentenced to death on September 18, 1954).

Finally, in the background of these changes, the urban landscape was profoundly changed. The end of the "Algerian years" meant the construction of tract housing, the growth of the suburbs, and a new (poor?) way of life. The first "hypermarket" (Carrefour) was opened in Sainte-Geneviève-des-Bois in 1963, while the suburbs developed, with Sarcelles (1961) as their emblem. Refrigerators and television sets (800,000 sets in 1958, 3 million in 1962) proliferated in homes.

Within that whirlwind, how could those who had "trudged" through the djebels, or who clung to the memory of a lost land, make themselves understood? Within the euphoria of "progress," everyone gave in to the pressure of the immediate, caught up in the avalanche of novelties and consumption.

How Distant the Aurès

Only ten years after the end of the Occupation, political space was determined less by ideological markers than by sociological ones: the upheaval of the agricultural landscape and end of the peasant world, the urban explosion on the periphery of the cities, the massive intrusion of television into homes, the beginning of the nuclear revolution. That nascent modernity concealed the issues born of the "Algerian years."

The attachment to the brand new comfort that this old country now enjoyed, the memory of two gigantic blood-lettings (the two world wars), whose traces were still visible, if not on the French landscape, then at least on every village square: everything joined together to lead to an entirely new approach to the problems of a war waged outside the Hexagon. Society knew, but was content to keep, the secret of an undeclared war. The relation to death was wholly private and excluded from public life: no funeral orations, no specific tombstones, no particular inscriptions on city and village monuments celebrated the merit of those killed "over there." That tendency to exclude and conceal death led people to renounce the effort to come to terms with that war. The age of consumer society and the society of the spectacle had sounded.

At the same time, the war served as a revelation. What was being born under the thick mask of indifference was hostility toward the man living in or coming from the south. That mysterious "other" had resisted, had wanted to obtain a nationality of his own; here was a man whose life, hopes, and history no one took the trouble to find out about. How very distant and strange the Aurès and their inhabitants seemed to the French. With the Algerian War, colonial racism began its crossing of the Mediterranean.

8

The Terrible End of War (1962)

The Franco-French War

In late 1961, the government of the Fifth Republic seemed to be running up against increasingly serious obstacles in the application of its new policy. The negotiations with the FLN ran aground over the Saharan question and had to be momentarily suspended. At the National Assembly on November 8, 1961, during the debate on the Algerian budget, several deputies in the center and on the right defended the idea of the OAS's representativeness and of the government's need to take its presence into account. The next day, during a study of the military allocations, the so-called Salan amendment received eighty votes. In certain circles of the police, the army, and the administration, it was well known that the organization benefited from multiple and sometimes significant acts of complicity. According to Police Superintendent Jacques Delarue, who was part of the struggle against the OAS, "we even know there was a mole in the Elysée Palace."

But, within Algeria itself, the OAS had to face repression conducted by law enforcement—hesitant at first, then increasingly firm—and especially, the actions of the parallel police networks (the notorious "secret agents" [barbouzes], who began to arrive in Algiers in October 1961) and the FLN networks. Often working together, they carried out a great number of individual attacks, answered terror with terror, and, in particular, resorted to abductions. The climate of violence became more acute, but, in the game of terrorism and counterterrorism, the OAS saw its very small ranks of combatants dwindle and its actions became more radical.

Lagging behind Algiers but using the same means, the OAS in Oran also got involved in terrorism, in spectacular strikes (bank or business holdups to procure funds), and in bloody expeditions against the Muslim Algerians. Thus, on January 13, 1962, six OAS men disguised as gendarmes appeared at the Oran prison where they got three FLN militants who had been sentenced to death released to them. They executed them a few moments later. The next day four other FLN prisoners escaped. The OAS gave chase, found them, and executed them. The activist organization produced pirate radio broadcasts, and, on February 6, published twenty thousand copies of a counterfeit issue of *L'Echo d'Oran*, condemning "de Gaulle's policy of abandonment." The OAS general staff could no longer count on the government to yield. The dream of a repetition of a "May 13"-type operation was now out of the question. Only one option remained: armed insurrection, which by maintaining a revolutionary situation might prevent the conclusion of the negotiations under way with the FLN.

In France the fresh outbreak of plastic explosive attacks in January and February 1962 may serve to illustrate that rise in violence: 40 attacks between January 15 and 21 (including 25 in the Paris region, 18 on the single night between January 17 and 18), 33 between January 22 and 28 (23 in the Paris region), and 34 between February 5 and 11 (27 in the Paris region). In Algeria, 801 attacks by the OAS, the FLN, and the anti-OAS were recorded between January 1 and 31, 1962, causing 555 deaths and 990 injuries, with 507 attacks recorded in the first two weeks of February, causing 256 deaths and 490 injuries (Kaufer 1986).

On February 5, 1962, General de Gaulle referred to these "incidents" in a speech and declared that, "as odious as they might be," they had only a "relative" importance. Nevertheless, he stated clearly that the OAS agitators "must be cut off and punished." The metropolis was proving increasingly hostile to the OAS: did these European insurgents want a French Algeria, or a *pied noir* Algeria on the model of South Africa?

The attack in André Malraux's apartment building, which cost a four-year-old girl, Delphine Renard, her eyesight, came on the heels of an attack on Jean-Paul Sartre and incited the indignation of a French public that had lost its patience. The left denounced "the fascist danger" and, on February 8, called for a demonstration of "republican defense."

At the appeal of the unions (the CGT, the CFTC, the FEN, and the UNEF) and the parties (the PCF, the Partie Socialiste Unifié, or PSU [Unified Socialist Party], and Jeunesses Socialistes [Socialist Youth]), five processions formed, headed for the Place de la Bastille. They collided with an imposing deployment of police. That morning, the Ministry of the Interior had reminded everyone that all demonstrations were banned on public thoroughfares. As during the Algerian demonstration on October 17, 1961, Maurice Papon was the prefect of police in Paris who coordinated the actions of law enforcement. That evening, the Charonne metro station became part of the collective memory of the left (as the Wall of the Federates had once been). The mob, panic-stricken, rushed into the metro entrance; a half-closed gate caught up the bodies of those who stumbled. On that human pileup, which completely blocked the entrance, witnesses saw a group of helmeted policemen "set to work." These officers struck at the pile with *bidules* (long wooden billy clubs, literally "thingamajigs"), and threw a café table and sections of cast iron torn from the fences protecting the trees. Amidst the shouts, the moans, the layers of tangled injured, eight dead bodies were pulled out. On Tuesday, February 13, the funerals of the eight victims of Charonne were attended by an impressive crowd estimated at 500,000. A general strike that day stopped trains, closed schools, and left the newspapers silent (Alleg 1981).

When on March 7, 1962, the new Evian talks began, the OAS commandos escalated their boldness and violence on Algerian soil: there were bazooka attacks on the barracks of mobile gendarmes, and booby-trapped cars caused havoc in Muslim neighborhoods. Horror followed upon horror. Algiers, and especially Oran, lived with death, as it had once lived with the Bubonic plague, as depicted in Albert Camus's novel *La peste*. On March 15, 1962, in Algiers, an OAS group murdered six leaders of the social education centers, including Mouloud Feraoun, a writer and friend of Camus. He had noted in his journal on February 28: "I have been locked inside my home for ten days to escape the Arab-bashing."

The Evian Accords and the "Scorched-Earth" Policy

On March 19, 1962, a cease-fire was proclaimed in Algeria. It was "peace" at last! The news spread over the telephone wires and the radio waves. Krim Belkacem affixed his elaborate signature next to those of Louis Joxe, Robert Buron, and Jean de Broglie, the negotiators named by General de Gaulle. Four weeks earlier, in a Council of Ministers, after Louis Joxe had given an account of the conclusion of the secret negotiations with the GPRA, Prime Minister Michel Debré had declared: "We are reaching the end of a painful ordeal. Malraux spoke of victory, but it is instead a victory over ourselves. Now everything will depend on what France will become" (Stora 1991a).

In Evian, the negotiators for the GPRA made a few concessions regarding the rights of Europeans (dual nationality for three years, then the option of Algerian nationality or the status of privileged resident alien), control of the

Sahara (preferential rights for French companies in the distribution of research and exploitation permits for six years, payment for Algerian fossil fuels in French francs), and the military bases (Mers el-Kebir was to remain French for a period of fifteen years and the installations in the Sahara for five years). In exchange, France declared itself willing to offer its economic and financial aid to independent Algeria, in particular, by continuing to carry out the Constantine plan launched in 1958, and to develop cultural cooperation. On October 3, 1958, General de Gaulle had chosen Constantine, a Muslim city for the most part, to make known the main lines of a new five-year economic and social program. He had then enumerated the provisions decided upon: the granting of sixty-two thousand acres of new land to Muslim farmers; the establishment of major metallurgical and chemical blocks; the construction of housing for a million people; regular employment for 400,000 new workers; schooling for two-thirds of children, with, in the next three years, schooling of all Algerian youth; and salaries and benefits equal to those in the metropolis.

Of the 93 pages of the Evian accords, of its 111 articles complemented by countless parts, sections, and appendices, the metropolis retained two passages in particular. First: "a cease-fire is established. It will put an end to the military operations and to the armed struggle throughout Algerian territory at twelve hundred hours on March 19." The war was thus acknowledged at the moment when the treaty marking its end was signed. And second: "The French citizens of Algeria will participate in public affairs in a fair and genuine manner. . . . Their property rights will be respected. No measure of dispossession will be taken against them without their being granted equitable compensation that has been fixed in advance."

But the signing of the Evian accords did not mark the end of the Algerian war (Ageron 1991; Pervillé 1991). In the aftermath of the negotiations between the GPRA and the French government, the OAS leaders, in a tract on March 21, 1962, proclaimed that the French forces were considered "occupation troops" in Algeria. The activist supporters of French Algeria took control of Bab-el-Oeud. They transformed the district into an enormous Fort Chabrol and attacked military trucks. The "battle of Bab-el-Oeud" produced 35 deaths and 150 injuries.

In the morning of March 26, the OAS command declared a general strike in greater Algiers. It appealed to the Europeans to gather, on principle unarmed, on the Glières plateau and at Laferrière Square. The objective was to then head for Bab-el-Oued to break through the encirclement around the district. Lieutenant Ouchène Daoud led the blocking of rue d'Isly, banning access to Bab-el-Oued from the center of Algiers. The orders from Paris were clear: do not yield to the disturbance. When

Ouchène Daoud and his superiors asked under what conditions they might make use of their weapons if necessary, the reply came to the headquarters of the Tenth military region: "If the demonstrators persist, open fire." At 2:45 p.m., a burst of Bren gun fire rattled toward the troop from the balcony of 64, rue d'Elsy. The regiment's command post gave the order to reply. At the corner of boulevard Pasteur and rue d'Isly, the machine gun mowed down the demonstrators. Forty-six dead and two hundred wounded (twenty of whom did not survive) were counted, almost all Algiers civilians. After the fusillade of rue d'Isly, the OAS began to recede. In April 1962, the Europeans of Algeria began to leave their native land en masse, headed for the metropolis (Lacouture 1985).

While Algiers was enduring these bloody hours, Oran was in a state of shock: General Edmond Jouhaud and his assistant Camelin were under arrest.

On March 28, Abderrahmane Farès, president of the Algerian "provisional executive body" set in place after Evian, settled with his team from the "administrative complex of Rocher-Noir." On April 8, a massive referendum vote held by the Elysée Palace (90.7 percent of voters approved the referendum, with 24.4 percent of eligible voters not participating) gave the president of the Republic the legal capacity "to establish accords and take measures on the subject of Algeria, on the basis of the government declarations of March 19, 1962." Far from appeasing the OAS command, the results of that referendum pushed it toward a frenzied escalation, the "scorched-earth policy."

In Oran on the morning of April 24, the OAS attacked a clinic belonging to Doctor Jean-Marie Larribère, a Communist militant who was very well known in the city. Two women, one of whom had just given birth, managed to escape the complete destruction of the building. The attacks by plastic explosives and machine gun occurred at a deadly pace. Mobile gendarmes were assaulted, and armored vehicles counterattacked with 20 and 37 mm cannons. Strikes occurred at random against buildings inhabited by Europeans. Airplanes joined the fray with their heavy machine guns. On April 23, 1962, the Oran Bar Association published a press release denouncing "these attacks against a civilian population, which would be contrary to the The Hague convention in wartime... . In peacetime, and among French people, they boggle the mind" (Paillat 1972).

In spite of OAS orders that prohibited the Europeans from leaving the country (the travel agencies were under surveillance), the exodus toward the metropolis began. On April 15, *Le Chanzy* disembarked a first contingent of the "repatriates" coming from Oran. The organization's attacks did not end. Terrorism can even be said to have been increasing in violence, with the murder of individual Muslims, manhunts, plastic bombs going off, mortar fire.

In late April, a booby-trapped car exploded in a market that was much frequented by Algerians in that holy month of Ramadan. It was the first of its kind (on May 2, the same method was repeated: a booby-trapped car exploded in the port of Algiers, causing 62 deaths and 110 injuries, all among Muslims).

In Oran in May, ten to fifty Algerians were slaughtered by the OAS on a daily basis. Things became so ferocious that the people who were still living in European neighborhoods left them in haste. They all barricaded themselves, protected themselves as they could. Some Muslims left Oran to join their families in the villages, or in cities that did not have a large European population. Others organized themselves into a sort of autonomous group in the Muslim enclave. Political representatives of the FLN surfaced, and a means of survival was set in place (supply operations, garbage collection). But, in this deadly cycle that went on and on, with bursts of automatic weapon fire reverberating here and there, day and night, what was to become of the European population, especially after the proclamation of independence, when the ALN troops would penetrate the city? The FLN leaders found it increasingly difficult to hold back an exasperated Muslim population which wanted to strike back.

However, the OAS leaders who were still free knew they had lost the struggle. The French army did not swing in their favor and morale was at its lowest after the arrests of Salan, Jouhaud, and Degueldre, and the failure of an OAS underground force in the Ouarsenis. Moreover, there was nothing to be expected from abroad. Then, too, there was the continuing exodus, the hemorrhaging. Beginning in late May, eight to ten thousand people, those who would later be called *pieds noirs*, left Algeria, hastily taking their most precious possessions with them.

June 7, 1962, was one of the culminating points of "the scorched-earth policy." The "Delta commandos" of the OAS burned the Algiers library, and set its sixty thousand volumes ablaze. In Oran, the city hall, the municipal library, and four schools were destroyed by explosives. More than ever, the city, where total anarchy reigned, was split in two: not a single Algerian moved around the European city any longer. The decision by Paris to open the border to ALN fighters stationed in Morocco caused even more panic among Europeans. In a state of fantastic disorder, Algeria was emptied of its managers and technicians. Worried about the general paralysis threatening the country, A. Farès decided to negotiate with the OAS through the intermediary of Jacques Chevallier, former vice-mayor of Algiers.

The accord with the FLN, signed in Algiers on June 18 by Jean-Jacques Susini in the name of the OAS, was rejected in Oran. On June 25 and 26, in a city covered with smoke from fires, OAS commandos attacked and robbed six banks. Following the announcement of Colonel Dufour (former leader of the First Foreign Regiment of Paratroopers and head of the Oranie OAS) that the OAS should lay down its weapons, it was making preparations to flee. On trawlers loaded down with weapons (and money), the last OAS commandos went into exile. During this time, the Europeans leaving Oran reached the scope of a tide of humanity. Thousands of distraught, bewildered people waited for the boats in a state of total destitution. Now that Algeria had been transformed into a hell, they had to flee as quickly as possible a country to which they would remain attached with every fiber of their being.

The Abandonment of the *Harkis*

In the June 1962 state of emergency, the embarkation of the *pieds noirs* took on the appearance of a stampede. But the ones who were truly forgotten, truly absent from that hasty exodus, were the pro-French Muslims, who would be designated by the general term *harki*. The first *harka* (an Arab word meaning "movement") had been formed in the Aurès in November 1954.

Before March 19, 1962, SAS officers had been preoccupied with transferring those who were threatened to the metropolis. But a telegram (no. 125/IGAA) of May 16, 1962, ordered them to stop: "The minister of state—Louis Joxe—calls on the high commissioner to remember that all individual initiatives tending to settle the Muslim French in the metropolis are strictly prohibited." Another directive from the same state minister, dated July 15, 1962, stated: "The auxiliary troops landing in the metropolis in deviance from the general plan will be sent back to Algeria." These officers later said: "We lost our honor with the end of that Algerian war" (Le Mire 1982).

How many of these "auxiliaries" to the French army were there? On March 13, 1962, a report transmitted to the UN assessed the number of pro-French Muslims at 263,000 men: 20,000 career soldiers; 40,000 soldiers of the contingent; 58,000 *harkis*, auxiliary units formed from the civilian self-defense groups, sometimes promoted to "hunt commandos," units that, provided at a ratio of one per military sector, were constituted in Kabylia, in the Aurès, and in the Ouarsenis; 20,000 *moghaznis*, police units constituted at the local level and placed under the orders of the SAS leaders; 15,000 members of the *groupes mobiles de protection rurale*, or GMPR (mobile groups of rural protection), later called mobile security groups and assimilated to the state security police (CRS); 60,000 members of civilian self-defense groups; and 50,000 elected officials, veterans, and functionaries.

The geographical area of recruitment, enlistment, and participation in the activities and operations of the French army by the auxiliary Muslim units was not confined to a single French department of Algeria, but extended into every region, constituting a heterogeneous space. Were these Algerians "manipulated" by French officers? Did they mobilize themselves spontaneously for the defense of French civilization in Algeria? Was that involvement only an aspect of the "wars" families waged among themselves, within a single village (one relative in the guerrilla forces, another in the *harkas*)? No doubt there was a bit of all that (Roux 1991).

In fact, the history of the *harkis* is inseparable from the fate suffered by the Algerian peasantry during the Algerian War. The work of Abdelmalek Sayad and Pierre Bourdieu (1963) has revealed the profound upheavals that marked traditional rural society during these years of war: the massive displacement of populations (more than 2 million rural people), the impoverishment, the marked disaffection with the peasant condition, the shift from a barter economy to a market economy, the withering of the peasant spirit, the high value given to nonagricultural jobs. The new psychological fragility born of social poverty and rootlessness made the concern to preserve one's patrimony, one's land, all the more keen. That dimension explains in great part the enlistment in the *harkas* and the rise in the ALN guerrilla forces: one's land had to be protected or recovered. At first sight what was at issue was not positive loyalty to a flag (French or Algerian). Violence, murder, the "settling of accounts" (sometimes within peasant families themselves), in short, the dynamic of war, hardened behavior and commitments. Then people got caught up in a chain of events. The Algerian nationalists needed to denounce the existence of "collaborators" to legitimate their conception of the unanimous nation; French officers needed *harkis* to show the loyalty of the now "pacified" native populations. In either case, the Algerian peasants found themselves transformed against their will into "faithful servants of France" or "absolute traitors" to the Algerian homeland. Several tens of thousands of them were massacred after Algerian independence, while others encountered enormous difficulties in becoming integrated into French society, living as outcasts.

The Algerian Victory, and the Divisions

The Evian accords marked a new stage in Algerian history. Independence was won, victory imminent. Yet, paradoxically, the period that followed the cease-fire of March 19, 1962, showed the weakness of the ALN-FLN within the country. The FLN leaders in the territory did not manage to control financial dealings, and a considerable volume of lands and buildings changed hands in the mass exodus of the European minority. Within a few weeks, the number of Algerian artisans and small tradespeople rose sharply, from 130,000 to 180,000. A few initiatives here and there attempted to check the speculative process, particularly via the creation of "management committees" on the lands left vacant by the colons. But, above all, the *wilayas* of the interior, which had no more than a few thousand "djounouds" before the Evian accords, subsequently "swelled" in record time.

The crisis within the FLN erupted publicly at the Tripoli Congress, held between May 25 and June 7, 1962. Nevertheless, a program was adopted unanimously there, almost without discussion, by the "Parliament" of the victorious nationalist movement, the CNRA (Harbi 1980).

In its principal points, the program subscribed to the populist ideology already expressed at the Soummam Congress in August 1956:

> The creative effort of the people has manifested itself largely through the organs and instruments it has forged for itself under the leadership of the FLN, for the general conduct of the war of liberation and the future construction of Algeria. The unity of the people, national resurrection, the prospect of a radical transformation of society, such are the primary results that have been obtained as a result of seven and a half years of armed struggle.

On the political level, the primacy of the FLN was reaffirmed against the GPRA, "which, with its birth, became confused with the FLN leadership, and contributed to weakening both the notion of the 'state' and that of the 'party.' The amalgam of state institutions and of FLN authorities has reduced the latter to nothing more than an administrative apparatus." This was a barely veiled attack against the GPRA, which had negotiated the Evian accords: "The Evian accords constitute a neocolonialist platform that France is preparing to use to establish and harness its new form of domination."

Thus, one current, formed around Ben Bella, and especially, around the general staff of the ALN, headed by Houari Boumédienne, stood opposed to the leaders of the GPRA: it proposed to transform the FLN into a party, and to create a political bureau. For their part, Ben Khedda and his friends wanted to preserve the GPRA until things were set up in Algiers. At night, between June 5 and June 7, 1962, Benkhedda left the CNRA without warning. The other participants dispersed in the confusion. On June 30, on the eve of the referendum, the GPRA met in Tunis, minus Ben Bella, who had hastily gone abroad. The GPRA then decided to dissolve the general staff, to officially dismiss Colonel Boumédienne and his two assistants, Ali Mendjli and Kaïd Ahmed. It ordered the *wilayas* "to tolerate no infringement on its authority by irresponsible elements whose activities can only culminate in fratricidal struggles."

Each faction had armed forces, militant troops on which it could rely. The war against the colonial power was followed by the war between factions of the FLN. Safe within its stronghold of Ghardimaou, on the border of Tunisia and Algeria, the general staff called the GPRA's decision "illegal" and "null and void." On June 28, 1962, Colonel Houari Boumédienne ordered his men—21,000 in Tunisia, 15,000 in Morocco—"to prepare to enter Algeria, in units formed within the region designated by the general staff." The first men and their heavy equipment would penetrate the country in the days that followed. The alliance between Houari Boumédienne and Ahmed Ben Bella managed to take root in the acquisition of power. Boumédienne finally thrust aside Ben Bella in a military putsch on June 19, 1965.

Independence

"Do you want Algeria to become an independent state cooperating with France under the conditions defined by the declaration of March 19, 1962?" On Sunday, July 1, 1962, in Algeria, 6 million voters answered yes to that question; a mere 16,534 said no.

The results, made public on July 3, showed a yes vote from 91.23 percent of registered voters, 99.72 percent of those actually participating in the poll. General de Gaulle drew the lesson of that predictable result. During a brief ceremony on July 3, at the administrative complex of Rocher-Noir, near Algiers, Christian Fouchet, high commissioner of France, handed over to Abderrahmane Farès, president of the "provisional executive body" formed after the Evian accords, the general's letter, which recognized Algeria's independence:

> France has taken due note of the results of the July 1, 1962, poll on self-determination and the application of the declarations of March 19, 1962. It has recognized the independence of Algeria. As a result, and in accordance with section 5 of the general declaration of March 19, 1962, the powers relating to the sovereignty over the territories of the former French departments of Algeria are, beginning this day, transferred to the provisional executive body of the Algerian state. In this solemn circumstance, Mr. President, I want to express to you in all sincerity the good wishes that I, along with France as a whole, have for Algeria.

"Seven years are enough!" That slogan, true for the majority of Algerians, spread through the cities and the countryside. They demanded an end to the bad times. The excesses, the bloody purges, the fighters-to-the-end, and the rumors of differences at the top were troubling. But nothing could spoil the return of peace and freedom. After the war, after the suffering and humiliation, victory entitled them to be joyful, and hence to forget.

Oran, the Final Tragedies

With the official end to the war, did the blood finally stop flowing?

On July 5, 1962, there was a tragic event in Oran. A mob from the Muslim neighborhoods invaded the European city at about eleven o'clock a.m. The first shots were fired. No one knew the causes of the gunfire. According to the reporters from *Paris-Match* present on the scene, "there is talk of an OAS provocation, of course, but that seems unlikely. There are no commandos left, or almost none, among the Europeans who stayed in Oran after July 1, which, in fact, is considered a date at least as fateful as 1940." In the suddenly empty streets, the hunt for Europeans was on.

On boulevard du Front de Mer, there were several dead bodies. Near boulevard de l'Industrie, shots were fired at motorists, one of whom was hit and collapsed at the wheel as his car crashed into a wall. One European woman who had come out onto her balcony on boulevard Joseph-Andrieu was killed. At about three o'clock p.m., the gunfire increased in intensity. Near the "Rex" cinema, one of the victims of that massacre could be seen hanging from a meat hook. The French, panic-stricken, sought refuge where they could, in the offices of *L'Echo d'Oran*, or fled to the Mers el-Kebir base, held by the French army.

During that time, General Katz, commander of the military installation in Oran, was having his lunch at the La Sebia air base. Alerted of the events, according to the historian Claude Paillat, he replied to an officer: "Let's wait until five o'clock to decide what to do." The French troops stood by, weapons at their feet, since the Ministry of Armies had prohibited them from leaving their quarters. At precisely five o'clock, the gunfire quieted down. In the days that followed, the FLN regained control of the situation and proceeded to arrest and execute rioters.

The toll from July 5 was high. According to the figures given by Doctor Mostefa Naït, director of the hospital complex in Oran, 95 people, including 20 Europeans, were killed (13 were stabbed to death). In addition, 161 were wounded. The Europeans told of scenes of torture, pillaging, and, above all, abduction. On May 8, 1963, the secretary for Algerian affairs declared at the National Assembly that 3,080 people had been listed as abducted or missing: 18 were found, 868 freed, and 257 killed (throughout Algeria, but especially in Oranie).

So ended the French presence in that "jewel of the empire," French Algeria. On July 12, 1962, Ahmed Ben Bella moved into Oran. Another battle began—the battle for power in Algeria.

On the other side of the Mediterranean, those who were henceforth to be called *pieds noirs* were preoccupied with finding their place in French society and with seeking out the sites of the lost memory of French Algeria. The "patroness" of Oran, Our Lady of Santa-Cruz, accepted the hospitality of the humble church of Courbessac, near Nîmes.

9

A War's Toll

Human and Material Losses

In his press conference on April 11, 1961, General de Gaulle declared: "Algeria is costing us—that is the least one can say—more than it is bringing in.... Now our great national ambition has become our own progress, the real source of power and influence. The fact is, decolonization is in our interest, and, as a result, it is our policy." We know, particularly through the work of the historian Jacques Marseille (1989), that, as the Algerian War was unfolding the colonial question was tending to become "a burden" for certain branches of French capitalism. The development of new forms of production, the pressure of international competition, the end of the peasant world, and the opening-up of the economy to the outside were all shifts that led certain participants in economic life to want to stop squandering considerable capital in the empire without any benefit. Yet there was an opposition between the "political" realm, which intended to maintain the strength of an empire, and the "economic" realm, which was more concerned with yield and efficiency.

That is why the Algerian War was still more costly to the French economy, even operating as a brake on the rapid modernization of society as a whole. That dimension cannot be included within the "accounting" of the war. The dispersed nature of the budgetary allocations and the indeterminate criteria for calculation make any assessment of the financial costs very problematic. In a study published in *Le Monde* on March 20, 1962, Gilbert Mathieu gave an estimate, solely for the duration of the war, of between 27 and 50 billion francs, that is, 10 to 18 percent of the gross domestic product of 1961. But ought we to consider only the military expenses incurred between 1954 and 1962? The various contributions of the French treasury to the Algerian budget, the "Constantine plan," which represented a financial commitment on the order of 2.5 billion new francs, and the responsibility assumed for the hundreds of thousands of repatriates between 1962 and 1965, estimated at a cost of 7.2 billion, must also be taken into account. And, above all, if we wish to establish an economic and social toll, how are we to "tally up" the cost of that war for Algerian society, via the massive displacement of populations, the impoverishment of the peasantry, and the destruction of economic potential by the "scorched-earth" policy?

During the early part of the war (1954–1958) the French army was content to string together long lists in press releases, conceived as veritable psychological campaigns of demoralization and attrition against the ALN/FLN. Its newspaper *Le Bled* regularly published lists of "rebel losses" in men and equipment (lists reprinted by part of the mainstream press). Hence, General Salan announced that for the first week of February 1957, "more than seven hundred rebels have been killed, and nearly two hundred taken prisoner; four machine guns, two mortars, several pistols, and five hundred war rifles were recovered during battles." For the same month, Robert Lacoste stated that "2,512 rebels [were] killed." This was the great era of an imminent and ineluctable military victory, the "last quarter hour." Let us note in passing that the number of wounded and captives was much lower than the number of dead.

The French army did not publish figures on its military losses. For example, there is not one line in *Le Bled* on the deadly ambush in Palestro on May 18, 1956, during which nineteen French soldiers were mutilated and massacred. It was not until General de Gaulle's press conference on October 23, 1958, that the first official war figures appeared:

You should know that, in the last four years in Algeria, about fifteen hundred civilians of French descent have been killed, whereas more than ten thousand Muslims—men, women, and children—have been massacred by the rebels, almost always by having their throats slit. In the metropolis, for the seventy-five people of French descent who lost their lives in attacks, one thousand seven hundred and seventeen Muslims fell to the killers' bullets or knives. How many lives, how many homes, how many harvests did the French army protect in Algeria! And to what slaughter would we be condemning this country if we were stupid and cowardly enough to abandon it! That is the reason, the merit, the result, of so many military actions in the form of men and exertions, of so many nights and days on guard, of so many reconnaissances, patrols, skirmishes. Alas! Seventy-seven thousand rebels have been killed in the fighting.

In his press conference on November 10, 1959, General de Gaulle gave different indications of the number of casualties. At that date he listed, "since the beginning of the rebellion," 171,000 dead: 13,000 French soldiers, 145,000 "rebels," 1,800 "civilians of French descent," and 12,000 Muslim civilians.

Thus, in one year, between October 1958 and November 1959, more than 6,000 French soldiers and 68,000 "rebels" were supposedly killed, that is, as many as during the first phase of the conflict. That hardly seems likely, despite the ferocity of the military campaigns (the "Jumelles" operations). A year later, on November 25, 1960, General de Gaulle declared to the managing editor of *L'Echo d'Oran*, "We have already killed 200,000, we are killing another 500 every week."

At the time the Evian accords were signed in March 1962, the total figure of French losses in Algeria was estimated by military authorities as follows:

—Killed: 12,000, including 9,000 of French descent, 1,200 legionnaires, and 1,250 Muslims. In addition, the auxiliary forces count 2,500 dead.

—Wounded: 25,000, including 18,500 of French descent, 2,600 legionnaires, and 2,800 Muslims, in addition to 3,500 wounded among the auxiliary forces. Moreover, accidents produced 6,000 dead, including 4,500 of French descent, 800 legionnaires, and 900 Muslims, and 28,700 wounded, including 22,000 of French descent, 2,000 legionnaires, and 3,900 Muslims.

—A total of 198 persons of French descent are still listed as missing. Nearly 7,000 wounded rebels are being cared for in French medical facilities.

Before moving on to the number of "rebel casualties," let us spend a moment on one figure, that of "accidental deaths." According to the official figures, one-third of French soldiers killed during the Algerian War died in accidents and not in combat. The accidentally injured represented two-thirds of the wounded. This included accidents of all kinds: mishandling of weapons, sentries who had fallen asleep, firing at random, mistaken targets, and, above all, motor vehicle accidents. Several campaigns were conducted by the military newspapers in particular in an attempt to reduce the rate of the slaughter.

The indications provided in a note from Renseignements Généraux (General Information Service) on March 9, 1962, based on French military sources, are the most surprising in terms of the "Algerian rebel losses."

Table 9.1 Muslim casualties of the Algerian War

FLN losses: Members of the ALN and auxiliaries	
Killed in battle	141,000
Victims of internal "purges"	15,000
Killed by the Tunisian and Moroccan armies	2,000
Total	158,000
Muslims killed by the ALN	
Soldiers killed in battle	3,500
Civilians missing (to March 13, 1962)	50,000
Civilians killed (to March 19, 1961)	16,000[a]
Total	69,000
Grand Total	227,000

[a]Rounded down from 16,378.

They are estimated at 141,000! That is, 4,000 fewer than in the figure given by General de Gaulle in his press conference held two and a half years earlier. At the time, no one noted the "anomaly."

The French army broke down the "Muslim losses" into two categories: disabled ALN/FLN troops and Muslim Algerians killed by the FLN/ALN.

As for the civilian population, there are no figures known for after March 19, 1961.

With these civilian figures, the total of Muslim Algerians killed by March 19, 1962, would thus rise to 243,378, according to the official French figures.

At the Tripoli Congress in June 1962, the FLN released the estimates that would be taken as definitive: "One million martyrs fell for the cause of Algerian independence." The *Charte d'Alger* (Algiers Charter, published by the FLN in 1964) certified that there were 300,000 war orphans, including 30,000 who had lost both father and mother, at the time of independence (p.

Table 9.2 Civilian losses in the Algerian War

	Killed	Wounded	Missing[a]
European descent	2,788	7,541	875
Muslim	16,378	13,610	13,296
Total	19,166	21,151	14,171

[a]As of September 1, 1962, the requests for searches received by the Red Cross rose to 4,500 Europeans, and 6,050 Muslims.

81), and "more than 1 million martyrs, nearly 3 million people forced from their homes and villages to be penned up in specialized centers created to that end, 400,000 refugees, primarily in Tunisia and Morocco, 700,00 migrants to the cities from the rural areas."

According to the most plausible estimates, the conflict produced nearly 500,000 dead (all categories combined, but particularly Algerians).

In the months following Algerian independence, the massacre of tens of thousands of *harkis*, the abduction of Europeans (especially in Oranie), the clashes for power between *wilayas*, added considerably to the already heavy toll of that "nameless war."

The Loss of the Empire
and the Crisis of French Nationalism

Forty years after the end of hostilities, the toll of the Algerian War continues to raise other problems of assessment and interpretation for historians, in particular, the crisis of French nationalism and the emergence and setting in operation of a "strong state" born of that war.

In his press conference on June 14, 1960, General de Gaulle emphasized that one had to turn one's back on the past: "It is altogether natural to feel nostalgia for what the empire was, just as one may yearn for the soft light of oil lamps, the splendor of the sailing-ship navy, the charm of the horse-and-buggy era. But what of it? No policy is valid apart from the realities." And he explained that the end of the Algerian War was an opportunity for France to point out a new path, to help the countries of the South. But that new epic was proposed at a moment marked by demographic uncertainty, industrial anxiety, and doubt about the nation's founding values. The end of the Algerian War weakened the army (eight hundred senior officers were discharged between 1961 and 1963); it divided the Church and broke the consensus resulting from the Resistance.

Only ten years after World War II, the kinship and participation in that unique history called "the Resistance" and "the Liberation" had been shattered. The rejection of the 1940 defeat and of the Vichy episode had restored the patriotic values that had fallen by the wayside. With the Algerian War, the pact on appropriate memories was broken. The Algerian War caused a true crisis in French nationalism, that is, in a certain conception of France, its role, its "civilizing mission" in the colonies. It led to this paradox: although the period brought about the construction of a strong state in 1958, it culminated in the crisis of French nationalism, of its centralized, Jacobin tradition. The approaching moment of Algerian independence accelerated the process of consciousness-raising and increased doubts. Traditional French nationalism found no way to express itself except as "the resistance to abandonment," the rejection of "decadence." In *Algérie française*, published in 1959, André Figueras wrote: "As long as we still have Algeria, we are great, we are strong, we are long-lasting. We have an incomparable destiny there."

Beginning in 1959, General de Gaulle, essentially through the magic of language, played a role in liberating public opinion from the haunting memory of "decadence" and "humiliation" and in leading the public to approve and accept Algerian independence. But the collapse of the empire in a climate of Algerian civil war led to a French crisis of conscience when the French were obliged to accept a decisive displacement of the French community. And this came at a time when the construction of Europe, still in its embryonic stage, was not having success in harnessing the fervor, the energy, left available by the end of the colonial adventure. In the tragic events that tore apart political, cultural, and intellectual "families," the French entrusted their harsh fate to the supreme magistrature. There was an insistent demand to resolve the tensions, to return to the Bonapartist tradition. The traditional French left also emerged seriously weakened by the Algerian War. A leftist government associated with the practice of torture and war; the distrust of a large portion of intellectuals, most of whom had embraced the left after the Liberation; the deterioration of the SFIO, which "rejected the false right of peoples to dispose of themselves in the name of human liberation" (in the words of Marc Sadoun); the true beginning of the internal crisis of the PCF, which did not allow itself to recognize any particularism apart from Communism— the profound upheavals experienced by the left at the time portended a real redefinition of its political values. That crisis weakened the foundations of republican ideology, the point of reference for the French Socialist and Communist left. And finally, between 1954 and 1962, successive waves of French soldiers, more than 2 million of them, went to Algeria to fight a war. During these seven years, one Republic had fallen and another had replaced it, hundreds of thousands of Algerians had died the victims of that conflict, and 1 million *pieds noirs* had left the country where their families had lived for generations.

Amnesty and Amnesia

French society rapidly assimilated the Algerian War era, much more rapidly than had been the case after World War II (when it was necessary to rebuild,

to live with ration coupons, to find housing). It did so at the risk of disturb-
ing, or even dislocating, the axis linking the present to the immediate past.
The memory of the Algerian War became encysted, as if within an invisible
fortress, not in order to be "protected," but to be dissimulated, like the un-
bearable face of a Gorgon. The succession of amnesties came to endorse
that dissimulation of the "Algerian tragedy" within a climate of indifference.
Things had to end one day: the remorse, the doubts, the painful shadows
that haunted the memory had to be dispelled.

On December 17, 1964, the first amnesty law associated with the "events"
in Algeria was passed. On December 21, 173 former OAS members received
a presidential pardon as a Christmas present. It would not be until 1968 that
"the account was closed." After the general strike on June 7, 1968, all OAS
members were pardoned. In the following days, they returned from exile
(Georges Bidault), or left prison (Raoul Salan). On July 24, 1968, the National Assembly passed a law that eliminated criminal penalties associated
with the "events" in Algeria. But this law did not stipulate any reintegration
into public duties (civilian or military), or the right to medals. On October
24, Jacques Soustelle returned to France after a period of exile resulting from
his activities for French Algeria. The law of July 16, 1974, eliminated all convictions that had occurred during or after the Algerian War. The law of November 24, 1982, passed under a leftist government did not confine itself to
amnesty; it rehabilitated the cadres, officers, and generals convicted or sanc-
tioned for having participated in subversion against the Republic. The
putschists of April 1961 once more became part of the French army.

Algeria, after enduring a terrible war, acceded to its independence. The
historical merit of the leaders who set off the insurrection in November
1954 is that they unjammed the colonial status quo through the use of arms.
They allowed the idea of independence to take shape among millions of Algerians. But, as the sociologist Abdelkader Djegehloul notes, "the war set in
motion a process of destruction of the capital of democratic experience and
modern politics, which the different political organizations had begun to accumulate before 1954." The strategies of exclusion, authoritarianism, and
hegemony took root within Algerian nationalism.

At the time of independence, hundreds of thousands of rural people, who
had just recently left the resettlement camps, filled Algerian cities. They
moved into the apartments that had been left vacant. This "peasant wave"
profoundly transformed the face of Algerian cities, and in a lasting manner.
In *Le fleuve détourné* (The Diverted River), the writer Rachid Mimouni de-
scribes the return of the soldier who opened his eyes to a new, alien world:
the troubling chaos, the keen lucidity, a new Algeria overwhelmed, the

river of its tradition diverted. Between an obedience to the former colonizer and an anonymous and collective submission to the new "administration," between the river diverted by foreign paratroopers or changed by autochthonous soldiers, was there any hope for a happy balance? The loss of a sense of duration accompanied the loss of political responsibilities. The economy seemed to dominate everything: battles about collectivization and self-management; the method of buying up and managing lands taken back from the French colons (the last lands were taken on October 1, 1963); the regulation and control of Algerian emigration to France, with the accords of May 29, 1963 (on family migration), April 25, 1964 (the first efforts to cut off immigration), and December 27, 1968 (the quota system); the nationalization of petroleum and natural gas product distribution companies, in none other than May 1968. Petroleum revenues and the various allocations of resources to parties favored by the regime allowed the latter to earn the goodwill of a large portion of the public. "Modernization," founded on industries difficult to master, sacrificed agriculture, hydraulics, and equipment.

Suddenly, Algeria's colonial past was completely transformed into a foil, a point of reference for the self-justification the social present needed. Everything about that past that was precarious, sordid, and merciless toward human life and labor was willingly pointed out. The reminder of all these defects served as camouflage; they helped to exorcise the traumatic changes and dissimulate the wounds of the present. Algeria wanted to advance, set aside the hundred and thirty-two years of French presence, undertake the construction of a new society. It wanted to maximize the resources and mobilize everyone: economic populism complemented political populism. Thus a state of mind gradually spread, one that contrasted a dark prewar colonial period to the just-ended reality of the glorious war and the hope for a radiant future.

Between 1962 and 1968, in both France and in Algeria the loud din of "modernity" that invaded the world also covered up the era of the Algerian War: the assassination of John F. Kennedy in 1963, then that of his brother Robert in 1968, the murder of Martin Luther King Jr. that same year, the impact of the Cuban revolution and the figure of Che Guevara, the police repression and the emergence of the youth movement in Europe and the United States, the Six-Day War (1967) and the invasion of Czechoslovakia (1968), the need to mystify history and the need to demystify it, the end of colonialism in Asia, and the shift to the war in Vietnam, which ended in 1975. These were years when history seemed to have vastly accelerated, with men who walked on the moon and the events of May 1968; the first oil crisis and the Yom Kippur War in 1973;

"stagflation" in 1975; the coup d'état in Poland in 1981, and the beginning of the end for Stalinist Communism.

Under these conditions, how can we fail to understand that the emergence from the Algerian "trauma" brought on a loss of consciousness, followed for a time by a confusional state? Yet, the poor "stockpiling" of memories never signified total amnesia, the massive forgetting of the facts.

Part 2

The History of Algeria since Independence

On July 3, 1962, Algeria became independent. The first French military forces were preparing to leave the territory. The country needed to emerge from the colonial state, underdevelopment, and to build a state that was now a full-fledged nation.

How did that large part of the central Maghreb, with its varied landscape, become a political region, then a nation? Or rather, how did Algeria, which was not a geographical necessity, become one in fact? The "invention" of Algeria with its present-day borders and language, the fluidity of its populated areas, the vitality of the cultural exchanges that united in spirit the mix of political social groups favoring independence, and the unifying role of Islam have already been studied in the first part of this book (see also Stora 1991a). We have seen how Algeria was born from a political will that appeared in the early twentieth century and that persisted through a long war of independence against French colonial power.

In part 2, the history of present-day Algeria, from its independence in 1962 to the aftermath of Mohamed Boudiaf's assassination in 1992, will be presented both in terms of its uniqueness and within a Maghrebian and Mediterranean perspective. The traditional chronology will be respected, as we study those periods when Ahmed Ben Bella (1962–1965), Houari Boumédienne (1965–1978), Chadli Benjedid (1979–1991), and Mohamed Boudiaf (1992) led the country.

The approach in part 2 is not meant to search for "revelations" about the last forty years. It is also not meant simply to see how history was made—with what aims and at what cost. There is no dearth of examples inviting us to decipher the historical mode of operation of Algerian identity, which borrows from republican, Islamic, and nationalalist models all at once: from the joy at independence in 1962 to the regime installed by the military in 1965; from the desire for social equality to the failure of the "industrializing industries" under Boumédienne; from the authoritarian management of society by the only party, the FLN (Front de Libération Nationale), to the violent riots of October 1988; from the desire for the emancipation of the citizenry to the irruption of political Islamism.

From 1962 to 1993 the organization of Algeria changed profoundly. The upheaval of the rural landscape, the advent of urban machinery that sucked up men long attached to their traditional lands, the demographic explosion and the human tides, the underground economic production (*trabendo*, or contraband), the popular art forms (rai music), the recomposition and loosening of family ties, and the historical diversity of the nation's geographical space have all been endlessly enriched by new differences, ways of reacting to transformations affecting Algerian society as a whole.

In 1962, Algeria had barely 10 million inhabitants. In early 1994 it had nearly 27 million, with three-quarters of the population born after independence. Most young Algerians did not experience the colonial era or the war against France, and they have only a distant relationship to the real history of their country. Nevertheless, the Algerian political regime has constantly appealed to history and has strongly preserved the imprint of the historical conditions under which it came into existence: the primacy of the military factor, the absence of democratic legitimacy, the violent exercise of authority. An executive power concentrated in the hands of the president of the Republic, relying heavily on the army's support and enjoying the advantages of a single-party system, lie behind the construction of an authoritarian state. Between 1962 and 1988, the regime sought legitimation and laid claim to the legacy of the struggle for independence; it also drew from other registers, including socialist-style economic development, "nonalignment" with the blocs in foreign policy, and state control of the values of Islam. Nationalist unanimism continued to undergird a fluctuating ideology. It became a remedy of sorts to the dizzying shifts in definitions based on identity; it attempted to erase linguistic and regional differences; and it was transformed into "reconciliation," the negation of social conflicts, as an apparent corrective to the ills of modernity. Society accepted this consensual reformism so long as a "redistributive" social policy, made possible by the petroleum windfall, was generating enormous revenues. The arrival on the scene of younger generations insensitive to the exclusive legitimation of the war of independence, and the drop in the value of petroleum income, have undermined the foundations of the established system.

The individuals and groups that make up Algerian society were placed in unprecedented situations with no points of reference in the past that would help them modify their behavior and hence have a sense that they are living in an unpredictable and arbitrary situation. Large numbers have been "uprooted" without the memory of their origins being abolished or their anxiety calmed with respect to an identity put to the test. The history of Algeria in the first decades after independence, when the country shed its long colonial past, looks like a major period of transition. In the construction—and anticipation—of a different future, that stretch of time has frustrated the desire to accede to new forms of satisfaction and to a greater number of material goods. At the same time there has been disillusionment, new ills, and a resurgence of nostalgia. Many Algerians are encamped on the fringe of a conquering "civilization" that bears with it a modernity that does not belong to them. And the society has found itself agitated by a feverishness presenting itself as a return to religious roots or a glorification of regionalism—of the "little homelands." Thus, "roots" and "modernity" are words spoken with violence and with renewed force.

10

Summer 1962

Guerrilla forces from the "interior" versus combatants from an army stationed "outside" the borders of Algeria; the first hunting down of *harkis*, the auxiliaries to the French army during the war of independence; the power struggles of factions within the FLN, and the assertion of the autonomy of armed groups in certain regions—the unity of the Algerian nation seemed seriously threatened in summer 1962. In addition, more than 40 percent of the population lived in the most abject poverty, and the economy, completely dismantled by a seven-and-a-half year war (1954–1962) and the massive departure of *pieds noirs*, was still closely linked to that of France.

A protracted civil war was barely averted. Ahmed Ben Bella, supported by Colonel Houari Boumédienne and his notorious "border army" (stationed in Morocco and Tunisia during the war), prevailed. He entered Algiers on August 3, 1962, with the aid of the "border army" forces.

The Proclamation of Independence

On July 1, 1962, a referendum took place. The accords ratifying Algeria's accession to independence were adopted almost unanimously by voters, Europeans and Muslims alike (5,994,000 out of 6,034,000 votes). On July 3, France officially recognized Algerian independence. Jean-Marcel Jeanneney was the first accredited ambassador, as the departure of Europeans—*pieds noirs*—for the metropolis proceeded at an accelerated rate.

The war against France was over. Above all, Tuesday, July 3, marked the arrival in Algiers of the GPRA, the provisional government of the Algerian Republic, which was formed in Tunis in 1958 by the FLN at the height of the struggle against France.

The Tunis-Air Caravelle landed at the Algiers airport. The members of the GPRA, led by their president, Ben Youssef Ben Khedda, made their triumphant entrance in Algiers. In the city, the crowd invaded the streets to display its joy. Algerian children, who were equipped with wood submachine guns and military caps, celebrated the holiday by imitating those they admired: the mujahideen, the underground fighters. Now Algiers was nothing but a giant village fair. The city, decked with thousands of green and white banners, echoed with the roars and whistles sounding five notes: *Ya-ya, Dje-za-ir* (Long live Al-ge-ria). Vehicles and tanks were decorated in a procession of floral floats. Automobiles and motor scooters, sporting Algerian flags, unrelentingly crisscrossed the city. Nevertheless, the appearance of the new leaders on the balcony of the Algiers prefecture caused a shock. The population had considered the international press's news of divisions, even a "crisis," within the FLN "colonialist propaganda." Doubt was no longer possible. The Algerians did not see two of the "historic chiefs" of the FLN, Mohammed Khider and, especially, Ahmed Ben Bella, who remained abroad. The intoxicating joy was accompanied by anxiety about the future. It was so intense that, in his speech to the assembled crowd, Ben Khedda asserted that "the popular will constitutes the most solid defense against the military dictatorship some are dreaming of, against personal power, the ambitious, the adventurers, the demagogues, and fascists of all stripes."

The target of this allusion was Houari Boumédienne, head of the "border army" installed in Ghardimaou on the Tunisian border. Two camps stood opposed as Algeria realized its dream of independence. On one side was the GPRA, which rallied around it the leaders of *wilayas* II, III, and IV, and the FLN's Fédération de France. On the other side, Boumédienne's general staff could count on *wilayas* I (the Aurés), V (Oranie), and VI (Sahara)—all of which, in fact, did not carry much weight at the military level—and, above all, on the border army. Ferhat Abbas, the famous pharmacist of Sétif, first president of the GPRA in 1958, and Ahmed Ben Bella (one of the leaders of the 1954 insurrection) had also opted to challenge the GPRA.

In the streets on July 5, the unions, young people, and militants from the FLN's autonomous zone of Algiers demonstrated in the capital. Ben Khedda spoke that day and demanded that the demonstrators return to

work. One must know how to end a party, especially when the social and political situation of independent Algeria is worrisome, even critical.

The Social Situation at Independence

In July 1962, Algeria was suffering from severe handicaps. The war had
been deadly and long (nearly eight years). For several months, between
January and June 1962, the OAS, composed of the supporters of French Algeria, had devoted itself to a scorched-earth policy. The economy had suffered greatly. Well before independence the signs of social decay were accumulating. Unemployment was high. The slums were multiplying around
the urban centers. Since the 1950s, a number of Algerian workers had gone
to France to seek employment, which was not available in their own country
(Stora 1992b).

In fact, in 1962 Algeria was heir to an outward-directed economy set up
in relation to the metropolis, and existed as a function of the million Europeans living there. In the first half of the twentieth century, the gradual integration into the French economy had brought about a rapid decline in local craft industries, which faced competition from French manufactured
products. A dual and largely agricultural economy took shape. Side by side
with a modern sector of large farm operations in the hands of the colons, a
traditional sector with low productivity attempted to provide for the local
population's subsistence.

In 1964, Pierre Bourdieu and Abdelmalek Sayad (1977) analyzed the
scope of the phenomena of marginalization, loss of class standing, impoverishment, the ruin of vast numbers of small peasants, and the displacement of
the rural population. They showed how that crisis in traditional agriculture
led to a calling in question of the "peasant spirit," a rupture in the link between the group and the land, and a collective rejection of the peasant way
of life. But, in 1962, Algeria was still an overwhelmingly rural society.

Until World War II, the exportation of agricultural products was the only
force driving Algerian growth. The importation of manufactured goods was
a condition for Algeria's being integrated into France, and all customs protection for eventual nascent industries was banned (Ageron 1979).

Thus industrialization was very slow in Algeria. It was really not until the
war of independence that France, facing social and political protest,
launched the Constantine plan in 1959–1960, the aim of which was to in-
dustrialize the Algerian economy.

In spite of that (belated) initiative, on the eve of its independence, Algeria remained an agrarian country. The industrial sector represented only

27 percent of overall production. Half of the sector consisted of the simple processing of agricultural products. The workers' rejection of agriculture was not adequately offset by their mobilization in industry. Demographic growth exceeded the local capacities for employment. The years 1961–1962 were characterized by a certain economic void. Nearly 900,000 people left Algeria (including 300,000 workers responsible for the administrative and economic management of the country). These Europeans procured half the revenue resources for the country; they consumed nearly 60 percent of imports and 40 percent of local production. In 1959, with the escalation in the conflict between the French army and the Algerian nationalists, the flight of capital became apparent. This trend continued on a vast scale until 1964, aggravated by the complete disintegration of the production apparatus.

The war further worsened the economic system. In particular, there was a significant loss of human capital, through the death of hundreds of thousands of Algerians, emigration, and the departure of nine-tenths of the European population, that is, most of the business leaders, managers, technicians, government employees, teachers, and doctors. In July 1962, the large agricultural operations were abandoned, the factories were closed, and many public establishments destroyed. At that time, in the Arab-Berber culture of Algerian society, only 10 percent of children of school age attended school.

It was in this precarious context that the new leadership team had to define a development strategy. Yet it found itself paralyzed by the struggle among factions.

Ideology and Power Relations within the FLN

Between the Evian accords of March 1962 and the proclamation of independence, the structures of the colonial state collapsed and confusion spread everywhere. The local structures of the FLN did not manage to control the new situation. Regionalist and clientelist practices set in, in anticipation of the arrival of the "counterstate," that of the border army located outside Algeria. The program adopted at the congress of the Conseil National de la Révolution Algérienne, which met in Tripoli, Libya, between May 27 and June 7, 1962, strongly denounced that emergence of "political feudalism, chieftaincies, and partisan clienteles," "the escape from reality"; but it was already too late. The FLN leaders were themselves very divided, and the confusion reigning in Algeria was also found at the summit of the organization.

At this Tripoli Congress, Ahmed Ben Bella attacked the GPRA team and had it voted out. Ben Youssef Ben Khedda, president of the GPRA, walked out on the congress and went to Algiers to assert the presence of his government there. For him, the latter government was the depository of national sovereignty until it could remit its powers to regularly elected representatives.

According to the Tripoli agenda, the "popular democratic revolution" was to be led "by the peasantry, the workers, and the revolutionary intellectuals," at the expense of the "Algerian feudality and bourgeoisie, whose ideology would set the stage for neocolonialism." With this agenda of Marxist inspiration, Algeria was to become a democracy founded on the socialization of the means of production. The religious dimension of the country's Muslim identity was emphasized: "For us, Islam, stripped of all the excrescences and superstitions that have smothered or corrupted it, is to find expression in two essential factors in addition to religion as such: culture and identity." All the same, the architects of the program hoped that a portion of the Europeans could find their place in independent Algeria: "The safety of those French people and of their possessions must be respected; their participation in the nation's political life must be ensured on every level. Many of them will move to France, but a large fraction will remain in Algeria, and the French government will encourage them by every means in its power."

On the economic level, the "democratic and popular revolution" adopted the objectives of an agrarian revolution focused on the free redistribution of land and the constitution of cooperatives based on free choice; a process of industrialization subordinated to the needs of agricultural development; the nationalization of credit institutions and foreign trade, with the nationalization of fossil fuel deposits envisioned for the long term. "For the moment, the Party must struggle to extend the gas and electricity system to the rural centers; to train engineers and technicians at all levels, in accordance with a plan that will put the country in a position to manage its own mineral and energy resources."

On the social level, priority was given to wiping out illiteracy, developing national Arab Islamic culture, promoting public medicine and women's liberation. Foreign policy was based on the principle of nonalignment.

The GPRA's dismissal of Colonel Boumédienne (head of the ALN's general staff at the time) after the Tripoli Congress precipitated the conflict. Ahmed Ben Bella immediately took the side of the general staff on the western front and formed a "political bureau" in Tlemcen "charged with taking Algeria's fate in hand." Clashes were unavoidable.

Summer 1962, the Battles for Power

Hence the GPRA was in Algiers, while the coalition composed of the general staff, Ahmed Ben Bella, and Mohammed Khider installed itself in Tlemcen. On July 22, Ahmed Ben Bella announced the constitution of the "political bureau." It was an institutional show of force against the GPRA. Various figures, such as Tewfik ed-Madani (head of the Association des Oulémas—doctors of law—and minister of cultural affairs in the first GPRA of 1958), Ferhat Abbas, and Yacef Saadi (former head of the FLN's autonomous zone in Algiers) supported the "Tlemcen group," which went on the offensive. On July 25, Constantine, the capital of eastern Algeria, was occupied. Blood flowed. The clashes produced 25 dead and 30 wounded. Salah Boubnider, nicknamed "Saout el-Arab" ("the voice of the Arabs"), head of the *wilaya*, and Lakhdar Ben Tobbal, the GPRA's minister of the interior, one of the "historic chiefs" of November 1954, were arrested.

The "Tlemcen group" imposed itself particularly as the party of physical military force. More and more clearly, it showed the true face of the future FLN regime. The occupation of Constantine produced a reflex of unity between historic nationalist chiefs such as Mohamed Boudiaf, Krim Belkacem, and Omar Boudaoud, who was active in immigration as the former head of the FLN's Fédération de France. In his own name, Mohamed Boudiaf made a declaration on the evening of July 25: "If, by some misfortune, the coup d'état were to succeed, it would mean the installation of a dictatorship of a fascist nature. The obvious goal of that attempt is to deprive the Algerian people of its victory for the sole end of satisfying the ambitions of certain men hungry for power."

Krim Belkacem's position was very close to that of Boudiaf in the crisis under way. Like Boudiaf, he launched an "appeal to all revolutionary forces in Algeria to oppose this armed show of force and any attempt at dictatorship." The two men announced the creation of a Comité de Liaison et de Défense de la Révolution, or CLDR (Committee of Liaison and Defense of the Revolution).

At the same time, Hocine Aït Ahmed, another leader of the 1954 insurrection, announced from Paris on July 27 that he was resigning from all the leading organizations of the revolution. Conspiracies and dissidence punctuated the organization and life of the increasingly splintered FLN, the victim of bitter power struggles. On August 2, a compromise was established between Mohammed Khider and the Belkacem-Boudiaf pair, which finally recognized the political bureau. That bureau was set up in Algiers. Ben Khedda, president of the GPRA, agreed to step down. On August 6, the FLN's Fédération de France, which until that time had supported the GPRA, gave its allegiance to the political bureau. Resistance continued, however, in *wilayas* III (Kabylia) and especially IV (Algiers), whose leaders demanded they participate in the designation of future candidates to the National Assembly. A compromise seemed at hand at the meeting of a mixed commission (political bureau and *wilayas*), which composed a list of 196 "candidates," most of whom were far from favorable toward the political bureau. On August 25, Mohammed Khider announced that the elections set for December 2 would be postponed and that the political bureau refused to continue its support of certain candidates.

Under the acronym "FLN," military and economic interest groups clashed. With the mass exodus of Europeans and the sudden rise of rural people in the political movement and throughout urban society, the return to the political forms born of the war itself accelerated: the trend toward the autonomy of the *wilayas*, factionalism, regionalism. *Wilayas* III and IV decided to maintain their councils "until the formation of a legally constituted Algerian state." Mohamed Boudiaf resigned from the political bureau, while the general staff declared itself ready to intervene.

In Algiers on August 29 Yacef Saadi's commandos attacked the units of *wilaya* IV. There were several deaths. The people of Algiers went out into the streets with shouts of "Seven years, that's enough." The UGTA, a union organization created by the FLN in 1956, attempted to intervene, but to no avail. The test of strength was definitively under way. On August 30 the political bureau gave staff troops and *wilayas* I, II, V, and VI the order to march on Algiers. The violent skirmishes in Boghari and El Asnam left more than a thousand dead.

That period of anarchy favored many "settling of accounts," which led to the execution of several thousand *harkis*, or pro-French Muslims (Hamoumou 1993), and abductions of Europeans, particularly in Oranie (1,800 "disappeared," according to the official figure). In *Le Monde* on November 13, 1962, the journalist Jean Lacouture announced that more than 10,000 *harkis* had been killed. The Vernejoul report of January 1963 inclined toward the figure of 25,000. In 1965, the Red Cross listed another 13,5000 former auxiliaries incarcerated in Algeria.

The civil war of summer 1962 accelerated the exodus, and paralyzed economic and administrative life.

The Wave of Migration to France

Since the 1930s, the era of the first wave of migration to what was then the "metropolis," the Algerian nationalist leaders had always established a link between the need for national independence and the resolution of the emigration question. According to them, Algeria had only to accede to independence for the departures to end and for the "return" of Algerians, who would come to build their country. The "myth of return" thus became deeply rooted in the Algerian community within France.

But once independence was achieved in 1962, the predictions of a "return" did not come true. On the contrary, the 1962 accords, which ratified Algerian independence, consequently defined the rights and duties of the citizens of the two countries. Fourteen articles were devoted to the rights of the French of Algeria, only two to the Algerians in France. According to articles 7 and 11, the Algerians, especially workers, possessed the same rights as the French, with the exception of political rights and certain union and associative rights; and they enjoyed freedom of movement between the two countries. History was to turn the predictions and accords on their head. The *pieds noirs* left Algeria en masse and the emigration of Algerian workers in the same direction increased. Seven and a half years of war, marked by destruction and the displacement of populations, the OAS's relentless efforts to destroy the country's infrastructures, the rapid mass exodus of the Europeans, the profound disorganization in Algeria that resulted, the sudden arrival on the labor market of tens of thousands of freed Algerian prisoners or demobilized soldiers, and the "civil war" for power were all factors that explain the resumption of emigration to France in summer 1962.

From September 1, 1962, up to and including November 11, 1962, the entry of 91,744 Algerians into France was recorded. These were entire families who arrived, settling by preference in departments in full economic expansion. As before, the Paris region was the most significant magnet.

Ben Bella Prevails

Despite the September 5 agreement, which made Algiers a "demilitarized city placed under the control of the political bureau," Colonel Boumédienne ordered his battalions to enter the capital on September 9, 1962. Now only *wilaya* III (Kabylia) was not under the control of the general staff. For the moment, the military intervention of the general staff gave a free hand to the political bureau to complete its appropriation of power and its elimination of potential counterbalances. Fifty-nine names were dropped from the single list of candidates to the National Assembly, and submitted to a plebiscite vote, which was approved by 99 percent of voters on September 30. The different components of the Tlemcen coalition divided the seats of power among themselves. Ahmed Ben Bella became head of the government, and Mohammed Khider, secretary general of the political bureau. The presidency of the assembly fell to Ferhat Abbas.

Nevertheless, the crisis continued. On September 27, Mohamed Boudiaf created the Parti de la Révolution Socialiste, or PRS (Socialist Revolution Party), which contested the legitimacy of the political bureau formed by Ahmed Ben Bella.

But the new political Algeria became "stabilized" with the army at the center of power and the single-party system, whose function was to legitimate that omnipresent army. For the sociologist Abdelkader Djeghloul, "this Algeria barely resembles the country envisioned by the first combatants of November, who, for the most part, are absent from the leadership of independent Algeria." In addition, most of the leaders of the FLN's Fédération de France found themselves out of power. Did they make the "wrong choice" in that summer of 1962 (in favor of the GPRA, and against the political bureau)? In any case, they were accused of not having fought on "national soil" (but how many did so from beginning to end?), were suspected of "Europeanism" because they had been under the influence of the French working-class cadres in the immigration movement in France. The new state inherited government workers, whom France had recruited and trained at an accelerated rate. On the eve of independence, elites—heterogeneous, but on the whole better-off, more urban, better educated, and more Gallicized than those who had initiated the armed struggle—had joined the FLN. That presence did not rule out other types of alliances in the state under construction, particularly with traditional religious circles, with which the regime apparently wanted to come to terms.

A powerful aspiration for change existed in Algeria, namely, a strong will for the rapid and radical improvement of the collective and individual conditions of existence.

How would the regime, built with the support of the new FLN that emerged after the crisis of summer 1962, face up to that demand?

11

Ben Bella's Algeria (1962–1965)

In the aftermath of the war of independence waged against France, the Algerian nationalists who took power adopted the official motto of "making up for the delay accumulated over the one hundred and thirty years of colonial domination." In a context marked by the emergence of the Third World countries on the international political scene, and by the development of "Arab nationalism" sustained by the strong personality of Nasser in Egypt, Algeria resolutely opted for a socialist path of development.

"Self-management" became the key theme for transforming and mobilizing Algeria. This practice was introduced by the regime "from above" in a country that was not prepared for it either politically or materially.

The Presidential Regime and Single-Party System

On September 25, 1962, the constituent National Assembly, elected on September 20, proclaimed the birth of the Democratic and Popular Republic of Algeria. By a vote of 159 to 1, it invested the government, which designated Ahmed Ben Bella premier.

There was not a single member from the last GPRA in that government. Conversely, five military men, including Colonel Houari Boumédienne, occupied key posts. This government proclaimed its desire to bring about a socialist revolution, agrarian reform, and an Algerianization of cadres. But the army (Boumédienne's stronghold), the FLN (which Mohammed

131

Khider, the new secretary general of the political bureau, was supposed to reorganize), and the Union Générale des Travailleurs Algériens (UGTA) remained outside its authority.

The notion of a single-party system, which had not really been put forward at the Tripoli Congress, gradually took root. The Parti Communiste Algérien was banned on November 29, 1962. The new FLN, emerging from the summer crisis, no longer had any competitors outside its ranks. Mohamed Boudiaf's Parti de la Révolution Socialiste (PRS) was outlawed in August 1963. Every party organization other than the FLN was denounced as indicating a division of the people, a fissure in the foundations of the state under construction. There could not be the slightest distance between the "people" and its FLN representatives. Everything would be played out within the Front. The debates, polemics, controversies (and oustings) within it cannot be considered the beginning of political pluralism.

For the most part, the FLN drew its legitimacy from the very recent history of the war of independence. It did not possess democratic legitimacy. As Jean Leca and Jean-Claude Vatin (1975) pointed out: "Neither the independence of Algeria nor the legitimacy of the FLN proceeded from a consultation of the populace, however formal it might be. Each was the result of the history of liberation. The legitimacy of the FLN as the only party is historical, elections played no role in it. The process of the FLN's investiture was perfectly alien to the mechanisms of classic democracy."

It proved difficult to bring into line the UGTA trade union, which hoped to remain independent of the party. During the first congress of the UGTA (January 17–19, 1963), Tahar Gaid, who presented the position report in the name of the national bureau, addressed the problems of relations with the Party as follows:

> Certain leaders of the Party who are not at all unionist—and probably for personal ends—have attempted to monopolize the UGTA. Thus the elected union bureaux were replaced by designated delegates. In certain guilds, they have gone so far as to create cells of the Party that, rather than complement the union's actions, have tended to eliminate it. (Weiss 1970)

As a result of the congress, the UGTA fell "under the aegis of the FLN, one of its national organizations," and had to withdraw from the International Confederation of Free Trade Unions (ICFTU). On April 11, 1963, Mohamed Khemisti, minister of foreign affairs, was the object of an assassination attempt (he would die on May 5). On April 16, Mohammed Khider resigned his post as secretary general of the FLN's political bureau. Ahmed

Ben Bella succeeded him and held concurrently the positions of head of state and of secretary general of the FLN's political bureau. He sought to bring about the militant and popular mobilization he so needed. But the Party had become an organization without real power, a symbol more than a truly effective political instrument.

On May 17, 1963, Colonel Houari Boumédienne was named vice-premier. The army imposed itself as the linchpin in the negotiation for power. On June 9, Hocine Aït Ahmed issued a brutal indictment of Ahmed Ben Bella and declared he was ready to lead a political struggle against the regime. With the constitution of the Front des Forces Socialistes, or FFS (Front of Socialist Forces) in Kabylia, he set out on that path in autumn of the same year. Ferhat Abbas resigned as Algerian premier on August 14 to mark his disagreement with the FLN's constitutional plan. The constituent assembly saw its role diminish in importance. The constitution itself was drafted outside it, since Ferhat Abbas and Krim Belkacem wanted to make it an instrument for control of the government. That constitution, presidential in nature and revolutionary in style, was adopted by the Algerian Parliament on August 28 by a vote of 139 to 23. It was approved by referendum on September 8 (by a vote of 5,166,185 to 105,047). On September 15, 1963, Ahmed Ben Bella was elected the first president of the Algerian republic, with 5,085,103 votes.

Algerian Socialism and Self-Management

On March 12, 1963, Ahmed Ben Bella came on the radio and television to present the decree regarding the organization and management of the industrial and agricultural operations determined to be vacant as a result of the departure of Europeans. On October 1 of the same year he announced the nationalization of the last properties belonging to French colons.

In 1963, Algerian Socialism primarily saw itself as the continuation of a peasant revolution. Ben Bella, the son of peasants from Marnia, where he was born in 1916, willingly looked to the rural areas and distrusted the attitude of dissent among city dwellers and workers. In January 1963, he declared to the congress of the UGTA: "We must refrain from the temptations that have surfaced here and there, and which bear a name: control by the workers [*ouvriérisme*].... That temptation of control by the workers, already seen in several African unions, would lead to creating a privileged category.... I am sorry there are not more fellahs at this congress." Some "vacant properties" were farmed by management committees composed of former agricultural workers. Other properties became "vacant" after the expulsion of the colons, while still others were occupied by the military and nationalized (particularly large "capitalist" holdings).

The socialist sector came into being through the reorganization of the former agricultural properties into large so-called self-managed units. At the same time, an Office National de la Réforme Agraire, or ONRA (National Office for Agrarian Reform) was created, which, managed heavy-handedly by the state, crushed the local committees' demand for autonomy without achieving a leadership role. The ONRA was dissolved in 1966 when it became apparent that the deficit in the socialist sector was growing with no end in sight.

In 1965, the self-managed agricultural sector included 5,711,332 acres and comprised nearly all "modern" agriculture. It had only 115,000 permanent workers in 1968, of an active agricultural population of 1,300,000. All the same, the "management committees" (which dropped from 2,300 in number to 1,650 in 1969) provided 60 percent of the gross agricultural product.

In the industrial and commercial sector, all the "vacant" businesses, as well as certain smaller ones belonging to French companies, were placed under the self-management system. A few businesses and Algerian properties were also placed under cooperative management (the self-managed industrial operations did not employ more than ten thousand workers). As for foreign trade, it was monopolized for the most part by a state office, the Office National du Commerce, or ONACO (National Office of Commerce).

In self-managed businesses, the power organization was in principle subject to so-called direct democracy. All the workers formed into a general assembly (*assemblée générale*, AG) constituting the supreme legislative organization. But the state remained the owner of the business property and assigned itself custodial power. The director, named by the government, had right of veto over any decision of the collegial organization that might be contrary to the goals of national economic central planning (Koultchizki 1974; Teillac 1965). The emphasis was placed on the revival of economic activity, on national development rather than the transformation of the relations of production (Duprat 1973).

The 1963 decrees did not serve to endorse a vast social movement that might have embraced self-management. After the harsh conditions of colonization, the poor peasantry aspired to break free of the old agrarian order and enjoy better working conditions. But nothing predisposed the colons' former laborers, uneducated and unskilled, to set in place forms of collective management. According to the sociologist Michel Launay (1963), the fellahs did not clearly opt for the self-management system. Some envisioned agrarian reform as a distribution of lands and private appropriation, others expected an improvement in their condition as wage earners within the framework of state farms managed by leaders named by the government.

Self-management was the political issue of the moment. The regime was torn between the UGTA militants, who pushed for the establishment of management committees, and the army, which intended to restore state authority. Gauthier de Villers (1987) notes: "In various respects, self-management constituted a temporary, conservative formula, more than it expressed a fundamental political choice."

Foreign Policy and the "Sands War"

The foreign policy of the "Democratic and Popular Republic of Algeria," which was admitted to the UN on October 8, 1962, was officially inspired by its geographical situation, but especially by the ideological choices of its leaders. "Algeria is an integral part of the Arab Maghreb, of the Arab world, and of Africa"; it practices "positive neutralism and nonengagement" (article 2 of the constitution).

Algeria's African vocation was expressed especially in positions taken in support of African peoples who were still under the sway of colonization (especially in Angola, Guinea-Bissau, and Mozambique) or racial domination (South Africa). As a result of the first pan-African summit meeting in Addis Ababa (May 22–25, 1963) with thirty independent states participating, the charter of the Organization of African Unity (OAU) was signed. Algeria's adherence to this charter earned it great popularity among black African leaders. Allegiance to the camp of "Arab nationalism" and Arabism, proclaimed by Ahmed Ben Bella, reinforced the solidarity between Algeria and Nasser's Egypt. But the reality of a unified Arab Maghreb, desired by the Algerian, Moroccan, and Tunisian leaders at the Tangier Conference (April 27–30, 1958), slipped away after various political and military conflicts. In January 1963, Habib Bourguiba, the Tunisian head of state, recalled his ambassador as a sign of protest against the protection granted by Algeria to the authors of the plot against the Tunisian regime. The conflict between Algiers and Rabat took on greater proportions and led to "the sands war" of October–November 1963. Ever since 1960, the Moroccans had hoped to see the Saharan border, which was drawn by France, modified in their favor, in compliance with an accord signed between King Mohammed V and the GPRA.

While negotiations unfolded in Oujda, skirmishes took place near the border on October 8, 1963, between soldiers in the Armée Nationale Populaire, or ANP (National Popular Army), and "uncontrolled elements" (according to the Algerians) or units of the Forces Armées Royales, or FAR (Royal Armed Forces)(according to the Moroccans). King Hassan II decided to dispatch Abdelhadi Boutaleb, minister of information, to Algiers, as troops were sent to the Saharan border. After the failure of the Boutaleb mission on October 10, the skirmishes multiplied. The Algerian government decreed the general mobilization of the former *djounouds* (fighters). The mediation of the Ethiopian sovereign at the Bamako Conference of October 29–30, 1963, led to a cease-fire agreement. The end of hostilities was to begin at midnight on November 2. A joint commission determined a withdrawal zone for the troops present.

Despite the cease-fire, the Algerians and the Moroccans were still fighting on November 2 over possession of the palm grove of Figuig. On November 5, the cease-fire was respected and the "sands war" ended with a return to the status quo.

To counterbalance its trade relations with France, which were judged too restrictive, Algeria sought to develop its economic relations with other states. The USSR provided loans and technical aid, but did little trade with Algeria. Algeria now did most of its trade with countries in the European Economic Community—about 70 percent of the total, half of it with France. The share in socialist countries remained low (less than 5 percent), while that in the United States and European states remained high (on the order of 10 percent). In 1970, France was still the foremost supplier of Algeria, but its role dropped after the 1971 crisis between the two countries.

The Worsening of the Economic Situation

Ben Bella, generous but ill-informed about the enormous tasks to be accomplished, introduced "self-management" in a country that was not prepared for it either politically or materially.

The social situation was worrisome. In 1963, Algeria had 2 million unemployed and 2,600,000 people with no resources. Various troubles born of poverty erupted: peasant revolts, especially in Constantinois; the spread of violent crime; sporadic but persistent demonstrations by the unemployed in the cities.

At least three causes lay behind this process: first, there was a lack of skilled labor and technicians able to run the colonial equipment abandoned by the Europeans; second, the deterioration of the plants had not been the object of any renovation at the approach of independence; and finally, the local production market, designed primarily to satisfy a demand of European origin, was shrinking. In addition, there was a grave crisis in agricultural exports because of the limitation in the outlets for local products (wine dropped by a third, vegetables by a quarter, and industrial crops by two-thirds).

The self-managed rural sector absorbed most of the allocations available, and it operated at a significant loss. Agricultural production did not improve, but consumer demand continued to grow. The average cereal production did not exceed 1.6 to 1.7 billion kilograms, while the need rose to 2.4–2.5 billion, and the population grew by 3 percent per year.

After the failure, then the official halt of the Constantine plan, the results in industry were alarming: in building and public works projects, for example, production dropped 55 percent between 1962 and 1963. Of two thousand public enterprises, fourteen hundred disappeared. In the mining sector, production dropped 20 percent; in metallurgy, 15 percent. The underuse of production capacities was very worrisome: 58 percent capacity in textiles, 14 percent in fish canneries, 40 percent in fruit production, and an almost total halt in sugar production. The fall in investments was even more abrupt than that in production: from 1,464 billion to 84 billion dollars between 1961 and 1963 in current prices, or, excluding petroleum, from 333 billion to 69 billion dollars. At the same time, nonproductive expenses grew, with an enormous expansion of public services. Between 1954 and 1963, the number of public employees went from 30,000 to 180,000.

The army was a significant burden on the operating budget. In early 1962, the Armée de Libération Nationale (ALN) had 880,000 soldiers on the borders and 6,000 in the guerrilla forces; in 1963, its strength rose to 120,000 troops, consuming 10 percent of the gross domestic product.

In 1963 the deficit was so high that Algeria was constrained to borrow 1.3 billion francs from France. It expected a whole series of decisions from France to shore up its economy: the completion of the works projects undertaken; the sending of voluntary technicians and national education *coopérants* (individuals performing their national service as social service abroad); export agreements on wine. The immigration of Algerians to France was favored during that period.

The Continued Emigration

The new waves of migration after Algerian independence shattered the provisions set out in the 1962 Evian accords. On either side of the Mediterranean, the Algerian and French governments envisioned establishing controls on the "flow." On January 9, 1964, the minister of social affairs in the Algerian government and the French minister of labor came to an agreement:

1. The two governments judged that it was in keeping with the interests of Algeria and France to normalize the flow of labor between the two countries; 2. Beginning immediately and until July 1 [1964], the entry into France of Algerian nationals will be determined as a function of the problems raised ... for the economies of the two countries; 3. Beginning on July 1 [1964], the entry of Algerian workers will be fixed as a function of the availability of labor power from Algeria and the capacities of the French employment market, which the French government will make known to the Algerian government three times per year.

This institution of a quota system did not prevent the expansion of emigration. In spring 1965 the threshold of 450,000 Algerians in France was passed.

The FLN's Algiers Charter, adopted in April 1964, recognized that "the causes of Algerian emigration to Europe, and more particularly to France, are closely linked to [Algeria's] level of development. It can be attenuated and slowed but will end only with the disappearance of its principal causes." In plain language, there was no possibility of stopping emigration as long as the country had not markedly developed. The appendix to the 1964 charter specified that "the French labor market will supply traditional outlets for unemployed workers in Algeria."

In fact, the Ben Bella regime recognized—against all the theories previously put forward—that it could not do without the safety valve that the employment market in France offered. Emigration was thus considered a "necessary evil." It was encouraged, in fact, by a state concerned to ease the pressure on the labor market and to improve the balance of payments (through the hard currency sent back to Algeria by the emigrant workers to financially support their families in that country).

Movement toward the Cities

The mass departure of *pieds noirs* (a term that, after 1962, designated the Europeans of Algeria) led to an appropriation of the spaces left vacant. The job vacancies led to a vast and abrupt shift of the population to the urban areas. These new migratory currents, composed primarily of landless peasants or fellahs without liquid assets, would mark the landscape of the cities in a lasting way (the old *medinas* filled up, substandard housing exploded, and slums were built close to new cities).

Between 1960 and 1963, 800,000 new residents arrived in Algerian cities, half of them in the Algiers area alone. The population of Algiers increased by

85 percent between 1954 and 1960. The population of the urban munici-
palities went from 3 million in 1959 to 4 million in 1966, out of a total population of 10 million. The appropriation of urban space did not wipe out
class differences; it even had a tendency to create some of them, especially
the opposition between the middle strata and the poor, uprooted peasantry,
sometimes composed of "rurbans" (Lacheraf 1965). The rural exodus led
only to unemployment, or, at most, to employment in unskilled service jobs
or odd jobs. The first years of independence also saw the consolidation and
broadening of the urban sector of the petty bourgeoisie: employees in the
civil and military administration, small tradespeople, artisans, small retailers.

Ben Bella's Political Isolation

Ahmed Ben Bella, a charismatic popular orator, increasingly cut himself off
from the economic realities, and, above all, from his former companions in
the nationalist struggle. On September 27, 1962, Mohamed Boudiaf,
though he too was one of the historical founders of the FLN, left that movement to create the Parti de la Révolution Socialiste (PRS), which contested
the regime's legitimacy. Ferhat Abbas, the first president of the GPRA in
1958 and of the constituent assembly in September 1962, also departed. On
April 16, 1963, Mohammed Khider, another "historic leader" of the November 1954 insurrection, resigned his post as secretary general of the
FLN. Other opponents (or those assumed to be opponents), if they did not
withdraw on their own, found themselves dismissed, or even incarcerated.
On June 25, 1963, Ben Bella officially announced that Boudiaf and three
others had been arrested for "plotting against the state." On September 29
of the same year, Hocine Aït Ahmed (Ben Bella's former prison mate during
the Algerian War) announced the creation of the FFS, which also went over
to the opposition.

On October 10, 1963, the ANP opened fire on troops from the seventh
region of Kayblia. The ANP entered National Fort in Azazga, in the Ouad-
hias, without encountering resistance. Colonel Mohand ou el-Hadj, Aït
Ahmed, and their supporters reached the guerrilla forces. On October 12,
Ben Bella ordered the police to recapture all the Kabylia centers. On November 12, an accord was reached between President Ben Bella and Colonel
Mohand ou el-Hadj. Aït Ahmed continued "resistance in Kabylia," which
took on the aspect of latent "civil war."

At the first FLN congress on April 16–21, 1964, Ben Bella, forcefully and
with conviction, asserted the primacy of revolutionary action over the tasks
of institutional construction and the reorganization of the country. In de-

nouncing the claim of the primacy of state construction, he was targeting the Boumédienne faction, even as the speech delivered by the president to this congress designated "elements linked to the bourgeoisie" as a threat to the country. This illustrates "the frequent use, during that period of Algerian history, of Marxist schemata of analysis with the goal of sublimating power skirmishes into class struggles" (Villers 1987).

But Ben Bella's shifting alliances, like his choice of self-management, led to an impasse. The shifting alliances did not allow him to establish his authority in an indisputable manner and consolidate the state in a lasting way; and the choice of self-management did not correspond to the state of social relations.

The Coup d'Etat of June 29, 1965

In the wake of Algerian independence, the attempts to base the reconstruction of a state and of the economy on the real society clashed with the power of the military apparatus. The historian Mohammed Harbi, who played an active political role during the war and the Ben Bella period, notes: "The inclination for abrupt and total change, the rejection of patient political action, Ben Bella's preference for irregular approaches to the conduct of public affairs—all these factors led straight to Boumédienne's coup d'état."

In 1964, an armed revolt erupted with Colonel Mohamed Chaabani at its head, supported by Mohammed Khider, who announced in August 1964 that he held "the FLN's secret funds." On October 17, 1964, Hocine Aït Ahmed was arrested in Kabylia. His trial took place between April 7 and 10, 1965. He was sentenced to death, then pardoned on April 12. Disorder was spreading, even at the summit of the state.

Ahmed Ben Bella, not daring to directly attack Houari Boumédienne, vice-premier and minister of defense (that is, head of the country's only organized force), sought to reduce the influence of the "Oujda group," named in memory of the time when Boumédienne had commanded the Oujda region. He instigated the resignation of Ahmed Medeghri, minster of the interior, by removing the prefects from his authority and linking them to the presidency. Similarly, he impelled Kaïd Ahmed to leave the ministry of tourism by taking the side of hostelry management committees in a conflict with their minister.

Seizing the opportunity of a reorganization of the ministries in December 1964, he considerably reduced the duties of Minister of Orientation Chérif Belkacem, a member of the "Oujda group," who had the Ministries of Information, National Education, and Youth under his authority. As president of the Republic, head of the government, and secretary general of the FLN, he assigned the duties of the Ministry of the Interior, Finances, and Information to himself. All the opposition forces were banding together against Ben Bella. Doctor Mohamed-Seghir Nekkache, minister of health, alerted him, feeling the imminence of the danger (Bourges 1967).

On May 28, 1965, while Boumédienne was representing Algeria at the conference of Arab government leaders in Cairo, Ahmed Ben Bella announced that he was relieving Abdelaziz Bouteflika, another member of the "Oujda group," of his duties as minister of foreign affairs. Bouteflika immediately alerted his "boss," Houari Boumédienne. The latter assembled his companions from the "Oujda group," who were then joined by those of the "Constantine group" (Tahar Zbiri, Saïd Abid, Ahmed Draia, Salah Soufi, Abdelaziz Zerdani). Everyone was for the overthrow of Ben Bella. The operation was meticulously planned.

On June 19, 1956, at 1:30 a.m., Ahmed Ben Bella was arrested. Tanks took positions at strategic points. Passersby thought it was the filming of *La battaglia di Algeri* (The Battle of Algiers), a film by Gillo Pontecorvo, which would receive the Golden Lion at the Venice festival in 1966. But, at 12:05 p.m., in a message signed by Colonel Boumédienne, Radio-Alger announced the creation of a revolutionary council that assumed all powers. The Afro-Asian summit was set to open five days later, during which President Ben Bella was supposed to appear as one of the principal leaders of the Third World.

The first president of the Algerian Republic remained imprisoned for fifteen years and was liberated only on October 30, 1980. His arrest did not incite large popular demonstrations, except in Annaba, where about ten deaths were reported, following bloody confrontations with the army. A new era had begun.

12

Boumédienne, the State, and the Institutions

Contrary to what has often been said, under Houari Boumédienne it was the army/state that really had a hold on the FLN Party, and not the Party that had a hold on the state. After the establishment of "communal" and "municipal" charters, the national charter of 1976 declared Socialism the "irreversible option," and set out the large-scale political, economic, and cultural orientations. The constitution of November 1976 organized the operation of the state apparatus and confirmed "Islam as the state religion." The first Popular National Assembly (*Assemblée Populaire Nationale*, or APN) was elected on February 25, 1977.

The Desire for a Strong State

Ahmed Ben Bella had scarcely been arrested when Houari Boumédienne published a communiqué/agenda to explain the reasons for the coup d'état on June 19, 1965. The text emphasized that the country "was on the brink of the abyss" and that, since the accession to independence, it had been "at the mercy of the intrigues and confrontations of currents and factions." He denounced "political narcissism," "publicity-seeking Socialism," and asserted that "the fundamental options are irreversible and the inalienable achievements of the revolution."

Boumédienne offered seats in the new revolution council to all members of the FLN's political bureau, with the exception of those who had been arrested. Only two refused: Hocine Zahouane and Omar Benmahjoub. All the ministers rallied as well (two of them, Ali Mahsas and Bachir Boumaza, resigned a year later). The government was formed on July 10, 1965. In September an underground network, the Organisation de la Résistance Populaire, or ORP (Organization of Popular Resistance), trained by former members of the Parti Communiste Algérien (PCA) and by independent Marxists who had been close to Ben Bella, was quickly dismantled by the new regime's political police.

Mohammed Brahim Boukharouba, known as "Houari Boumédienne," was officially born on August 23, 1932, in Heliopolis (near Guelma) in eastern Algeria. He was the son of a poor peasant who had a hard time supporting his seven children. Beginning at age fourteen, Boumédienne received training in Arabic, attending in turn the *medersa* Kitania in Constantine, the Zitouna in Tunis, and finally, as of 1951, the University of Al Azhrar in Cairo. He was head of *wilaya* V during the war of independence, and established his headquarters in Oujda, Morocco, before becoming chief of the ALN staff (Francos and Serini 1976).

Boumédienne, a secretive and inflexible man, as well as an austere and willful ideologue, left a strong imprint on the contemporary history of Algeria. He had a "Jacobin" and centralizing side, and it has often been said that he wanted to make Algeria "the Prussia of the Maghreb" and the unifier of the region (Balta and Rulleau 1978). He had little consideration for the FLN, which he believed had become a "body without a soul." To govern, he relied primarily on the army. With the help of the formidable military security (political police), he eliminated any inclination to mount an opposition. Mohammed Khider was assassinated in Madrid on January 4, 1967. Krim Belkacem, former vice president in the GPRA during the war of independence and the foremost Algerian negotiator in Evian, was found strangled on October 20, 1970, in a Frankfurt hotel room. Hocine Aït Ahmed and Mohamed Boudiaf lived in exile abroad, where they attempted to organize opposition movements.

The revolution council itself, set in place after the coup d'état on June 19, 1965, dwindled away over the years. After the departures of Ali Mahsas and Bachir Boumaza, Abdelaziz Zerdani broke with the regime in 1967 on the issue of self-management. He was joined by Colonel Tahar Zbiri, who launched an unsuccessful attempt at a putsch. On December 15, 1967, President Boumédienne discharged Zbiri and took over the command of the Armée Nationale Populaire (ANP).

The Oujda faction, a team of senior officers who had become associated in 1956 during the war and who had aided Boumédienne in his rise to power, was disintegrated in the 1970s. In December 1972, a presidential communiqué relieved Kaïd Ahmed of his duties as head of the FLN. Minister of the Interior Ahmed Medeghri died under mysterious circumstances in 1974, supposedly by "suicide" according to the official version. Chérif Belkacem, a state minister, was dismissed in 1975. Abdelaziz Bouteflika was the only one in the "Oujda faction" to keep his job. Between 1964 and 1979, he remained the irremovable minister of foreign affairs.

In 1975, ten years after the coup d'état, the revolution council had only twelve of its twenty-six original members. Most of the "founders" of the council were dismissed in favor of high officials and administrators. Their names were Belaid Abdesslam, Sid Ahmed Ghozali, Mohammed Liassine. After 1976, the regime attempted to reintegrate a portion of the intellectual elites. In April 1977 the last government constituted by Houari Boumédienne included such men as Mostefa Lacheraf, Mohamed Benyahia, and Rheda Malek.

The most significant evolution of the Algerian political system set in place after the 1965 coup d'état was thus the amplification of the authoritarian character of the state, which relied on the army. That process occurred in several stages.

The Framework of Society: Communes, *Wilayas*, Business Enterprises

After independence in 1962, the structures of the new Algerian regime remained those of the former colonial power. It was only on July 5, 1975, that an order officially abrogated the law of December 31, 1962, which had renewed until further notice the French legislation in force. A few institutional rules had been set down in 1962, among them, the preeminence of the Party, the rejection of the separation of powers and of political pluralism. This was especially the case after the coup d'état on June 19, 1965, which was later baptized "the revolutionary recovery."

The communal charter of January 18, 1967, conferred the responsibility for managing the affairs of each commune on the popular communal assemblies (*assemblées populaires communales*, ACP), or on the "municipal councils," which were originally elected for four years by direct universal suffrage on a motion by the Party. The charter elaborated its own local economic program and, in compliance with the national development plan, defined the economic actions likely to ensure communal development.

The *wilaya* charter of May 25, 1969, created a popular *wilaya* assembly (*assemblée populaire de wilaya*, APW), elected for five years by direct universal suffrage on a motion by the Party; it was assisted by an executive council placed under the authority of the *wali*, named by the central government and charged with carrying out the assembly's deliberations. Like the commune, the *wilaya* had considerable economic powers. In particular, it participated on the local level in the management of national businesses and of those from the socialist sector. The wali also held a key role both in relation to the commune over which he had administrative and financial oversight, and in relation to the *wilaya*. In particular, he assessed whether the acts of the local organizations complied with "revolutionary legality." He was both "governor" and "supervisor."

The institutional imposition of Houari Boumédienne's regime was shored up by the "socialist turn" of 1971.

The order of November 8, 1971, concerning "the agrarian revolution," affected one-fourth of the agricultural land and about 120,000 beneficiaries, who were organized into cooperatives of various types (shared operations, collective production, polyvalent and specialized services). The best lands were already under public control (the so-called self-managed holdings).

The order of November 16, 1971, organized the Gestion Socialiste des Entreprises, or GSE (Socialist Management of Enterprises), and applied to all businesses "whose wealth is constituted entirely of public property." Its base was formed of the workers' assembly, elected for three years by the collective of the workers' group, from among the unionized workers proposed by a tripartite electoral commission (made up of the Party, the union, and the administration). But the real power was held by the leadership council. It included one or two members of the assembly elected by that assembly, but it was presided over by the general director, named and removed by the overseeing authority (the state) on a motion by the general director. The latter, who "acted under the overseeing authority," was "responsible for the general operation of the business" and "exercised hierarchical authority over personnel."

This general model reproduced, on the scale of business, the political system as a whole. The "citizen workers," who were the base of power, supervised by the union and the Party, were mobilized to participate in the proper operation of the different "republics" (communes, *wilayas*, cooperatives, business enterprises) under the control of "revolutionary power" (for recruitment) and of state power (for execution and oversight).

Through these measures, Boumédienne sought a new political balance by redefining his orientations and alliances. He demonstrated signs of openness toward the "progressive intelligentsia." In particular, he included, though in a nonpublic manner, the Parti d'Avant-Garde Socialiste, or PAGS (Avant-Garde Socialist Party, composed of Communists) in the formulation of ideological themes for mobilizing power.

The National Charter of 1976

For the tenth anniversary of the coup d'état, on June 19, 1975, Houari Boumédienne announced the drafting of a national charter and the election of a national assembly and a president of the Republic. On April 26, 1976, the first draft of the National Charter was made public. A vast campaign of public debates was organized in neighborhoods and workplaces in town and in the country. But the procedure adopted for the drafting of the definitive plan was such that the regime retained control of the process of public discussions and amendments. The initial text underwent very little modification.

The National Charter, adopted by referendum on June 27, 1976, with 98.5 percent of the vote, constituted "the supreme source of the nation's policy and the laws of the state," according to the constitution presented after the fact (article 6). It was the object of the oath the future president of the Republic would take, which indicates its importance.

In that charter, Algeria was presented as a country divided into various classes and groups, but not into different ethnic groups or "nations." Algeria was "not an assemblage of peoples in a mosaic of disparate ethnic groups." The Berber question was not mentioned in this document.

Algeria was an organic totality in which socialism was rationally developing what the war of national liberation had begun: the rebirth of the nation and the total reorganization of society. It followed that social pluralism ought not to be expressed as a political pluralism that would be exercised through voluntary and politically autonomous organizations. The general interest had to be sought out via social integration, resulting from the action of a strongly focused political power.

The Algiers charter adopted by the FLN in 1964 criticized the state institution and the bureaucracy by asserting the preeminence of an "avant-garde party profoundly linked to the masses." By contrast, the National Charter of 1976 asserted: "To restore national sovereignty, construct socialism, struggle against underdevelopment, build a modern and prosperous economy, and be vigilant against external dangers requires a solid and constantly fortified state, not a state invited to die out, when it has barely reemerged from the void." This text thus led to an extolling of the role of the state: the symbiosis between the people and the revolution led to the people's being embodied in the Party, and the Party in the high leadership of the state. The state, heir to the struggle for national liberation, was the expression of the will of the nation and of the people. Now that independence had been won in a lasting manner, the state was also the "principal agent of the restructuring of the economy and of social relations as a whole."

The charter laid claim to the fusion of the political, economic, and religious spheres. Every Algerian had to be at once a militant of the socialist revolution, a producer in an industrial society, a consumer in the national market, and a believer in the state religion.

Islam was in fact an integral part of the state ideology, as a "fundamental component of the Algerian personality." In addition, it was the "state religion" (since "socialism is not a religion" the charter said), but, consequently, it was the state that defined its political import. The charter explained that "Islam is linked to no particular interest, to no specific clergy, and to no temporal power" and concluded that "the erection of socialism is identified with the blossoming of Islamic values." The constitution, as the first application of the charter of which it was the legal expression, became the "keystone" of the institutional edifice. It was officially approved on November 19, 1976, by 7,080,904 Algerians, out of 7,708,954 eligible to vote and 7,163,007 actual voters (99.18 percent of the vote).

The Constitution and the Parliament

The preamble to the 1976 constitution recalled that Algeria owed its independence to a war of liberation, "which will remain one of the greatest epics in history to have marked the resurrection of the peoples of the Third World," and asserted the socialist choices of the country. It emphasized that the aim of the institutions set in place, beginning June 16, 1965, was to "transform the progressive ideas of the revolution into concrete realities."

The 1976 constitution consecrated the presidentialism of the Algerian political system and the preeminence of the state and of the government over every other representative organization of a partisan or elective nature (Cubertafond 1979). It attributed a "leading role to the FLN" only in the sense that power fell to its leadership, which was indistinguishable from that of the state. Article 98 of the constitution stipulated, in fact, that the leadership of the Party was called upon to shape the general policy of the country within the framework of a "unity of the political leadership of the Party and that of the state"; article 102 stipulated that "the decisive positions of responsibility at the state level are held by members of the Party leadership."

The head of state was the supreme leader of the armed forces. He determined, directed, and executed the general policy of the nation. He named and removed the members of the government, who were responsible only to him. He had the power to initiate laws in the same capacity as the assembly and legislated by order during parliamentary recesses. He held the statutory power from which the application of the laws stemmed.

On Saturday, December 11, 1976, Mohamed Benhamed, known as "Abdelghani," minister of the interior, proclaimed the results of the presidential election. President Boumédienne, the sole candidate nominated by the FLN, officially received 99.38 percent of the vote. On Friday, February 25, 1977, the Popular National Assembly was elected. As premier, it chose Rabah Bitat, the last of the "historic chiefs" of the Algerian revolution still in power.

The constitution conferred legislative power on the APN, which it shared with the president of the Republic, since the latter could legislate by order between sessions. The twenty-six items of article 151 set out the principal realms in which the assembly exercised its activities. In particular, it was up to the assembly to define the principles of economic, social, and cultural policy, to vote on taxes and the budget, to adopt the plan and set guidelines for the management policy of the territory, the environment, and of the quality of life.

The candidates for the National Assembly, the commune assemblies, and the *wilaya* assembly were selected by the Party and the politico-administrative regime. These elected officials were, in fact, more functionaries and supporters of the regime than true representatives of the people able to criticize the supremacy of the presidency and of the government apparatus. In the leaders' minds, the aim of the institutionalization of the regime was to bring about the formation of intermediate elites who represented the state in relation to the populace, and not the reverse. The objective was thus not at all to secure the foundations of a lawful state, or to introduce pluralism and political alternation, but to "integrate" the society into the system built by the regime of June 19, 1965 (Leca and Vatin 1975; Leca and Vatin 1977).

13

Economic Choices and Foreign Policy (1965–1978)

The true turning point in Algerian economic policy occurred in 1971. That year, Boumédienne nationalized natural resources, particularly fossil fuels (oil and gas). The authoritarian military regime, which came about in a coup d'état, attempted to obtain its political legitimation via a redistribution of the "oil windfall." It also hoped, by way of the vast revenues generated by oil and gas, to set a new model of development in place.

Algerian "Developmentalism"

The head of state, surrounded by a small team of voluntarists, believed it was possible to move rapidly, by forced march as it were, from underdevelopment to an industrial phase. Proclaimed "the highest of priorities," industrialization was supposed to be the "locomotive" that would pull agriculture forward.

In the early 1970s, the theory of "industrializing industries," inspired primarily by the French economists François Perroux, and especially Gérard Destanne de Bernis (professor at the University of Grenoble), became the key reference for the Algerian development strategy. François Perroux defined industrialization as a "cumulative process structuring the society as a whole via the intensive use of systems of machinery and allowing the increase in objects beneficial for the human race at decreasing cost." Following Perroux, de Bernis analyzed industrialization as

151

a total, complex phenomenon where the technological, the economic, the social (social restructuring, flexibility of social and socioeconomic structures), the political (political structures are profoundly transformed by industrialization) and the psychosocial (behaviors) are closely interwoven. The links between phenomena always occur in both directions, each being at once the condition for the realization of the others and the result of the realization of the others. (Destanne de Bernis, 1969)

Gérard Destanne de Bernis described the socioeconomic system bequeathed to the dependent countries at the time of colonization as outward-directed and inwardly disorganized. As a result, the aim of the development approach set in place after independence was to bring about the integration and refocus of the national production system. To create an internal dynamic of development, a certain primacy had to be granted to industrialization. According to this model, an efficient strategy had to grant a privileged role to "driving firms," to types of industrial investment that exerted "propulsion effects" on the entire economic and social environment. These basic industries, called industrializing industries, were to reinforce the integration of the national economy through the effects they produced "upstream" (supply) and "downstream" (outlets). In addition, they were supposed to raise productivity and allow the cadres and workers to become trained in a modern and technologically advanced environment. And, above all, they were supposed to be industries that produced equipment and, in particular, machine tools (Benhouria 1980; Benissad 1979).

At the turn of the 1970s, other authors influenced Algerian leaders as they established the development strategy and model, among them, André Gunder Frank, Charles Bettelheim, Immanuel Wallerstein, Emmanuel Arghiri, F. H. Cardoso, Celso Furtado, and Samir Amin. For these authors, only the state can achieve the model in which industry serves as a driving force within a national framework.

The idea that the accelerated setting in place of heavy industry was a necessary foundation for development was shared by a number of observers and analysts. The "Algerian path" represented by this economic choice was at first perceived as a desirable national choice for "planning the country's future." For the Boumédienne regime, development (obtained rapidly and by the means generated by oil revenues) was above all a way to assert (and legitimate) the state and the nation. The power of the production apparatus was supposed to consolidate the state's political independence, and increase the capacity to "achieve Socialism."

The Fossil Fuel Strategy

The Evian accords recognized Algeria's sovereignty over the Sahara and its natural resources. A breach opened in the French interests on December 31, 1963, with the creation of the Société Nationale de la Recherche, le Transport, la Transformation, et la Commercialisation des Hydrocarbures, or Sonatrach (National Company for Fossil Fuel Research, Transport, Processing, and Marketing). At the time, however, the Algerian state held only 4.5 percent of the exploration perimeters, while French interests were as high as 67.5 percent (Blin 1990). After the Arab-Israeli War in June 1967, Algeria decided to nationalize the refining and distribution activities of Mobil and Esso, and Sonatrach signed an agreement with Getty Oil on October 19, 1968. The US company returned 51 percent of its interests in Algeria to the Algerian company. Protests against the French companies became more urgent.

On February 24, 1971, President Boumédienne began the "decolonization of petroleum." The old concession system was replaced by a seizure of a 51 percent share of French petroleum companies. The oil and natural gas pipelines were nationalized. Only Total agreed to continue its activities; the other oil companies left Algeria. France boycotted Algerian oil as the dinar broke free from the franc zone.

The process of nationalizing foreign oil interests indicated a radicalization of the strategic choices of the regime at the political level. The effect was to increase the resources that the state hoped to mobilize to strengthen its control over the principal means of production and trade.

In late 1973, the first oil crisis tripled oil and gas receipts. The Algerian development strategy granted a major role to oil and gas as the principal source of financing for industrialization. It privileged on-site processing of mining and petroleum resources. This "industrializing" character of oil and gas was therefore supposed to contribute to the realization of a coherent production system.

Over the years, half of industrial investments went toward increasing the

Table 13.1 Oil and gas revenues for the state (in millions of dinars)

1967	1969	1971	1972
880	1,320	1,659	3,200

Source: Jacquemot and Raffinot 1977.

capacities of oil and gas production, funds needed to purchase from abroad the large equipment required for the adopted strategy (Rafot 1982).

A large share of petroleum resources thus served to forge the means for producing more oil and gas. In 1982, Algerian oil production—about 50 million metric tons per year since 1972—did not exceed 2 percent of world production. The volume of extraction was stabilized in 1982 at about 40 million metric tons in order to conserve that unrenewable strategic resource. The reserves in 1982 were estimated at 1.2 billion metric tons, or about twenty years of extraction (beginning in 1992) at that rate. With 3,000 billion cubic meters of reserves, Algeria held 4 percent of world reserves. Production in 1992 ranged from 14 to 16 billion cubic meters per year.

The Production System and Its Results

The years 1962–1965 was a phase that saw the nationalization of the "modern" European agricultural sector and the creation in 1964 of the Algerian dinar (the dinar, long equal in value to the franc, was worth approximately 1.20 francs between 1973 and 1980). Between 1969 and 1978 a second phase occurred, that of "industrialization."

It was characterized, first, by a wave of nationalization that allowed the state to control the instruments of economic power. On May 8, 1966, mining operations came under public control. Then, on May 31, the state established a monopoly on the insurance business. Esso's and Mobil's distribution network was nationalized in August 1967. In May–June 1968, a large wave of nationalization was carried out. On May 13, 1968, that of the distribution of petroleum products to the Algerian market occurred (fourteen foreign distribution companies); on May 21, twenty-two companies were nationalized in the sectors of construction materials, fertilizers, and metallurgy (including Rhône-Poulenc); in June it was the turn of about fifty cement works, paint plants, oil works, and metallurgy companies (including Ripolin, Lafarge, and Lesueur). In August 1968, a series of operations gave Sonatrach (a public petroleum trust) the monopoly on the marketing of petroleum products throughout the petrochemical sector.

The wave culminated on February 24, 1971, with the nationalization of all the deposits of natural gas and crude oil and of all the oil and gas pipelines, and with the exercise of state control over 51 percent of the French oil companies ELF (Erap at the time) and CFP (Compagnie Française des Pétroles). On November 15, 1974, the end of the nationalization process was announced. The assigned objective was to build in the shortest time possible an independent and integrated economy. As in the USSR, very high rates of investment were sought out, with priority given to basic industries (iron and steel, chemical engineering) and to the use of the most recent technologies. The development of heavy industries was supposed to pull along the economy as a whole. Consumer industries were to be developed in a second phase, to respond to the increase in demand generated by the new revenues resulting from the increase in production.

Priority was therefore given to basic industries and to industry at the expense of agriculture. The industrialization of agriculture (mechanization, increase in the use of chemicals) was set as a condition for its expansion (the creation of jobs, products for consumption, the achievement of alimentary independence for the country).

Until 1966, the banking sector had remained dominated by foreign (especially French) banks. Between 1966 and 1967, three large banks took over former institutions: the Banque Nationale d'Algérie (BNA) on July 1, 1966; the Crédit Populaire d'Algérie (CPA) on December 29, 1966; and the Banque Extérieure d'Algérie on September 12, 1967. And, beginning with the first development plan (the three-year plan for 1967–1969), a complete nationalization of the banking sector came about. The first four-year plan (1970–1973) set in place financial central planning (the BAD, the Conseil de Crédit) for the financing of investments.

Would the objectives set in place for the Algerian production system be achieved?

In the first place, what about central planning? The state planning office, which was supposed to ensure the overall coherence of this mechanism, confined itself in fact to collecting the plans of the large national companies and their supervisory ministries. In matters of equipment it was there that the true decision-making power lay.

Despite the enormous investments approved, growth remained excessively slow. Where investments represented 21 percent of the gross domestic product (GDP) in 1963, 42 percent in 1973, and 50 percent in 1977 (that is, some of the highest rates in the world), the GDP increased by an average of 6.4 percent per year over the period 1971–1980.

The gross domestic product reached 36.6 billion dollars in 1981, that is, $1,917 per resident, which placed Algeria far behind Libya ($8,640), but well ahead of Tunisia ($1,242) and Morocco ($722).

The production of raw steel rose from 400,000 to 1.2 million metric tons between 1977 and 1982. The manufacture of tractors, which began in 1974, reached 4,900 units in 1979. The production of electricity went from 4,000 gigawatt-hours in 1977 to 6,000 gigawatt-hours in 1980, and that of manufacturing industries increased 9.9 percent per year between 1970 and 1979, but with many anomalies.

The overconcentration of sources of financing in the oil and gas sector (about 30 percent of total investments between 1967 and 1977) aggravated the situation of the production goods sector, which turned to the importation of Western technologies and to international credit. The objective of economic independence quickly appeared out of reach.

The massive investment in industry (64.1 percent of total investments between 1974 and 1977), and the political weight of state control prevented essential connections from being made: those between public and private sectors, between the production apparatus and the distribution system, and between agriculture and industry. Hence, difficulties in realizing the industrial plans accumulated.

The industrial production units were set up primarily as "turnkey" plants, which were supposed to accelerate development. But the difficulties in mastering and managing sophisticated technologies were largely underestimated. The rise in production of the new factories often took a very long time. The volume of production remained uncertain once they were set in operation. The plans, based on the prospect of very rapid growth, were often overextended, and production units often operated at 30 to 40 percent of their capacity. The hoped-for economies of scale turned into cost overruns. The inadequacy of the stockpiling infrastructures and the total lack of ideas in the marketing system increased the regional imbalances in favor of the industrial poles. The systematic appeal to foreign firms translated into deep debt: Algeria's foreign debt went from 2.7 billion dollars in 1972 to 23.4 billion dollars in 1979 (that is, respectively, a servicing of the debt equal to 12 percent, then 25.6 percent of exports) (Ecrement 1986; Rafot 1982).

Finally, agriculture experienced a rapid aging of its active population, and its low productivity proved incapable of meeting alimentary needs.

The Agrarian Question

The "agrarian revolution," instituted by an order of November 8, 1971, applied to 2,818,000 acres (noncolonial agrarian land) between 1972 and 1975 and was founded on a system of cooperatives: 5,261 cooperatives of different types were formed, with an average size of 536 acres, affecting 90,000 peasants, versus 170,000 in the "self-managed sector" (state farms). Only 10 percent of private property was state-run. The "agrarian revolution" did not elicit great enthusiasm; in fact, a significant proportion of the those receiving allotments would withdraw. The peasant population, estimated at 7 million in 1973, did not feel involved in that authoritarian transformation of agriculture, which remained subordinated to the dictates of the state (Burgat and Nancy 1984).

After the experiment of self-management at the initiative of workers, poor peasants, and some militants (Laks 1970) in 1962–1967, the agricultural sector was supposed to provide industry with a part of its outlets. The objectives assigned to agriculture were various: improve the revenue-production balance to guarantee a decent income to the poorest peasants; diversify and intensify agricultural production to respond to the alimentary needs of the country; and consolidate and improve Algeria's position on the international market in terms of the exportation of agricultural products (Bedrani 1981).

Despite formal statements recognizing the importance of the agrarian sector, however, the latter was sacrificed, and industrialization became the sole priority.

According to the economist Abdellatif Benachenhou, the overall ratio between the investment made and that normally required simply to maintain and replace the production apparatus in the self-managed sector during the 1966–1974 phase was 38 percent. In general, agriculture's very small contribution to the GDP continued to drop: from 31 percent in 1963 to 18 percent in 1965 to 13 percent in 1970. It received only 12 percent of investments for the period between 1970 and 1973, and 7.4 percent between 1974 and 1977, which did not always allow material replacement of the existing means of production. Agrarian reform lacked coherence. For the political scientist Bruno Etienne (1977), what drove the process was "a certain submission of the peasant and of the rural world to the logic of the industrialization of the economy, and, more generally, the imposition, by a power dominated by urban categories, of an urban-industrial conception of development."

In fact, the increasingly unequal urban-rural exchanges served to finance industrial growth. For more than ten years, prices and "salaries" remained frozen in the agrarian sector in order to supply the cities at the lowest possible cost. Factories were set up on more than 370,000 acres of good agricultural lands and drew off the youngest and most skilled labor. The radical devaluation of agricultural work led to a rural exodus that increased on the order of 100,000 people per year.

Agricultural production progressed little. The cereal harvest was on average 1.98 billion kilograms for the period 1979–1981, versus 1.93 billion for 1970–1973 (2.3 billion for 1954–1957) (Benamrane 1980).

The level of alimentary self-sufficiency, which was at more than 70 percent in 1969, was only 30 percent in 1980. Half of the cereal consumed was imported, as was 80 percent of the oil, two-thirds of the legumes, and almost all the sugar. In 1984, Algeria was importing 60 percent of its alimentary consumption (one-quarter of the value of the country's total imports). This rate was constantly on the increase.

The Increase in Emigration

On August 8, 1966, the Algerian head of state, on the occasion of a "first seminar on emigration," cited the industrial accomplishments of Annaba and Arzew, which, according to him, would be able in time to offer jobs to "emigrants planning to return."

But the propaganda on "the return" poorly concealed the migratory pressure toward France that continued to exist. The Franco-Algerian accord of December 27, 1968, limited the freedom of movement set out in the Evian accords. Border control chose to be stricter, more selective than in the past.

On January 12, 1973, at the opening of a "Conference on Emigration," Boumédienne harshly denounced "the insults, provocations, murders, and other discriminatory measures" of which the Algerians in France were the victims at that time, as a result, according to him, of decisions by the Algerian government to nationalize petroleum resources. The Algerian national residing in France, he said, ought to be proud "of his Arab Islamic authenticity," which, Boumédienne added, "protected him from any desire to become integrated into the receiving society."

In fact, in the 1970s, the mobility of the population continued to increase. The agricultural crisis, demographic pressure, and the accelerating rate of urbanization produced even greater displacement. Although migration occurred primarily between Algerian cities within a single rural area, it is also true that the Algerian presence in France continued to grow.

A population of Algerian origin settled in France in a lasting manner, with no plan to return. It retained solid ties with its society of origin on the economic and sociocultural level.

Table 13.2 The Algerian population in France

1968	1975	1982	1988
471,020	710,690	795,920	820,900

Source: *L'Etat du Maghreb* (Paris: La Découverte, 1991).

The Great Third World Plan

Boumédienne achieved his greatest successes on the regional and international scene. Third World intellectuals, but also European ones, hastened to admire "the Algerian miracle." The fourth summit of nonaligned countries was held in Algiers from September 5 to 9, 1973. At the time, the image of Algeria was that of a revolutionary state supporting the political and economic "liberation movements."

The principles set down from the beginning by "the Soummam charter" of 1956 and the "Tripoli agenda" of 1962— constantly reasserted in various international meetings—had the objective of producing and promoting the various common interests among the Third World states. That search for common interests was based particularly on an economic approach to international relations. For the jurist Jean-Robert Henry, Algeria's political vision was "fundamentally economistic, adapted to the means of the country—which did not allow an excessive arms build-up—and to the issues that presented themselves in turn: emerge from the neocolonial system, promote development, find a place in the world economic order" (*Le Monde*, July 3, 1982). In that spirit, the first words of the National Charter of 1976 indicated that "foreign policy must reflect domestic policy."

Algeria was basking in the aura conferred upon it in the eyes of many Third World peoples as a result of its war of liberation, and supported by a team of "diplomat militants"—which led people to say that Algeria had a "diplomacy of freedom fighters" (Balta, Duteuil, and Rulleau 1981). Under the direction of Houari Boumédienne and Abdelaziz Bouteflika (minister of foreign affairs), it sought to broaden its international role.

After the cancellation of the Algiers conference scheduled for summer 1965 following the Boumédienne putsch, diplomacy was revived through the adoption of the so-called Charter of the 77 in October 1967. The so-called 77 group, which brought together developing countries within the framework of the UNCTAD (United Nations Conference on Trade and Development), insisted on the internal efforts that developing countries had to make. Then Algeria applied itself to ironing out its disputes with its Maghrebian neighbors. The signing of a treaty of "fraternity, neighborliness, and cooperation" with Morocco (the Ifrane treaty), on June 15, 1969, included a recognition of Mauritania. An identical accord was signed with Tunisia in January 1970. At the same time, the thorny problem was raised of relations with the old colonial metropolis. France dismantled the Reggane atomic base in the Sahara in 1966, evacuated the Bizerte military base on January 1, 1968, and the Bou-Sfer base on December 28, 1970. The crisis between Algiers and Paris reached significant proportions when oil and gas deposits were nationalized in 1971. It was via the conflict with its French partner that Algeria then attempted to involve the Third World countries in a concerted action to reform the world economic order. Emphasis was placed on the issues of raw materials, including fossil fuels, national economic independence, and the need for a new world economic order (Grimaud 1984).

After the Algiers conference in September 1973, at which a "list of grievances" was established, and the Arab-Israeli War in October of the same year, Algeria tested "the petroleum weapon." Boumédienne worked to maintain the difficult cohesion of OPEC (Organization of Petroleum Exporting Countries) and to prevent its richest representatives from joining the camp of the "wealthy" and thus from cutting themselves off from the Third World. In April 1974, the Algerian president defended the new international order before the UN General Assembly, convened at his request, in the name of the nonaligned countries. In March 1975, Algeria took the initiative by calling the first OPEC "summit."

But Algeria's great Third World plan ran up against the hostility of certain Western countries, got bogged down in discussions internal to the Third World, received rough treatment during the conflict in the Western Sahara, and suffered the consequences of the new international power relations set in place after 1973, resulting from what has been called the "first oil crisis."

The Conflict in the Western Sahara

After the 1963 "sands war" (see above, chapter 11) and the 1969 Ifrane treaty, Algeria made peace with Morocco and Mauritania. Hassan II, the king of Morocco, in his encounters with Boumédienne and Moktar Ould Daddah, who ruled Mauritania, subscribed to the principle of self-determination for the Spanish Sahara. He had no doubt that a vote by the populations concerned would be only a formality, destined to consecrate their attachment to Morocco. The population of the Western Sahara under Spanish domination was composed of about twenty tribes, which were attached to four large groups: the Reguibat, the Tekna, the Maquils, and the Ouled Delim. The census taken by the Spanish in 1974 estimated that population at seventy to eighty thousand. This figure did not take into account the Saharans who had fled to the bordering countries or those who were nomadic. The Polisario Front (Popular Front for the Liberation of Saguia el

Hamra and Río de Oro), created on May 10, 1973, estimated that the number oscillated between 250,000 and 300,000.

Beginning in 1963, Spain had exploited phosphate deposits (discovered in 1947) in Saguia el Hamra in the Western Sahara. At 75 kilometers long and between 1 and 15 kilometers wide, these deposits extended over 250 square kilometers. The reserves were estimated at 10 billion metric tons. Elsewhere, the substratum also contained iron, copper, uranium, and natural gas. Along the coast lay one of the richest fish "reservoirs" in the world.

In 1973, Morocco, which intended to increase its economic power in phosphates by reclaiming the Western Sahara, became concerned. Spain wanted to arrange for an independence agreement for the territory that would preserve its interests in the region. And, above all, the Polisario Front, led by a handful of young militants assembled around a twenty-five-year old academic, El Ouali Mustapha Sayed (he would die in June 1976), launched the first military operation against the Spanish on May 20, 1973. Algeria, for its part, opted for an independent, nonaligned Western Sahara. On August 20, 1974, Hassan II announced that he was opposed to any referendum that might lead to the independence of the disputed territory. In late October, he interested the Mauritanian president in an eventual division of the Western Sahara and concluded a secret agreement with him. In April–May 1975, a UN investigative mission went to the site and recommended that the principle of self-determination be applied. On October 16, the international court of The Hague, seized by Hassan II, also recommended self-determination. The king of Morocco then wagered everything. He rallied the Moroccan opposition to his side (with the exception of certain far left groups, especially the Marxist-Leninist organization Ilal Amam) and persuaded the organization to hold a "green march." Beginning on November 5, it assembled 350,000 demonstrators, who marched toward the Sahara.

The Spanish regime was impressed. On November 14, 1975, the Madrid accord consecrated the division of the Western Sahara between Rabat and Nouakchott.

Isolated at first, Algeria set in motion an intense diplomatic campaign. On February 27, 1976, the majority of members in the Organization of African Unity (OUA) were ready to recognize the Polisario Front as a "liberation movement." The front immediately proclaimed a Sahrawi Arab Democratic Republic (SADR), with Mohamed Abdelaziz, then age thirty-one, at its head. The supreme organ of the SADR was the executive committee, or command council of the revolution, composed of nine members. It ensured the control of 60 percent of the territory and announced that it had ten thousand soldiers, including three thousand permanently stationed at the front. The Polisario Front was supported militarily by Algeria and financially by Libya (Barbier 1982). It was often said at the time that all-out war might erupt between Algeria and Morocco. In the end, the tension was handled skillfully by both sides.

On May 1, 1977, the Polisario Front, which focused most of its military efforts on Mauritania, received widespread media attention by killing two French citizens and abducting six others in Zerouate. On November 25, the French military intervened. Tensions ran high. Morocco sent out an expeditionary force of twelve thousand men. The men in the Polisario Front attacked the mining centers that ensured the export of iron, the principal source of Mauritania's revenues.

On July 10, 1978, Lieutenant-Colonel Mustapha Ould Salek overthrew Moktar Ould Daddah, the Mauritanian head of state, and proposed to extricate the country from the war. On July 12, the Polisario Front decreed a cease-fire with Mauritania. It concentrated its attacks against the Sharifian kingdom, which was impelled to build a very long protective "wall." In Morocco, the burden of military expenses contributed to the deterioration of the economic and social situation.

When President Boumédienne died in December 1978, the conflict in the Western Sahara was not yet settled. For a long time, it continued to poison relations between Algeria and Morocco, with Rabat accusing Algiers of hegemonic ambitions in the Maghreb (Assidon 1978).

14

Society and Culture in Algeria (1962–1982)

When Algeria achieved independence in 1962, it lacked both financial means and cadres. To win the wager of economic autonomy, it needed competent men and women. Within only twenty years the cultural and social landscape was profoundly changed.

The Challenges of Education and Training

In 1961, French young people were educated at a rate of 100 percent, Algerian children at less than 15 percent. The number of Muslims registered in primary classes was barely 700,000. In 1970, it was already close to 2 million and, in 1980, over 4.5 million. At the beginning of the school year in 1982, 250,000 young people were attending high school, and 80,000 students were at university (there had been 2,800 in 1963).

In July 1962, there were only 1,700 Algerian teachers in primary education. At independence, 1,000 of them were called upon to organize the new administrations. Thousands of "monitors" were recruited, aided in their tasks by *coopérants*. A total of 11,000 French teachers would come over the years to offer their help. In 1982, the number of instructors, all Algerian, in educational activities was twenty-seven times what it had been twenty years earlier, rising from 1,700 to 19,000.

School was an integral part of the Algerian landscape in the large cities and from the Aurès to the oases of the Sahara. Groups of children trudging along roads with school bags on their backs or in their hands were an omnipresent sight (Haddad and Khenniche 1981).

Between 1970 and 1980, the disparity between the schooling of girls and that of boys dropped. Girls represented about 40 percent of those attending primary and secondary school. At the university level, that rate stagnated at 25 percent beginning in 1978.

Nevertheless, the progress in the rate of education among girls signified the changes produced by the "schooling revolution," especially in the relations between the sexes. Co-education took root on school benches, toppling conformism and prejudice. Large numbers of young Algerian girls, who had abandoned the *haik* (traditional veil) en masse and who wore slacks, became part of the skilled labor force. They were found especially in education; women magistrates, lawyers, and doctors were more unusual. Nevertheless, modernization, brought about by urbanization and schooling, did not touch all sectors of society related to women: arranged marriages continued, family tradition still carried a great deal of weight, and women and men did not mix openly in public (Khodja 1985; Maschino and M'Rabet 1972; M'Rabet 1979; Vandevelde 1980).

The "basic schooling" plan was set in place at the beginning of the school year 1980. From that time on, pupils had to take a nine-year curriculum divided into three integrated cycles of three years each. The basic cycle (for six- to nine-year-olds) was devoted to learning the fundamentals (reading, writing, arithmetic) by active methods. The intermediate cycle (for ten- to twelve-year-olds) was to reinforce the first achievements and also introduced the teaching of French at a rate of ten hours per week, out of a total course work of twenty-seven hours and thirty minutes. Finally, the advanced cycle (thirteen- to sixteen-year-olds) allowed for specialization, and dealt with the scientific disciplines, the social sciences, and "polytechnical education." The classes educated between 1970 and 1981 produced 33,000 intermediate school teachers and 500 school inspectors. Logistical structures were also set in place, such as the National Pedagogical Institute, which printed 21 million volumes for the single year of 1982.

At the university level, the following provisions were made in the 1970s: the university year was replaced by semesters, the traditional Faculties were complemented by institutes, vacations were shortened, teaching modules were set in place, and the separation between disciplines was eliminated. This system was inspired by the American model, while "basic schooling" was suggested instead by the model in force in the Eastern countries. In both cases, this was a break from the educational tradition bequeathed by the French presence. The results were not very convincing. More than 200,000 students left school every year between the age of six and thirteen.

The success rate at the *baccalauréat* exam hovered around 25 percent in 1982. Recourse to foreign assistance remained very high. In the early 1980s, nearly one-third of primary school teachers were French, Russian, Romanian, Syrian, and especially, Egyptian *coopérants*. In secondary education, priority was given to general education. For the school year 1975–1976, the secondary education students were divided as followed: 93.4 percent in general education, 7.6 percent in technical education.

The university graduation rate was low. Only slightly more than seven thousand degrees were awarded in 1980–1981. Studies lasted an unusually long time. The imbalance, already very visible in secondary school, between general studies and scientific pursuits, persisted. (Nearly 40 percent of students were in the literature, economics, and law tracks.) Although the number of students rose considerably after independence, their supervision and technical training were not adapted to the imported technologies. The training of cadres led to a priority being given to the operations of management at the expense of a mastery of technology. The role assigned to cadres required a diploma as the unimpeachable right of access to a position, rather than knowledge indispensable for future technological mastery.

In addition, the Algerian educational apparatus, in spite of the enormous efforts in schooling, came up against two problems: demographic growth and questions of identity in the gradual Algerianization of the schools.

The Demographic Problem

The health care revolution, via effective medications, vaccination campaigns, and the massive distribution of chemical products to prevent infections and epidemics, produced a drop in the mortality rate in the Maghreb. The average life expectancy, which was barely thirty years in 1920, ranged between sixty-six (Tunisia) and sixty-one (Morocco) in 1980. That decline in the mortality rate was not accompanied by a drop in the birth rate. Beginning in the 1970s, Algeria had one of the highest population growth rates in the Maghreb and among developing countries, as the table below indicates.

In 1974, during the international conference on population, Algeria classified itself as one of the anti-Malthusian countries, and claimed that "the best contraceptive is development." Locked within the Third World pro-birth ideology, it was approaching a world record, with 8.1 children per woman in 1975. The country, with a resident population estimated at 18,666,000 on July 1, 1980, and with 46.5 percent of its population under

Table 14.1 Population growth rate in the Maghreb (1950–1990) (in average annual percentages)

	1950–1955	1955–1960	1960–1965	1965–1970	1970–1975	1975–1980	1980–1985	1985–1990
Libya	1.8	3.6	3.7	4.0	4.0	4.0	3.8	3.6
Tunisia	1.8	1.8	1.9	2.0	1.8	2.6	2.1	2.3
Algeria	2.1	2.1	2.0	2.9	3.1	3.1	3.0	3.3
Morocco	2.5	2.8	2.7	2.8	2.5	2.9	3.2	3.1
Mauritania	2.0	2.2	2.35	2.45	2.6	2.8	2.9	3.1
Average for developing countries	2.1	2.1	2.3	2.55	2.4	2.1	2.0	1.9

Source: L'Etat du Magbreb (Paris: La Découverte, 1991).

the age of fifteen, in 1980 produced 19,000 more newborns than France, whose population was three times as great (819,000 versus 800,000).

In 1983, a new awareness of the problem expressed itself in the adoption of a national program to control population growth, which occurred at a time when fertility was already beginning to drop: 6.1 children per woman in 1984 (the mean was 4.8 in 1987).

That drop in fertility went hand in hand with the schooling of girls and became more pronounced with a greater participation by women in economic life. But did not that drop in fertility face possible pressure from the Islamist movements, given their conception of the place of women in society?

Although Algeria, like the other countries in the Maghreb, entered a phase of "demographic transition," a time of falling fertility, the statistics are nevertheless "mind-boggling": Algeria had 26.6 million residents on January 1, 1993, versus 8.5 million on the eve of the war of independence. According to the Algerian National Office of Statistics, the population grew by 640,000 in 1992, which is a birth rate on the order of 3 percent. The population curve predicted more than 50 million residents by 2025.

The demographic situation influenced the strategy of social development in employment, housing, education, and health. Demographic policy was also concerned with the scope of migration (hence, for the years 1975 and following, approximately 170,000 people definitively left the rural areas). Rapid urbanization led to the development of substandard housing on the outskirts of the big cities.

Table 14.2 Demographic indicators

	1970	1980	1992
Population (in millions)	13.7	18.7	26.3
Density (in residents per square kilometer)	5.8	7.9	11.0
Annual growth (%)	3.0[a]	3.1[b]	2.7[c]
Mean fertility (number of births per woman)	7.4[a]	6.8[b]	4.9[d]
Infant mortality (per thousand births)	139.2	97.6	61.0[d]
Life expectancy (in years)	52.4	58.0	66.0[d]
Urban population (% of total)	39.5	43.4	52.0[e]

Source: *L'Etat du monde* (Paris: La Découverte, 1994).
[a] 1965–1975.
[b] 1975–1985.
[c] 1985–1991.
[d] 1990–1995.
[e] 1991.

Social Questions

The considerable rise in the urban population came about within a context of weak social structures and a deterioration in living conditions: rapid growth in the occupation rate per lodging, deterioration of housing for workers (Benamrane 1980), the development of regular agglomerations of substandard housing around the large industrial cities (the process of "slumification"), and inadequate health coverage for families (despite the free care established in 1973).

For the first time, in 1977–1978 the population of urban workers was greater than the population employed in the rural areas (at least if the official statistics on the active population can be trusted, which took little account of female and child labor). The decade of the 1970s, in fact, underwent a significant development in blue-collar jobs in the industrial sector: the share of industry and of construction work in overall employment rose from 21 percent in 1967 to 37 percent in 1983, and, excluding agricultural and service workers, the number of blue-collar workers rose from 240,000 in 1969 to about 1,100,000 in 1983, a growth in the employed population from 13 percent in 1967 to 30 percent in 1983. The division of workers by industrial branch shows a predominance, in the late 1970s, of fossil fuel industries, iron and steel, metallurgy, and mechanics, whereas, in the late 1960s, the alimentary industries, textiles, construction work, and transportation employed the largest share of the labor force. Industrialization also produced a significant spatial redeployment of activities in Algeria (primarily Annaba in eastern Algeria and Oran/Arzew in the west). Saïd Chikhi (1989) notes that "the coastal *wilayas*, which accounted for 56 percent of public industrial labor in 1970, represented only 29 percent in 1982." That increased dispersion of the industrial plants relativized somewhat the appearance of industrialization in its beginnings, which primarily affected the coastal areas.

At the same time, great inequalities appeared between the wage earners in the public sector and those in the private sector. Between 1967 and 1980, though there was little progress in the purchasing power of workers, that of private entrepreneurs increased by 56 percent (Thiery 1982). That shift led to an increase in the number of strikes, even in public enterprises where they were theoretically prohibited. According to Ministry of Labor statistics, the number of workers "directly affected by strikes" represented 9.6 percent of the total work force in public and private enterprises in 1964, 6.9 percent in 1972, and 11.3 percent in 1977, the year of the major transportation strike in Algiers. Officially, the number of strike actions rose from 521 in 1977, with 72,940 strikers, to 768 in 1981, with 117,254 strikers. In 1969, strikes affecting public enterprises represented less than 3 percent of the total; in 1977, 36 percent; in 1980, 45 percent; and in 1982, 63 percent (Saadi 1982; Touati 1982). More than the strikes, daily conduct at work (relaxed pace, negligence, absenteeism) attested to the fact that the wage relation was not yet "normalized." In addition, urbanization contributed to a severing of traditional ties, and the rural exodus prevented workers from identifying with their community group of origin. The spread of education also imposed different cultural models. Access to consumer goods offered workers the possibility of changing their way of life. Everything moved very quickly in Algeria in the years 1975–1980. That "de-symbolization" (Chikhi 1989) of the traditional universe, the "forced-march" modernization of an entire society, made Algeria's experience of identity problems more acute.

Algerianism, the Linguistic Questions

The Algerian revolution intended to re-Arabize Algeria, which was "de-personalized by colonialism." Beginning with independence that desire for Arabization gradually took root in education. Under the presidency of Houari Boumédienne, these efforts accelerated and the battles for Arabization took on an ideological aspect. One had to definitively turn the page on French colonialism. In 1973, Minister of Information and Culture Ahmed Taleb, or Ibrahimi—son of Sheikh Bachir Ibrahimi, president of the Association des Oulémas Algériens—wanted to demonstrate that "France killed Algerian culture by cutting it off from all lifeblood, and by keeping it outside the moment of history. That is a real murder" (Taleb-Ibrahimi 1973). In 1972, Abdelmajid Meziane described the model desired by France as a de-culturation of the Algerian populations. This plan led "to generalized rootlessness; there was no longer any refuge, any anchor; religion itself was colonized. The oral tradition of the roving poets saved what could be saved (the recollection of ancient glories, the legendary eras of the heroes of Islam, the idealization of traditional values)."

For them and for others the history of Algeria was battered, violated by the colonial system; it was never perceived as the bearer of any kind of modernity.

For those who had been dispossessed of their culture, the long and exacting task consisted not only of recapturing a lost ancestral patrimony, but also of radically breaking with the tradition inherited from the French presence. The notion of "wiping the slate of the past clean" set in. It was practiced primarily in the realm of Arabization, in the battle against the perpetuation of the French language. For Ali Ammar, head of the "studies and concepts department" of the FLN at the time, "in 1974 Algeria, people more often spoke, and on a vaster scale than in the past, the language inherited from colonialism. Almost instinctively, two people who met for the first time began their conversation in French. That meant that the Algerian of 1974 identified more easily with the dominant culture (and hence the dominant ideology) than in the past" (Stora 1991b). With bilingualism considered only "circumstantial," Algeria thus refused to associate with the Francophone movement and advocated in its stead the use of the Arabic language. Unlike the situation in other Mediterranean nations such as Lebanon, Egypt, and Turkey, French culture had become implanted in the Maghreb as a result of a violent act of colonization. Yet, particularly in Algeria, it is nevertheless true that French culture had rapidly taken root in the local reality, even becoming an instrument of struggle against French political domination. Moreover, Arabization was a long and difficult task. Classical literary Arabic remained a "foreign" language for the majority of Algerians. Bilingualism, despite the progress of Arabic, remained an established fact. The daily newspapers in the Arabic language, such as *Ech Chaab* (The People), were read less often than the papers written in French, such as the daily *El Moudjahid* or the weekly *Algérie-Actualité*. That tendency still existed in the early 1990s. In addition, the democratization of education paradoxically multiplied the number of French speakers.

The problems of identity experienced by the Algerians were highlighted by the confrontation in the 1970s between the advocates of total Arabization on one side, and the champions of Arabic, Algerian, and Berber "popular cultures" on the other. The crisis, in fact, was not only linguistic but cultural, and even political in the broad sense of the term. This was particularly clear at the time of the eruption of the "Berber spring of 1980" (see below, chap. 15).

In practice, the Arabization of education in basic schooling and in certain sectors of higher education (especially the social sciences) was completed in 1982. Arabization hardened the distinction between Arabophone elites and Francophone elites, a distinction, moreover, that the educational system continued to reproduce (medicine and technology were still taught in French).

At the ideological level, the spread of the classical Arabic language made it possible, via foreign *coopérants*, to increase the influence of the pan-Arabist currents, particularly Baathism (currents of Arab nationalism originating in Syria and Iraq), and very active currents of political Islam from the Middle East (especially Egypt, with the "Muslim Brothers" movement).

State Control of Islam, the First Islamist Opposition

Superimposed on the battle for an Arab identity was the battle for an Islamic identity. The desire to Islamize Algerian society from above was set in place by a whole series of measures and initiatives. A decree was promulgated on August 16, 1976, that a day of rest be imposed on Friday (which is considered the holy day in Islam) instead of Sunday; on March 12, 1967, gambling and the sale of alcoholic beverages to Muslims were banned; on February 27, 1979, a decree was promulgated banning Muslims from raising hogs; a decree of February 9, 1980, asked the Ministry of Religious Affairs to "concern itself with promoting an understanding of Islam, while explaining and diffusing the socialist principles of the government." Seminars on Islamic thought took place every year after 1968, in the presence of official public figures and religious and political representatives.

The constitution and the National Charter, as well as the statutes of the FLN, defined the place and role of Islam in the institutions. The National Charter of June 27, 1976, stipulated that "Islam is the state religion" (article 2), and added that the president of the Republic had to be of "the Muslim faith" (article 107); it required "that he take an oath ... , respect and glorify the Muslim religion" (article 110), and stated that "no proposal for a revision of the constitution may target the state religion" (article 195).

All the private schools were nationalized; the only kind of school that existed was denominational. The number of mosques increased from 2,200 in 1966 to 5,829 in 1980. In the twenty years following independence, religion was used as an instrument to contain possible advances in the secular and democratic currents, and, above all, as a weapon for the legitimation of power.

In *L'Islamisme radical*, Bruno Etienne (1987) aptly demonstrates that Algerian Islam is a monist Islam (a philosophical system in which there is only one sort of reality on the religious level). That version expressed itself in the state monopoly on religious affairs and the repression of beliefs and practices judged deviant in relation to official norms. All the same, the state seems to have tolerated what Henri Sanson, in *Laïcité islamique en Algérie*, calls an "internal pluri-denominationalism": in Algeria, Sunnite Islam of the Maliki school coexisted with that of the Hanifi and Ibadite schools. Moreover, despite the centralization of the politico-religious field, popular practices, such as the cult of local saints, remained strong and were combined with the practices of Islam established by the state (Sanson 1983).

The Islamist movement that began in the 1970s, isolated within secrecy and exclusion, operated underground, developing a language that rejected the state's monopoly on religion. Thus, in Morocco in 1974, Sheikh

Soltani, close to the traditional ulama, published a virulent critique of the Socialism of the Algerian leaders, and of Boumédienne's Socialist choices, under the title *Le mazdaquisme est à l'origine du socialisme* (Mazdakism is the Origin of Socialism), which is considered the first manifesto of the Islamist movement in Algeria. He denounced moral decay and "the destructive principles imported from abroad." The association *Al Qiyam* (The Values), formed in 1964 around the figure of Hachemi Tidjani, presented itself as the instrument for restoring the authentic values of Islam. It called for "action ... within the framework of the party of God, as opposed to the party of Satan," recommended "an Islamic policy drawn from the divine revolution," and envisioned the formation of a "single state with a single leader, founded on Muslim principles" (Lamchichi 1990). The association, dissolved by decree on March 16, 1970, opened the way for other currents of Algerian Islamism (Deheuvels 1992). These developed using the linguistic debates of the 1970s. Students in the Arabized tracks, frustrated by the lack of openings and the inadequacy of their training, were receptive to the protests that championed the value of Arab Muslim culture (Burgat 1988).

The Reconstruction of the Past and the Legitimation of Power

After the 1965 coup d'état, power became concentrated in the hands of a single man. "It was necessary both to articulate the three structures—state, army, and FLN—with one another to make them a functional triangle, and to 'nationalize' them to make people forget their 'original illegitimacy,'" notes the sociologist Abdelkader Djeghloul (1989).

A military bureaucracy seized power and organized society in an authoritarian manner on the pretext of preventing any scission in the national structure. But nothing was more dangerous for this regime established by force than the lack of "legitimacy." The FLN thus became the site of symbolic legitimation. The Party ideologues deliberately opted for a history encapsulated in the lapidary formula, "by the people and for the people," which, in reality, consisted of eliminating all the protagonists in the national movement (before and during the war) that the canons of the system did not embrace.

For the Algerian military, which took power in 1965, this entailed rewriting Algerian history to make people forget the role of the guerrilla forces within the country. It also entailed making them forget, via that fictional history in which the military played a central role, certain moments in the partisan history of Algerian nationalism. Among other functions, the commemorative frenzy under way eliminated the intervention of the peasant (August 1955) and urban (December 1960) masses, the role of the immigration movement and hence of the FLN's Fédération de France, and finally, the advantageous use of international relations to win the war. "The border army," headed by Houari Boumédienne, entered Algerian history in force. That "writing of history" began in June 1966, when a decision was made to establish a measure of sovereignty by "nationalizing" the teaching of history via Arabization. The libraries, and especially, the bookstores, were controlled by the monopoly on foreign trade. In 1974, the system was perfected through the creation of the National Center for Historical Studies, or NCHS. An order published in the *Journal Officiel* a few years later limited historical research not authorized by the NCHS. At the time, it was common to read in the official Algerian press articles against foreign researchers, who were accused of exploiting the history "of the Algerian revolution for mercantile aims." Were Algerian researchers therefore encouraged to set to work? The answer to that question oscillated between two extremes.

On the one hand, the response was that it was still too early to do objective work: the writings of Mohammed Harbi (*Aux origines du FLN* [Bourgois, 1975] and *Le FLN, mirage et réalité* [Editions Jeune Afrique, 1980]), Ferhat Abbas (*Autopsie d'une guerre* [Garnier, 1980]), and even Major Azzedine (*On nous appelait fellaghas* [Stock, 1976]) were dismissed. Professor Mahfoud Kaddache's imposing *Histoire du nationalisme algérien* (*History of Algerian Nationalism* [NPDC, 1980]) set out the premises of the war. During a "seminar on the writing of history" in Algiers in 1981, he said: "However partisan the analysis of these authors, whatever reproach one might make of their investigative method, it is nevertheless true that their works constitute important testimony, which, as objects of scientific criticism, will allow us to advance in the writing of that history."

On the other hand, people were encouraged to produce episodes in a revolutionary chanson de geste that projected the mythic image of a Manichaean universe, with the roles of heroes and traitors, liberators and oppressors, well defined. Slimane Chikh, author of *L'Algérie en armes* (Economica/OUP, 1981), criticized that conception of the "writing" of history: "The word, so long contained, is fairly apt to bay in becoming liberated. Thus the history of the armed struggle often adopts the tone of the triumphalist hymn, which sees itself as a just tribute to the martyrs, hagiography rather than history."

Paradoxically, never was the history of "the Algerian revolution" so celebrated, so commemorated, as during the period 1965–1980. But what history was at issue? A sanitized history with, as its central motto: "A single hero, the people." An anonymous history, since the names of the protagonists in that war of liberation were disappearing from school manuals and street signs. Only the dead were fully accepted. The traces of the terrible "settling of accounts" between Algerians (which had produced thousands of victims, particularly among the émigrés) were effaced (Stora 1992b). The existence of political pluralism, at work in the long march of Algerian nationalism before 1954, with Messali Hadj's pro-independence radicals, who had opposed Ferhat Abbas's "reformists" and the religious ulama, was concealed. In contrast, History (with a capital H) in the present was written in a uniform manner, rejecting any plural approach. Under these conditions it is not surprising that Algerian youth struggled with "gaps in memory" and became once more depoliticized.

A cliché-laden language set in, especially in the official media. On the particular subject of historical writing, the terms of the debate were redefined early in the presidency of Chadli Bendjedid. In the 1984 issue of the journal *Ath Thaquafa*, Nasreddine Saïdouni pleaded "for a new conception of our Algerian history." He envisioned "reappropriating the past" by ridding oneself of "all conceptions contrary to the authenticity of the Algerian nation, which stand as an obstacle to the development of society in its *Islamic and Arabic crucible*, and which do not conform with the foundations on which the modern Algerian state rests." To erase 132 years of French presence and to return to the mythical purity of an Arabic and Islamic state entailed re-creating a "sovereign Algerian state," which Charles X's soldiers had supposedly destroyed in 1830. That state was said to have been resurrected in 1962. As a result, official historiography transformed the French colonial period into a continuous, permanent insurrection, and by-passed the modern voluntarist dimension of Algerian nationalism in the years preceding the November 1, 1954, insurrection against France.

Publishing, Literature, Film

The National Publishing and Distribution Company, or NPDC, was created in 1967. Major state subsidies (2.5 billion dinars in 1981) covered all costs other than those incurred in printing and distribution, which made it possible to market books at an average price of between 20 and 30 dinars per copy. The same financial efforts were approved by the state for imported books, in order to reduce the bookstore price by 25 percent for works of a scientific or technical nature, which, along with ordinary books, represented two-thirds of orders from abroad.

In 1973, the creation of the Office of University Publications, or OUP, placed under the supervision of the Ministry of Higher Education and Research, complemented the activities of the NPDC. The OUP attempted to provide a university system under development with the manuals, courses, and basic works, while at the same time ensuring the publication of certain research works.

In 1975 an impressive industrial printing and graphic arts complex was built in Reghaia, near Algiers. It began operation in 1978, and, on principle, could produce up to 12 million volumes per year.

Despite the establishment of that publishing house and manufacture, most Algerian writers, and especially the French speakers, published abroad, particularly in France. Of the 1,800 works on Algeria published between 1962 and 1973, the NPDC published only 555 (287 in Arabic, 268 in French). In great part censorship and bans of all sorts explain the "flight" of authors. There was, in addition, the weight and effect of the bureaucracy. Manuscripts sometimes sat in a drawer for several years without the authors even being informed of the fate of their manuscripts. Literary life was almost nonexistent. The Writers' Union, created in 1963, was considered a "professional" organization and, as a result, placed under the aegis of the Party. The novelists Mouloud Mammeri and Kateb Yacine did not belong to it. The journals, such as *Novembre* (run by Mourad Bourboune), *Promesses* (launched by Malek Haddad), *Deux Ecrans* (run by Abdou B.), and *Cahiers Algériens de Littérature Comparée* (run by Jamel-Eddine Ben-cheikh) disappeared in the 1970s. After Algerian independence, however, several writers exemplified the explosion, the combative vitality of a body of literature: its creative impact is still being assessed and its original internal architecture admired. Side by side with the "old hands" such as Kateb Yacine (*Le polygone étoilé* [Seuil, 1966]), Mohamed Dib (*Le talisman* [Seuil, 1966]), Mouloud Mammeri (*L'opium et le bâton* [Plon, 1965]), stand Assia Djebar (*Les alouettes naïves* [Julliard, 1967]), Mourad Bourboune (*Le Muezzin* [Bourgois, 1968]), Rachid Boudjedra (*La répudiation* [Denoël, 1969]), Nabile Farès (*Yahia pas de chance* [Seuil, 1970]), and Rachid Mimouni (*Le fleuve détourné* [Laffont, 1982]). Although each of these writers has his or her own style and individual ambitions, common themes can be found when they denounce antidemocratic regimes and colonialist ambitions, excoriate racism in France, or quite simply, defend their cultural identity with their pens (Achour 1985; Dejeux 1982; Dejeux 1993). The great Arabophone writers Abdelhamid Ben Hadouga (*Laid Bare*) and Tahar Ouettar (*The She-Mule's Wedding*) belong to the same worldview, as did the poet Jean Senac, who was murdered in Algiers by religious fanatics on September 4, 1973.

The attention given to cinema as a combat weapon and as a witness began with the creation of the GPRA in 1958 and made possible the formation of a small circle of technicians during the war of independence. The National Office for Cinematographic Commerce and Industry, or NOCCI, created in 1967, obtained a monopoly on production and distribution in Algeria. The traditional periodization of the young history of Algerian cinema (Boudjedra 1971) posits three major phases between 1962 and 1982. The first phase, lasting until 1971, was the armed struggle for independence and its continuation; its high point was 1966 with the international recognition of *La battaglia di Algeri* (Gillo Pontecorvo, winner of the Golden Lion in Venice), and *Vent des Aurès* (Mohamed Lakhdar-Hamina, winner of the Cannes prize for first film). In addition, there were other war films such as *Décembre* (M. Lakhdar-Hamina, 1971) and *Patrouille à l'est* (Amar Laskri, 1971). The second phase, beginning in 1972, was the agrarian revolution, with three notable films: *Le charbonnier*, by Mohamed Bouamari, *La corde*, by El Hachemi Chérif, and *Nous*, by Abdelaziz Tolbi (Maherzi 1979).

The third phase dealt more with daily life and corresponded to the era following the adoption of the 1976 National Charter. That phase is illustrated by such films as *Omar Gatlato* by Merzac Allouache (1976), or *La nouba des femmes du mont Chenoua* (1977) by Assia Djebar. In the latter film, the war of liberation is revisited through the memories of a group of women, whose recollections as fighters collapse into an often-frozen present.

This very schematic classification, of one theme within one period, does not account for the complexity of the relationship the filmmaker maintains with society. Many films lie outside that necessarily arbitrary chronological and thematic categorization. Scarcely five years after the end of hostilities, the theme of the war of independence could elicit laughter in *Hassan Terro* (M. Lakhdar-Hamina, 1968); Tewlik Farès depicted the popular memory with *Les Hors-la-loi* (1969), which celebrated the great deeds of the bandits of honor. Off the beaten path, Mohamed Zinet created an astonishing film about Algiers in *Tahia ya didou* (1971); in 1967 the Cannes Film Festival's Palme d'Or was awarded to *Chronique des années de braise*, by M. Lakhdar-Hamina; and, in 1982, Okacha Touita's *Les sacrifiés* showed that, in the war of liberation, the enemy was not only the French police, but might also be a "brother."

In literature, on movie screens, in the street, and in certain newspapers, there was a constant effort to exercise freedom of expression. The Algerians, hungry for culture and passionate about the debate of ideas, felt the need for a revival, especially since at the time of Boumédienne's death on September 27, 1978, nearly 60 percent of the population had never lived under colonization. Neither the "bahis" (young people excluded from the school system and unemployed) nor the "Tchi-tchi" (the cream of young people from the best neighborhoods) nor the "hittistes" ("wall-holders," the idle young who leaned against walls) identified with the populist ideology spread by the regime. Animated by contradictory motivations—to move into cultural

Table 14.3 Cultural indicators

	1970	1980	1992
Illiteracy (%)	75	55.3[a]	42.6[b]
Number of doctors (per thousand residents)	0.13	0.36	0.51[c]
Schooling 12–17-year-olds (%)	30.8	47.7	64.7[b]
Schooling advanced studies (%)	1.9	6.2	11.8[b]
Television sets (per thousand residents)	29.1	52	74[b]
Books published (number of titles)	289[d]	975	718[e]

Source: *L'Etat du monde* (Paris: La Découverte, 1994).
[a] 1982.
[b] 1990.
[c] 1987.
[d] 1968.
[e] 1984.

modernity or to rediscover their roots, to guarantee themselves a stable job or to be able to leave Algeria—Algerian young people asserted themselves in the 1980s and 1990s as an explosive social and political force. The calling into question of the official culture, again carried out by the young, expressed itself best in the realm of music. The revival of Kabyle song found expression in Aït Menguellet, Idir, and Djamel Allam, who were anti-establishment in relation to the regime; and also in rai music, originating in Sidi-Bel-Abbes, which used dialectal Arabic and expressed the discontent and frustrations of young people living in the cities. Such singers as Cheb Khaled and Cheb Mami would become "stars," representatives abroad of the new Algerian music.

15

The Jamming of the System (1979–1988)

In the 1980s and 1990s several major processes developed in the Maghreb and began to resonate with Islamism, a political current that in the previous years had had a "low profile," at least on the public stage.

The Maghreb was confronting Europe. Very complex ties, often the result of the conflictual relations born of colonial history, were established between the Maghreb and Europe. The desire to close the borders, expressed by the countries of Western Europe beginning in 1974–1975, and even more clearly by France in 1986 with the introduction of visas, which banned de facto the very intense movement between the Maghreb and France, reinforced the Maghreb's retreat into identity ("Europe is closing, let us be ourselves"). The rise of nationalism in Europe was accompanied by a crisis in the Maghrebian nation-states.

These nation-states were constructed on imported models, and primarily on the French, Jacobin, and centralizing model. Even though the propaganda, the speeches, and the official ideology denied that debt, it was certainly that model that came to be imposed on the historical situations of Algeria, Tunisia, and Morocco. Yet three questions arose in these countries: must a modern nation-state be constructed on an already-existing imported model? Ought one to embrace an Arab identity, Arab nationalism? Or ought one to embrace Muslim nationalism, the Islamic *umma* (community of believers)? These questions, which were pervasive in Maghrebian societies, proved that the state no longer had the monopoly on national feeling.

179

In that conceptual ambivalence of the nation, breaches and fractures appeared into which the Islamists could insinuate themselves. They would seize hold of national aspirations to contest and challenge the state.

Maghrebian societies in the 1980s were also confronted with a greater affirmation of individual autonomy that expressed itself in a greater frenzy for the consumption of media images, a greater desire to move about freely, a tendency toward and demand for independence of the press, the exercise of rights, and a desire for more openly displayed creativity. That evolution led to a crisis in the family and community model central in these societies. Unquestionably, a shift came about, a desire to move from a subject constantly subjugated to the imperatives of family, religion, and tradition, to a subject who was master of his own human destiny. In Algeria, Islamism presented itself as a response to this very profound unrest, especially since the single-party political system was blocking the development of society.

The Arrival of Chadli Bendjedid

Houari Boumédienne died of an illness on December 27, 1978, before reaching his fiftieth birthday. The emotion of the crowd at his funeral proved that, in the end, he had become popular. On the army's recommendation, Colonel Chadli Bendjedid was designated to succeed Boumédienne by the FLN, the only existing party, by virtue of his status as "the oldest officer of the highest rank." Would he be simply a "transitional president"? Chadli Bendjedid, elected president of the Algerian Republic on February 7, 1979, later received two additional five-year mandates and remained in power until January 1992. Like Houari Boumédienne, he was from the eastern part of the country, Constantinois. Born on April 14, 1929, in Bouteldjia, near Annaba, to a family of poor peasants, he was a noncommissioned officer in the French army when the insurrection erupted in November 1954. He joined the ALN in 1955 and rapidly moved up the hierarchy. He became a member of the general staff established in Ghardimaou under the authority of Colonel Boumédienne. During the crisis in the summer of 1962, Chadli stood behind his leader and against the GPRA. In June 1964, he took over the leadership of the second military region (Oranie), which he held without interruption from 1964 to 1979. Although he was a member of the council of the revolution in 1965, he lived on the fringes of the major political decisions. When Boumédienne died, he prevailed over his two principal opponents, Mohamed Salah Yahiaoui and Abdelaziz Bouteflika, who were also former members of the general staff, thanks especially to the support of Kasdi Merbah, the coordinator of the Algerian security services and the head of military security (political police). The "barons" of Boumé-diennism (Tayebi Larbi, Abdelghani, Ahmed Draia, Benchérif) were ousted and replaced by a new generation of senior officers (Abdi, Blin, Redjala, and Stora 1992).

Chadli depended on several concentric circles to exercise his power: military security, his close friends in Annaba and Constantine, his family entourage, and the FLN's political bureau. Most of the real decisionmakers in Algerian policy were originally from the geographical triangle located in the eastern part of the country, Biskra-Tabessa-Skikda (BTS), with the cities of Khenchela and Batna overrepresented. Did the arrival of that unassuming man, less a "revolutionary" than an administrator, mark the beginning of a new era for Algeria? Chadli Bendjedid wanted economic liberalization and intended to free up Algerian politics. He eliminated exit visas required to leave Algeria and had Ahmed Ben Bella liberated on October 30, 1980. The new regime very quickly ran up against the "Berber spring" in Kabylia, a true cultural explosion that put linguistic plurality (Arabic, Berber, and French) on the agenda in Algeria.

The Crisis of the "Berber Spring"

In the 1970s the conception of the nation that took root strongly was that of Arab Islamism. Ahmed Taleb-Ibrahimi, minister of information and culture, did not hesitate to write in 1973: "In reading everything that has been written on the Arabs and the Berbers in Algeria, we realize that a real effort was made to undermine and divide the Algerian people. To advance, for example, that the Algerian population is composed of Arabs and Berbers is historically false" (Taleb-Ibrahimi 1973).

The National Charter of 1976 not only omitted all reference to Berber language and culture, it also specified that "the generalized use of the Arabic language and its mastery as a creative functional instrument is one of the primordial tasks of Algerian society."

On March 19, 1980, the government banned a conference at the University of Tizi-Ouzou, presented by the writer Mouloud Mammeri, on the use of the Berber language. Teachers and students occupied the university as a sign of protest. A general strike began in Kabylia in April 1980.

The "Berber spring" of April 1980 profoundly shook Algerian ideological institutions. In the first place, it raised the problem of the diversity of the population and of cultural definition in Algeria (Durand and Tengour 1982); in addition, it made possible the restoration of another dimension of Algerian history. In December 1983, in the journal *Tafsut*, Salem Chaker and

Saïd Sadi, two of the leaders of that "Berber spring," explained that "since independence, the ideological currents of the regime, and especially, Arab Islamism, have exerted a monopoly on the cultural and intellectual life of the country, founded on censorship and authoritarianism. They have elaborated an explicit desire to stifle and liquidate the Berber dimension and all autonomous thought."

The effect of the "Berber spring" was to produce, for the first time since independence and from within Algeria, a public counterdiscourse of real import, in a country operating on the principle of unanimism. In that compact universe, where society and state, private and public mingled together in a single bloc, the blossoming of autonomous popular associations and organizations gave texture to Algerian society. The appearance of cultural, democratic pluralism allowed conflicts existing "within the people" to be expressed and resolved by political means.

The Berber "riots" were harshly repressed throughout Kabylia in April and May 1980.

The Party and the Army

Houari Boumédienne's successors inherited the single-party system. At first, they timidly attempted to open things up politically (former president Ahmed Ben Bella was liberated), and reduced the role of the security services and of intelligence. But they did not tackle the single-party system, promoted by the army to check the progress of the political and social "void."

On May 3, 1980, the third session of the FLN's central committee, in its organic resolution published on May 14, granted full powers to President Chadli to proceed with the readjustment of FLN structures. The special congress of the FLN met on June 15, 1980, with 3,998 delegates, 3,339 elected and 659 appointed. The concentration of powers in favor of the head of state (president of the Republic, secretary general of the Party, and minister of national defense) was confirmed. The Algerian institutional system, installed in 1965 and "constitutionalized" in 1976, looked in 1980 "like a state power invested by the military leadership" (Koroghli 1989); other authors have called it variously "Sultanism" (Leca and Vatin 1975), "Bonapartist" (Ammour, Leucate, and Moulin 1974), "military-bureaucratic" (Nair-Sami 1982), and "bureaucratic capitalism."

On December 24, 1980, during the fourth session of the FLN's central committee, the cadres of the "mass organizations"—the UGTA, the Union Nationale de la Jeunesse Algérienne, or UNJA (National Union of Algerian

Youth), the Union Nationale des Femmes Algériennes, or UNFA (National Union of Algerian Women), the Union Nationale des Paysans Algériens, or UNPA (National Union of Algerian Peasants), and the Organisation Nationale des Moudjahidin, or ONM (National Organization of Mujahideen)—and members of the elected assemblies were obliged to join the FLN beginning on January 1, 1981, in application of article 120 of the Party's statutes. President Chadli proceeded to designate the thirty-one secretaries of the *mouhafadhats* (subdivisions of the FLN at the *wilaya* level). Each of these thirty-one men would preside over a coordination council composed of the commander of the sector of the Armée Nationale Populaire (ANP) and the president of the popular *wilaya* assembly. The FLN was increasing its control over society. By application of article 120, it subjugated the youth organization and the unions. In his "state of the nation" message on January 10, 1983, Chadli Bendjedid declared: "It is my will that the Front de Libération Nationale Party be a powerful party, capable of assuming its full role in all realms of national life."

The FLN, which gradually lost the historical legitimacy resulting from the war of independence, had long been discredited for its bureaucracy, money-grubbing, and careerism. That bureaucratization prevented it from carrying out "moralization" operations against those who had diverted funds. On April 21, 1983, *El Moudjahid* announced that about one hundred court clerks and agents in the penitentiary system would be handed over to disciplinary commissions for misappropriation or abuse of power. On May 7, the Audit Office fined Ahmed Benchérif 47,000 dinars for incurring expenses in an irregular manner in 1977, when he was minister of hydraulics. On March 13, 1984, the supreme court charged two former walis from Bechar with diversion of public funds. On August 8, Abdelaziz Bouteflika declared to the AFP agency that he was ready to face "the political debate behind the accusations of diversion of funds; [and that] he had always acted on the instructions of President Boumédienne." On October 24, 1984, a judgment of the Audit Office implicated Belaïd Abdesslam and Liassine, former minister of industry under Boumédienne, in mismanagement. Tayebi Larbi, former minister of agriculture, was accused by the office of diverting public funds.

Most of the procedures were hushed up. Despite several "clean-up" campaigns under Chadli Bendjedid's tenure, corruption reached unparalleled proportions. The practice of "commissions" for establishing foreign companies on Algerian territory developed on a grand scale.

The personalization of the regime, through the concentration of executive and legislative duties, always occurred under the vigilant eye of the army, which was the true governing structure. The army was reorganized in

November 1984. Colonels Abdallah Belhouchet and Mustapha Benloucif were awarded the rank of major general, and eight colonels were promoted to generals. A general staff of the ANP was created, headed by Mustapha Benloucif with the aid of generals. Khalded Nezzar emerged from that group as a leading figure.

Mohamed Chérif Messaadia, the man behind the notorious article 120 of the Party's new statutes, occupied the post of permanent secretary of the FLN's central committee until the 1988 riots. He was to be the focus of the popular discontent.

The Crisis in the Production System

Despite the successes of the economic policy, which gave Algeria a production system mirroring that of semi-industrial countries (an average annual growth rate of 7.5 percent and an 8.1 percent annual growth in industrial production between 1970 and 1980), the difficulties inherent in the introduction and operation of the industrial units (cost overruns, low usage rate of production capacities, lack of mastery of imported technologies) led to serious problems (Ecrement 1986).

In the late 1970s the huge flaws in the successive development plans became apparent, revealing the gaps in the strategy adopted, in particular regarding the priority given to heavy industry at the expense of agriculture and the production of alimentary goods. The expense of importing alimentary goods (2.2 billion dollars in 1980) made Algeria dependent for more than 60 percent of its needs.

That crisis situation led to a sort of "pause." In June 1980 the new five-year plan (1980–1984) attempted to remedy the imbalances produced by the "industrialist" strategy.

The new strategy elaborated under Chadli Bendjedid included a recognition of the role played by the private sector. Beginning on December 10, 1979, a conference on the exploitation of petroleum recommended increasing participation in the research effort by foreign companies and countries. As the result of a meeting of the FLN's central committee, on January 2, 1980, a housing charter was promulgated, encouraging families to acquire private property. On January 6, 1980, the aims adopted for development were made public. These aims, which were supposed to serve as the basis for the five-year plan (1980–1984), recommended in particular a revision of the petroleum policy and a deceleration of the industrialization process. By a decree published in the *Journal Officiel* on May 7, 1980, Sonatrach was "split apart" into four enterprises. Other measures were taken in 1982–1983:

Table 15.1 Algerian foreign trade of commodities

	1970	1980	1992
Foreign trade (% of GDP)	24.4	29.1	21.6
Total imports (in billions of dollars)	1.3	10.8	8.5
Agricultural products (% of total)	16.6	24.2	32.1[a]
Mining products and metals (% of total)	1.9	1.7	2.5[c]
Manufactured products (% of total)	79.3	71.7	62.6[c]
Total exports (in billions of dollars)	1.0	13.9	12.1
Agricultural products (% of total)	20.5	0.9	0.3[a]
Oil and gas (% of total)	70.5	98.5	95.9[a]
Mining products and metals (% of total)	2.5	0.5	0.5[b]
Principal suppliers			
EEC (% of imports)	72.0	67.9	64.2[a]
France (% of imports)	42.4	23.2	26.3[a]
United States (% of imports)	8.0	7.1	8.8[a]
Principal clients			
EEC (% of exports)	80.2	43.4	67.7[a]
France (% of exports)	53.5	13.4	15.1[a]
United States (% of exports)	0.8	48.1	16.8[a]

Source: *L'Etat du monde* (Paris: La Découverte, 1994).
[a] 1991.
[b] 1989.
[c] 1988.

credit was reissued to entrepreneurs in industry and services, and to farmers in the private agricultural sector; authorization was given to private entrepreneurs to freely import spare parts. The central planners sought to develop certain sectors that had been neglected until then (housing and light industries). The privatization of agriculture was encouraged. By virtue of the liberalization of real estate transactions after the 1983 law, and especially, the restructuring of the socialist sector, 1,700,000 acres were transferred from the socialist to the private sector (the "agrarian revolution" had affected 2,883,000 acres). The private sector covered 55 percent of the useful agricultural lands in 1980, rising to 62 percent in 1985: it represented more than 50 percent of production (Cote 1983).

The new economic phase also sought to stimulate private savings and the acquisition and preservation of family wealth: the purchase of land, trade, importation of vehicles, and, after August 1986, the ability of Algerians to open "hard currency accounts" in Algerian banks, regardless of the origin of the funds deposited.

The private sector was at the center of the economic reorientation. The wager was to develop a strong industry in consumer goods, and to reintegrate the unemployed by creating large numbers of jobs. The results fell far short of the announced intentions. The private sector produced few jobs, compared to the public sector.

The more intense search for financial profitability led to a slowdown in hiring. During the first two years of the plan (1980–1981), no more than 280,000 employment positions were created. That reflected a halt in the absorption of the labor force (in 1976, 250,000 new jobs were created annually). The million unemployed already existing from the early 1970s still had to be absorbed, and every year 200,000 more young people came onto the labor market.

Few jobs were directly productive. Strictly speaking, industry represented only 20 percent of new jobs created, plus another 20 percent in construction and public works, versus 33 percent in the already heavily bureaucratized administration.

In agriculture, the private sector provided most of the products, and yields were still very low. The price of Algerian agricultural products was significantly higher than prices worldwide, and it seemed more "profitable" to import. In 1984, the country imported 40 percent of its national consumption of cereals, 50 percent of dairy products, 70 percent of fats, and 95 percent of sugar.

Finally, Algeria remained very dependent on its fossil fuels. This sector represented 32.3 percent of the GDP in 1976–1979, and 37.5 percent in 1980. Industry still represented only 10 percent of the GDP in 1982, that is, a share equivalent to that of 1962, and industrial exports did not always manage to penetrate the world market. The export of fossil fuels counted for 92 percent of the total value of exports for the period 1975–1982 (88 percent in 1972). The fall in oil prices in 1983, and again in 1986 (the correction following the oil crisis), worsened the situation of an economy that was financed almost completely by the international valorization of fossil fuels.

The Burden of Debt

During the 1970s inadeqate savings within the country meant that energy profits and foreign loans were responsible for the vast program of industrialization and the growth of the wage-earning population. In the early 1980s, that translated into a deepening of foreign debt, which represented 35.5 percent of the gross domestic product in 1981.

Inasmuch as the financing of industrialization relied on the revenues from the international valorization of fossil fuels, the drop in oil and gas prices led to an increase in the servicing of the debt.

In the first half of the 1980s, the cost of a barrel of oil fluctuated between 30 and 40 dollars. Beginning in 1986 there was a drop in revenue from the

Table 15.2 Foreign debt of the countries of the Maghreb

	1982	1985	1988	1992
Debt, expressed as percentage of GDP				
Algeria	40.2	32.5	46.8	68.0
Morocco	84.9	136.6	99.5	75.0
Tunisia	48.1	61.6	70.3	55.0
Servicing of debt, expressed as percentage of exports of goods and services				
Algeria	30.7	35.7	78.7	77.0
Morocco	43.2	33.2	26.1	28.5
Tunisia	16.2	25.0	21.8	19.0

Source: World Bank; national data; *Conjoncture* (November 1993).

sale of fossil fuels. A barrel of oil fell to about 15 dollars by 1993, and oil and gas revenues accounted for 97 percent of the country's hard currency receipts. This made the financing problem insoluble. Algeria had to reimburse its creditors, import alimentary products and pharmaceuticals, and, at the same time, buy spare parts and equipment for industry.

The debt, 80 percent of it in private credit at short-term high interest rates, imposed an enormous sacrifice on the country. In 1989 the servicing of the debt reached 6.5 billion dollars, absorbing in itself three-quarters of export receipts.

To a certain extent, the Algerian leaders had opted to "underplay" the foreign debt, which was truly a state secret. Now that "ostrich policy" was no longer possible. The darkest forecasts predicted that Algeria, which had always paid its debts "cash on the nail" (by starving its businesses), would take in 55.5 billion francs in oil revenues in 1994, when the payment for servicing the debt (capital and interest) would cost exactly the same amount. The financing of imports thus looked impossible.

The situation was so grave that, after paying its creditors more than 32 billion dollars between 1989 and 1993, Algeria faced the specter of suspension of payments for the first quarter of 1994. The restructuring of the debt, long a taboo political issue because of political nationalism, was now on the agenda.

Foreign Policy and Relations with France

In foreign policy matters, Chadli Bendjedid confined himself to the traditional Algerian policy axis in his travels: he visited several Arab states first, then made a long tour of Africa (March–April 1981), which allowed him to visit eleven countries, ranging from Mali to Congo. Algeria continued to convince the international scene of its capacity for organization and its "seriousness."

Two actions demonstrated Algeria's authority in diplomatic matters: first, its "goodwill mission" in the delicate negotiation for the liberation of the American hostages held by Tehran from November 1979 to January 1981; and second, its attempts at mediation in the Iran-Iraq war, which were abruptly cut off by the tragic death in an airplane accident, on May 3, 1982, of Mohamed Seddik Benyahia, Algeria's minister of foreign affairs, and of his thirteen companions (including several directors in his ministry). After Benyahia, Ahmed Taleb-Ibrahimi took charge of Algerian diplomacy. But, in the early 1980s, Algeria seemed to be hesitating between assuming its ambitious geopolitical legacy and withdrawing from the game in the world-wide economic disorder. Although preserving the vocabulary of the great Third World plan, the country shifted to a "realist" policy when the first cracking noises began to be heard in the Soviet empire (considered a "natural" ally to the Arab world). The country attempted to establish economic and technological relations with the United States and other Western countries. The experiment of negotiations with France indicated that desire to move to a more realistic policy.

In the early 1980s, the contentiousness between Algeria and France was primarily focused on three points. In the first place, there was emigration. The 820,000 Algerian emigrants (including 360,000 workers) in France could not be sent back home "like parcels," said the Algerian authorities. Second, there was the problem of the "Beurs" (second-generation immigrants). According to French law, the children of Algerians born in France were French. But were they really? said the Algerian authorities, who considered them "nationals." At the time, the question affected 160,000 young people. And finally, there was the social security issue. Since 1965, Algeria had been demanding that France make back payments of 1 billion francs. France refused to acknowledge that startling figure. The relations between the two countries improved with the French left's accession to power. On November 30, 1981, François Mitterrand, while visiting Algiers, proposed that Franco-Algerian relations be "a symbol of the new relations between North and South." On February 3, 1982, the natural gas agreement was signed. Minister of Energy Belkacem Nabi obtained an indexation of the price of Algerian natural gas with that of crude oil.

For France, Algeria was the Algerian state, and certain interlocutors were privileged within that state. The country remained a large "reserve," an economic partner with natural gas and oil. The postulated homogeneity of Algeria, organized around its state and supported by the army and the Party, led to a refusal to examine other forces, other social or political movements. France's attitude manifested itself particularly when Ali Mecili, a member of the Algerian opposition belonging to the Front des Forces Socialistes (FFS), was murdered in Paris on April 7, 1987. The French authorities extradited the alleged killer, Amellou, thus indicating their desire to bury "the Mecili affair" in order not to compromise relations between the two states (Aït Ahmed 1989; Naudy 1993).

Cracks in the "Official History"

During President Chadli Bendjedid's tenure, the war waged against the French colonial presence remained the central moment of symbolic legitimation for the nation, but also for the state. That era was represented as the unification of an entire people without social, political, or cultural distinctions. The presentation of a unanimist memory laid the foundations for a powerful populism (which attempted to mask all social differences and opposing political views) at work in the official ideology.

The era of a complete concealment of Algerian history in all its complexity under the presidency of Houari Boumédienne was followed in the 1980s by that of "the writing of the history" of the war of independence. Memory—lived, preserved, and formulated—became a rallying sign for the entire generation of the upheaval, the memory of victory through independence. That, at least, was the intention of various "seminars in the writing of history" that were organized by the FLN beginning in 1982–1984.

The vast operation of collecting and recording verbal accounts of the different phases of the Algerian revolution, decided on by the authorities, occurred within a clearly defined point of view: "Nothing can allow us to remain spectators of a history that others may write and that some have attempted to falsify on the basis of their political views or their immediate interests" (*Algérie-Actualité*, October 28, 1982).

The presentation of the armed struggle in a heroic mode (where the military chanson de geste served to justify the army's role in the state following independence) was expressed particularly in the genre of biography. Colonial society, a nonegalitarian society, naturally did not conceive of biographies as the lives of the humble and obscure. Thus these obscure people now had to take center stage. For example, with the approach of November 1, 1984, the thirtieth anniversary of the insurrection, obituaries proliferated in the Algerian press.

All these biographies had to do with men who died in battle with weapons in hand. The function of this ceremonial discourse, where praise was the dominant mode of expression, was to celebrate the building of the Algerian state through the intermediary of "heroes" set forth as examples. In the establishment of a collective memory, the repertoire of heroic figures also played a central role in intensifying that memory, in struggling against forgetfulness in a country that was emerging from a "long period of colonial occupation." "To Arm Our Youth via History with the Patriotism of Its Elders"; "The Force of the Past"; "To Restore the Great Deeds in Their Truth"; "In the Living Memories of Those Who Made Revolution"—such were a few of the titles found in the Algerian press to mark the studies from the second seminar on the writing of the history of the revolution in May 1984.

Within this framework, history could become an instrument for providing information but also a means to refashion the past as a projection of present power relations. In the ceremony/commemoration, some figures appeared, others disappeared.

On October 24, 1984, the formal reburial of Krim Belkacem and eight former leaders of the FLN took place in Algiers. On November 1, for the thirtieth anniversary of the outbreak of the insurrection, a presidential decree posthumously pardoned and rehabilitated twenty-one personalities. Was the role of the various participants in the war finally going to be clearly stated? On July 8, 1985, a special issue of *Algérie-Actualité*, devoted to the Organisation Spéciale, or OS (the underground organization set in place by the pro-independence nationalists in 1947), was seized from the newsstands. Several thousand copies were destroyed. That ban can be explained by the fact that the articles mentioned Hocine Aït Ahmed, Ahmed Ben Bella, and Mohamed Boudiaf (leaders in the OS underground organization of the nationalist movement and founders of the FLN, who had all gone over to the opposition). That spectacular example of censorship illustrates the limits of the practice of the Center for Historical Studies, set up by a decision of the only existing party, the FLN. The aim of the commission was not to research and understand a complex past, but to obey the orders of the regime and the demands of the present. It was used in that way in the FLN's internal political debates.

The official history established points of reference, constructed its own legitimacy, and effaced any pluralist approach. In fact, it fabricated forgetting (Stora 1991b).

In July 1987, the weekly *Algérie-Actualité* published a major poll of young people on the history of Algeria and its memory. The names of Krim Belkacem (one of the principal leaders of the GPRA), Abbane Ramdane (organizer of the Soummam Congress), and Didouche Mourad (head of Constantinois in 1954) were rarely mentioned. The commentator on the poll noted: "The heroes are those shown most often on the front pages of newspapers and on television: Amirouche, Larbi Ben M'Hidi, Si Haouès, Zighoud Youcef.... . The only real hero is a dead hero." In effect, the best-known men were those who had died in battle before independence.

The Algerian writer Rachid Mimouni observes: "In Algeria, 60 percent of the population is under twenty. They know that the war existed, of course, but for them it is an old story with mythical aspects."

It was those young people who would be found in the streets in October 1988.

Islam, The Family, and State Fundamentalism

The February 9, 1980, decree relating to the duties of the minister of religious affairs stated that he had the task of "explaining and diffusing the Socialist principles contained in social justice, which constitutes one of the essential elements of Islam." Islam manifested itself in the personality of Algeria and found its full expression in the Socialist Party. The state was the guarantor of both, hence also the guarantor of Islam. The state set in place "a public religious order," but only to the extent that Islam was the religion of Algerian Socialism.

Islam's submission to the official values was reaffirmed in the National Charter of 1986, a new ideological point of reference: "Islam brought to the world a noble conception of human dignity that condemns racism and rejects chauvinism and the exploitation of man by man; the equality it champions is in harmony with and adapted to each of the centuries of history."

The state nationalized Islam without wishing to modify it. The political movement of Islamism came about through a refusal to subordinate Islam to the state, especially since the Algerian state did not have religious legitimacy, unlike, for example, Morocco (Leveau 1993).

The first violent incidents erupted between "Islamist" and "secular" groups at the university housing complex of Ben Aknoun, in the hills of Algiers, on November 2, 1982 (a "progressive" student was killed with a saber). In April 1985, 135 Islamists, accused of belonging to an underground organization, the Islamic Movement of Algeria, or IMA, were put on trial. Their leader was Mustapha Bouyali who had taken to the hills and for five years had defied the police in his home region (Larb'a, near Algiers); he was sentenced in absentia to life in prison and was brought down in January 1987. The Islamist movement made its public appearance during the funeral of Sheikh Adbdellatif Soltani at the Kouba cemetery on April 16,

1984. Thousands of people came for the ceremony, which devolved into clashes, then arrests (Lamchichi 1990).

Through the Ministry of Religious Affairs, the state closely controlled the naming of *imams*, based on a decree of August 6, 1983, which centralized the training of the religious leaders, ordered the creation of a major university of Islamic science at Constantine (it would open its doors in September 1984), and oversaw the construction of mosques, whose number rose to nearly six thousand in 1986. That growth in the number of mosques produced an increasing need for religious workers. The "free imams," close to Islamist circles, took advantage of that shortfall. They belonged to various currents: the traditional ulama, with Mohamed Sahnoun and Abdellatif Soltani, the association *Al Qiyam* (The Values), and Malek Benabi's current. Others were part of the current originating in the Arab East and were associated with the Association of Muslim Brothers, created in Egypt in the 1930s by Hassan el-Banna. Their preachers in the "private" mosques fed the Islamist mobilization. They directed a campaign for the moralization of a society they considered impious. They found a source of encouragement in the diffusion of their ideology through the debate on "the code on the status of the individual and of the family." In spite of numerous protests, and after the bill was put off several times beginning in 1962, the code was adopted by the National Popular Assembly on May 29, 1984. The continuation, though in a limited manner, of polygamy, the prohibition on women marrying a non-Muslim, the fact that women, even as adults, needed a matrimonial guardian, were in contradiction with the 1976 constitution, which proclaimed equality before the law. Many women's associations, particularly those of female veterans of the war of liberation, considered the code a significant regression with regard to the real changes that had come about since independence in the relations between the sexes. The Islamists, for their part, took advantage of the code to demand full application of the shari'a (Islamic law).

Social Movements and the Jamming of a System

Twenty-five years after independence, the economic, social, and cultural landscape of Algeria had been radically transformed. Large modern industrial complexes appeared in Skikda, Annaba, and Arzew. Algeria had a vast iron and steel complex in El Hadjar, oil refineries, fertilizer factories, and natural gas liquification plants. The number of wage-earning jobs rose from 700,000 in 1963 to 2,300,000 in 1981.

The country's center of gravity shifted from the rural areas to the cities.

The population had doubled and become very urbanized (the urbanization rate rose from 30 percent in the early 1960s to nearly 50 percent in 1988).

The continued emigration to Europe, the displacement of the population toward the city, and the movement of rural young people toward wage-earning jobs illustrated the extraordinary mobility of Algerian society. That upheaval was not only geographical but also social and cultural. Millions of Algerians rapidly adjusted to city life and discovered different modes of consumption. Yet the abrupt urbanization produced an "urban crisis." In 1982, the housing situation was catastrophic, since 1 million housing units would have had to be built within ten years merely to reduce the scarcity to its 1973 level. The inadequacy of hydraulic equipment was severe, and this translated into water rationing in most of the large cities. The housing crisis curbed the autonomization of the nuclear family at a time when the old extended family was falling apart.

The new wage earners were now recruited from the large mass of young people, most of them from the cities. Although they had spent more time in school than their elders, they had no social or political memory. They had not experienced the harsh working conditions of the colonial era and the first years of independence. They grew up in a society where the dominant discourse promoted the state's taking charge of the public welfare. But, in the 1980s and 1990s, the state was less able than ever to keep its promises of access to the greatest number of consumer goods, leisure, education, and stable and well-remunerated work. Yet, as the Algerian sociologist Abdelkader Djeghloul (1989) notes, "until the beginning of the 1980s, the strength of populism in the Algerian political regime unquestionably lay in the fact that it was not only an ideology, a discourse of self-legitimation, but a group of effective practices for integrating the majority of the Algerian population into the channels of salaried work and the urban area."

In the late 1970s, the number of unemployed began to grow more quickly, and affected primarily the young. In 1985, nearly 72 percent of those looking for work were under twenty-five. With the crisis in unemployment, housing, and education, a certain disenchantment toward the ideological model grew, especially its industrialist aspect, which had been the foundation of the regime's legitimation and of national consensus in the previous phase. The desire for consumer goods collided with austerity. Algeria was trying to find itself between the old structures, which had been shattered (the familial and social model), and the new ones, which were not yet codified. "Resourcefulness" and individualism developed. The state's deployment of oil and gas revenues was no longer sufficient to finance the vast programs of public investment in industry and services. In addition, there were institutional and political roadblocks. The single-party system, founded on clientelism, curbed any inclination toward autonomy on the part of wage earners, and prevented the younger political generation from taking over for its elders.

Thanks to its oil revenues, Algeria had been spared the "bread riots" that shook Morocco and Tunisia in 1984. But the population was increasingly exasperated by the display of wealth and the arrogance of a new privileged caste. A chasm opened between two societies. Frustrations of every kind accumulated, especially among the young (65 percent of the population).

In 1985, oil prices abruptly collapsed, a counterreaction to the oil crisis. Hard currency became increasingly scarce. Algeria adopted a draconian austerity plan: reduction of social expenses, imports, and the state budget. Equipment and basic necessities began to be scare. The rural exodus continued, and the urban housing crisis deepened. The young were victims of unemployment; deprived of a real cultural life and of big projects to rally behind, they were a potentially explosive force.

The Islamists developed their networks in a clandestine manner. In April 1985, a trial opened for 135 militants accused of belonging to underground organizations. At the same time, demonstrations erupted in the Casbah of Algeria, demanding improvement in housing conditions. The next year, in November 1986, the capital city of eastern Algeria, Constantine, was also affected by violent youth riots. The FLN and the political class in general were implicated. Discontent grew, culminating in the bloody demonstrations of October 1988.

In the end, the economic and political system, the source of the weakness of democratic culture within the society, went into open crisis: there were workers' strikes, culturalist protests, the creation of organizations for the defense of human rights, and the rise of political Islamism.

16

The Crisis of October 1988
and Its Consequences

In October 1988, one year before the fall of the Berlin Wall in November 1989, Algeria experienced the collapse of the single-party system, which, along with the army, had organized Algerian society as a whole in an authoritarian manner. The race began to see which side—a "democratic pole" or an "Islamist pole"—would fill the vacuum left by the FLN Party. That battle got under way just as the outline of a "new world order" was taking shape. In 1991 the Gulf War led to the effacement of the political role played by the USSR (which would disappear as a state entity the same year) and the assertion of the United States as the superpower within the UN. The Maghreb and the Arab Muslim world in general were pervaded by a nationalist or identity-based fervor. After a brief moment of democratic euphoria, Algeria was about to become caught in the tragic web of violence.

The October Riots

On the evening of October 4, 1988, demonstrations, composed primarily of children and young people, erupted in Algeria in protest against the widespread rise in prices and the growing scarcity of basic necessities. In the working-class neighborhood of Bab-el-Oued, cars were trashed and store windows shattered. The next day the demonstrations turned into riots. The main commercial artery was devastated, as was the cultural com-

195

plex of Ryad el-Feth. The rioters targeted public buildings, airline head-quarters, and a nightclub. The FLN's political bureau blamed "irrespon-sibles," who were supposedly "manipulated by secret partners." The army stationed itself at strategic points in the capital, and on October 6 a state of siege was decreed. Despite the armored vehicles, the demonstrations continued. Flaming barricades were set up and shots were fired, causing several dozen deaths and injuries. The newspaper *El Moudjahid* ran the headline, "Stop the Vandalism"; and, on October 7, the unrest spread to the major Algerian cities. Three hundred arrests were officially an-nounced in Algiers. In an interview on *Radio-Beur*, in France, Ali Ammar, president of Amicale des Algériens (Algerian Association, an FLN organi-zation) in Europe, declared: "It's just a racket made by kids who have lost control, that's all it is." The same day, the major new element was the Is-lamists' entry on the scene. In the Belcourt neighborhood, after Friday prayer, a procession of seven to eight thousand Islamist sympathizers clashed with the police. The next day in Kouba, the army opened fire near a mosque, causing about fifty deaths. On October 10, in Bab-el-Oued, as a bloody repression was striking the Islamist processions (33 dead), Presi-dent Chadli received three leaders of Algerian Islamism: Imam Ali Benhadj, one of the preachers most heeded by the young, Mohamed Sah-noun, and Mahfoud Nahnah. They handed him a list of grievances. That evening, Chadli Bendjedid gave a speech on television. A voice offscreen interrupted him: "Thirty-three dead in Bab-el-Oued."

One week after the riots, a provisional toll listed five hundred dead in Al-geria (including between two hundred and fifty and three hundred in Al-giers). Thousands of arrests had been made.

The crisis of "October 1988" profoundly shook the Algerian state and its society. The Islamist activists had demonstrated their importance in the mo-bilization of the population and the charisma of some of their leaders. But they were not the initiators of the movement, which was largely sponta-neous. At the other extreme, a democratic pole was attempting to constitute itself. Thus, on October 10, a collective of seventy Algerian journalists, in a press release to Agence France Presse, denounced the ban on the objective reporting of events, the lack of respect for freedom of the press, and the attacks on human rights. On October 22, in a press release disseminated by the official agency Algérie-Presse-Service (APS), Algerian attorneys protested the arrests and pronounced themselves in favor of an independent legal power. A national committee against torture, created in late October, brought together academics and trade unionists. The protests addressed the need for profound reforms of the political system, the end of the single-party system, and the guarantee of democratic freedoms.

The shock wave of "October 1988" marked the end of an era. The upheaval was so great that the shift to a multi-party system quickly got under way.

The Multi-party System and Political Turmoil

On October 10, 1988, President Chadli Bendjedid announced a referendum revising the 1976 constitution, and setting in place the principle of the government's responsibility to the National Popular Assembly. That first breach was followed, on October 23, by the publication of a plan for political reform that, in theory, further undermined the FLN's monopoly on political organizations and expression. It entailed three points: the separation of the state and the FLN, the freedom of candidacies in municipal and legislative elections, and the independence of "mass organizations."

On November 3 the referendum to modify the constitution was overwhelmingly approved (92.27 percent of the vote, with a participation rate of 83.08 percent).

Given the "black October" Algeria had just lived through, the time had come for methodical exploration and historical stock-taking. The following lines appeared in the weekly *Algérie-Actualité* on November 24, 1988:

> The children of October strangely resemble those of May 8, 1945, those of November 1954, those of December 1960.... Among all these children, there is not just a resemblance, there is an identity in their demands, unless we deny the history of the contemporary national Algerian movement. The lucid examination of our history, the humble study of the facts, of all the facts, beyond any act of exorcism, will certainly allow us to solve our problems. Yet we must recover our memory, all our memory, without "filters."

The sixth congress of the FLN (November 27–28, 1988) endorsed the reforms, particularly the separation of the Party and the state. But that did not prevent it from designating Chadli Bendjedid as the sole candidate for the presidential election. And, over the weeks, "the independence of the mass organizations" was transformed into a classic "organic autonomy," still under the aegis of the FLN. On December 22, 1988, Chadli Bendjedid was reelected president.

Disappointment and bitterness were accumulating in a society weary of the quarrels within the FLN, where factions clashed over whether the existing political system needed to be "liberalized" or "locked in." The army, which actively participated in the October repression, emerged weakened by the shakeup of October 1988. On February 5, 1989, the Algerian press published the text of the new constitution, which no longer made any reference to socialism or to the FLN. In its article 40, the legislation opened the way to a multi-party system. The popular referendum on the new constitution was approved on February 23 (73.4 percent of the vote). Progress was made, and new political parties came into being. The Union for Culture and Democracy, or UCD, created by Saïd Sadi on February 9 at the national meeting of the Berber cultural movement in Tizi-Ouzou, was legalized. The UCD set down the principle of the separation between the religious sphere and society, while recognizing the Muslim dimension of Algeria. In contrast, on the political and cultural chessboard, the Islamic Salvation Front, or ISF, headed by Abassi Madani and Ali Benhadj, championed the installation of an Islamic republic in Algeria. It was legalized by Mouloud Hamrouche's government on September 14, 1989.

In the meantime, the military leaders were demanding that the president of the Republic relieve them of the duties they held within the FLN. All the senior officers left the FLN's central committee on March 4, 1989. In the period of uncertainty, social turmoil, and political unrest, the army, which still held the real power, was apparently refusing to commit itself.

Parties that had formerly opposed the FLN, whose leaders lived in exile, obtained their political legalization. On December 15, 1989, Hocine Aït Ahmed returned to Algeria, after his party, the Front des Forces Socialistes (FFS), had obtained official recognition on November 20, 1989. Then, on September 27, 1990, Ahmed Ben Bella, head of the Mouvement pour la Démocratie en Algérie, or MDA (Movement for Democracy in Algeria), returned after ten years of exile.

In 1989 and 1990, forty-four parties came into existence, a good number of which were to participate in the legislative elections planned for the end of June 1991. Human rights leagues, independent women's organizations, and cultural movements developed. A new political sphere formed, which attempted to elude state authority. With it, certain bans began to be dropped, and critical and individual arguments on public questions developed. The formation of public opinion was linked especially to the circulation of the written word. Six national dailies existed in 1990, among them, *El Watan* and *Le Matin,* which rapidly supplanted the traditional *El Moudjahid* in sales and distribution (Brahimi 1990).

Of the new independent weeklies, let us note *Le Chroniqueur,* composed in Algiers and printed in Oran; *Le Nouvel Hebdo,* which competed with *Algérie-Actualité; Maghreb-Sports,* conceived in Oran, composed in Algiers, and printed in Constantine; the economic weeklies *Perspectives* and *Le Défi Economique,* with the latter publishing two editions, one in French, the other in Arabic; *Le Temps du Constantinois, Ouest-Hebdo,* and *Centre-Ouest,* weeklies of regional life; and *Parcours Maghrébins* and *Variétés Magazine*, which reviewed cultural events. Several independent publishing houses attacked the monopoly on the publication of books. With that information effort, which extended from politics to religion and from culture to economics, Algerians were becoming subjects of history, and not only subjects of a regime. The democratization process was real, even though the FLN remained a dominant party/state, one of the two arms (with the army) of presidentialism. Under the governments of Kasdi Merbah (November 1988–September 1989) and Mouloud Hamrouche (September 1989–June 1991), the exercise of power fluctuated between opening democratic spheres (freedom of association and of the press) and repressing the "dangerous classes," especially marginalized young people in the cities, who monotonously moved back and forth from soccer match to television to the mosque. Although Chadli Bendjedid grieved over the victims of October 1988, those responsible for the repression, and particularly for the torture, were never brought to trial or even named.

The Economic Questions

Kasdi Merbah's government, established in the wake of the October 1988 riots, intended to reform business operations and restart growth within the framework of the law of finances and the annual plan of 1989. The composition of the government, in terms of economic posts, is revealing. The four principal ministries of an economic nature were entrusted to men with practical experience, most of it directly in business operations. Thus, Sid Ahmed Ghozali, named minister of finances in 1989, had long been head of Sonatrach and possessed a certain credibility on the international financial market.

Sixty-seven public enterprises were targeted for "autonomy" on February 1, 1989. After two decades of massive industrialization, the objective was to make the power of businesses autonomous in order to protect against the many shortcomings of the public sector and the crisis of the Algerian economy. The leaders also intended to encourage the private sector by means of the mobilization of savings and productive investments, while proclaiming that it wanted to oppose activities assumed to be of a speculative and exclusively mercantile nature. That profound revision of economic policy ran into several difficulties: the challenge of learning the new methods of management; the absence of a stock exchange; the scarcity of means for making foreign debt payments, which the pretense of a "hard currency budget" would at most allow to gloss over; the lack of social consensus; the lack of an economic and democratic culture within civil society; and the blocking of reforms by the deputies, who all belonged to the FLN, previously the only party.

Algeria was still counting on oil and natural gas for its advancement. The Sonatrach-Gaz de France accord, signed on January 12, 1989, allowed the state to set a compromise price of about $2.30 per million BTUs. A total of 9.5 billion cubic meters of natural gas were delivered per year until 1990, and Sonatrach recovered 850 million francs in arrears, since the accord applied retroactively beginning on November 1, 1987. In addition, France granted Algeria 7 billion in credit with advantageous conditions. The de facto devaluation of the dinar, however (30 percent between 1986 and 1987, 20 percent in 1988), did not succeed in stimulating exports. Prime Minister Mouloud Hamrouche's team, formed on September 10, 1989, intended to accelerate the shift to the market economy. The Algerian leaders estimated that, for the economy to become efficient once more, the real value of the national currency had to be restored to it through the standardization of its exchange rate relative to the parallel market. They estimated that the state's contributions also had to be lightened and prices allowed to fluctuate with demand. In short, a series of adjustments had to be made to balance public accounts; the Algerian economy had to regain its credibility on the international scene; and help had to be given Algeria to enable it to join the international market. But the rapid end of the Gulf War in 1991 lowered the price of oil, which was now barely 18 dollars a barrel. Algeria was thus led to readjust its request from the International Monetary Fund (IMF) and the World Bank and to make greater concessions to them.

The question of restructuring or refinancing the debt arose. Sid Ahmed Ghozali's government, formed on June 5, 1991, did not decide that question; that of Belaïd Abdesselam, formed on July 8, 1992, rejected the restructuring out of political and economic nationalism. It tended to encourage the return to a self-maintained economy. But the populist and pro-independence state control of revenues, the legacy of the "Boumédienne years," had long ago reached its limit.

The IMF made its aid contingent on a program of draconian adjustment: a sharp drop in the number of public enterprises and administrations, privatization, a rise in charges for public services, a rise in interest rates, and, above all, a devaluation of the dinar.

The hypothesis of growth in agricultural work was not conceivable. The experience of the 1980s and 1990s showed that, because of a lack of mastery over natural conditions, and in the absence of a modern peasantry capable of increasing the value of the investments made by the state, the increase in production and agricultural productivity remained low.

Thus, the economic reforms begun in 1989 ran into enormous difficulties. Apart from the prices of a few basic necessities, which remained frozen, all consumer and industrial products increased in price by between 50 and 200 percent in 1990.

In the meantime, the dinar lost more than half of its value in relation to the French franc. Purchasing power had greatly deteriorated. Social discontent ran deep. The general strike launched by the UGTA (Union Générale des Travailleurs Algériens) on March 12 and 13, 1991, was observed by more than 90 percent of civil service workers and employees in public enterprises.

The demographic pressure produced a constant growth in the demand for common consumer goods (which further worsened alimentary dependence), but also in the demand for housing, school and medical equipment, and leisure activities, and the authorities were unable to respond. The increasing frustration of an ever-growing proportion of the young and penniless population thus continued, seriously threatening the civil peace and feeding all sorts of protests.

From Pan-Arabism to Islamism

The collapse of the FLN and the ISF's rise to power lay in the continuing failures of pan-Arabism and the development of political Islamism.

The Arab defeats by Israel (in 1967 and 1973) led to the crisis in Arab nationalism. The volatile mixture of Islamism and oil led to new conflicts, while the state apparatus originating in Arabism defended itself with concessions and repressions. Given the Iran-Iraq war (1980–1988) and its parade of atrocities, the persistence of underdevelopment, the lack of resolution of the Palestinian question, and the Israeli invasion of Lebanon in 1982, people in the 1980s were troubled by a queasy sinking sensation and the certainty that the collapse of values would ineluctably be punished. Gradually, for some, the hope of a return to original Islam was carved out. The new power acquired by the Gulf states (especially Saudi Arabia) after the oil crisis appeared to many faithful as a sign of divine providence. Compared to the patent failures of the secular states, which had fashioned their industrial development model on that of Eastern Europe, the international weight acquired by Riyadh gave fundamentalism a new credibility.

In the early 1980s, the landscape of the Maghreb was transformed. With the urban riots in Morocco in 1981 and 1984 and in Tunisia in 1984, and the Algerian outbreak in October 1988, social frustrations were laid bare. The organs for controlling and organizing societies were no longer adequate to stifle their expression. The rise of the individual and the slow acquisition of personal freedoms were translated into the creation of associations (the human rights leagues, for example) and public demonstrations to demand new rights.

That approach required the end of the single-party system, which had failed in its curious mixture of universalism and specificity (Islam and national socialism). The Algeria of 1990, with the multi-party system and elections planned for 1991, opened the way to the nation/society's appropriation of the freedoms until then confiscated by the party/state. That desire for democracy, which opposed the "forced modernity" proposed by the military, fractured the vision of Arab nationalism, especially since every state baldly obeyed its own logic, its own interests. In practice, every instance of nationalism developed at the expense of pan-Arabic propaganda. The borders, even the most artificial ones coming out of colonization, produced the same state allegiances in the territories they circumscribed, the same networks of sympathies and behaviors that gradually became fixed and institutionalized. Positions were taken, choices made, which the bureaucratic cadres in the states were reluctant to abandon.

Political Islamism emerged as a major factor, and took its place in the void left by Arab nationalism (*Peuples méditerranéens*, 1990). The populations were barely gathering up the detritus of modernity. They felt that yawning gap— between the rulers and the ruled, between the very rich and the very poor, and between the "North" and the "South"—as an injustice. The rise of Islamism, experienced as the hope for a return to ethics, in combination with the bankruptcy of the single-party system, brought about a need for individual responsibility, which would go hand in hand with the search for a new kinship.

At the same time, the crisis of "Arab Socialism" made a need for personal freedom, or individualized responsibility, appear. Human rights leagues, but also new unionist organizations, women's movements, cultural associations, and a series of journals began the work of criticism: how could the state become disengaged from the economy? How could individuals assert themselves as political subjects and as citizens? How could the culture, and in particular the representations of Islam, transform itself? That reflection on democracy was still very fragile when the Gulf crisis erupted, with Iraq's invasion of Kuwait on August 2, 1990.

The Singularity of the ISF

In 1989, for the first time since independence, Algeria was engaged in a process of democratization. Several parties were legalized, in particular, the

Islamic Salvation Front (ISF). That too was a great innovation: for the *first time*, an Arab and Muslim country authorized a party that had Islam as its foundation, and the installation of an "Islamic republic" as its openly announced goal. The army chiefs thought that the legalization of an Islamist party was a mistake in a country where religion played such a strong role and constituted one of the levers of national cohesion. Others, like Chadli Bendjedid and his prime minister, Mouloud Hamrouche, felt that institutional guarantees were enough to ward off any subversive threat.

The democratization experiment was blocked by a series of maneuvers and manipulations (the FLN acted to make itself appear as the only alternative to the ISF), and of errors in calculation (the regime underestimated the power of Islamist troops), which led to open crisis. On December 15, 1989, Hocine Aït Ahmed returned to Algeria. His party, the Front des Forces Socialistes (FFS), with deep roots in Kabylia, decided not to participate in the next scheduled elections, saving itself for the legislative elections. On May 31, 1990, 100,000 of his supporters paraded in Algiers. But, for the most part, it was the Islamist movement that occupied the foreground of the Algerian scene.

On June 12, 1990, at the municipal and regional elections, there was a massive rejection of the FLN, and a landslide for the ISF, which ran away with almost all the municipal councils in the large cities. Of 12,841,769 registered voters, and 8,366,760 participants in the vote, the FLN obtained 2,245,798 (18.3 percent of voters and 17.5 percent of those registered) and the ISF 4,331,472 (54.3 percent, and 33.7 percent, respectively). For its part, the Front des Forces Socialistes (FFS) had decided to sit out the election.

At the time, the government thought that economic and social measures would allow it to limit the ISF's influence. This was again a misunderstanding of the significant grassroots work done by the Islamist militants; but, above all, it was a poor judgment of what made the ISF strong: its conception of the nation as exclusively Muslim and rid of all foreign influence. The Islamists rejected democracy as a product of French colonial history and a value imported by the West, which was permanently demonized. Their discourse had a huge impact on young people in search of an identity and of memory. Henri Sanson (1983) refers to that dual desire of Algerian society as a whole "to have Islam as the transcendent norm or even as a principle of membership, of reference, of justification, of finality on the one hand, and, on the other, secularity as a practical norm or even a principle of action, with all that entails in terms of appeals for independence, freedom, reason, and conscience." This interpretation is essential for grasping the reality of Algerian society. But other explanations have been formulated to explain the

Islamist landslide in the municipal elections of June 1990, and in the first round of legislative elections on December 26, 1991: it has been seen as a protest vote, as a vote by default, and as a hedge vote.

Might it have been a protest vote, since voters sought to punish one party, the FLN, which had held the reins of power exclusively since independence in 1962? Or a vote by default, since the parties calling for democracy in Algeria, Ahmed Ben Bella's MDA, and especially, the Front des Forces Socialistes (FFS), led by Hocine Aït Ahmed, did not participate in the election? Or finally, might it have been a hedge vote for one party—a religious movement that had been able to capture (not to say hold captive) the current of feeling produced by the bloody massacres of October 1988?

Though very pertinent, all these explanations have the shortcoming of depicting the ISF as a new party, emerging almost ex nihilo within the specific construction of the Algerian nation.

In fact the ISF was accused of calling into question the cohesion of the "single nation" held together since its origins by Algerian nationalism. Had not the ISF refused to participate in the traditional November 1 ceremonies in 1989 (marking the anniversary of the outbreak of the anticolonial insurrection)? In situating themselves outside the founding era that based consensus on the sacredness of origins, in resolutely placing their vision within the national sphere, beyond the borders inherited by the war of independence, in constantly referring to an "Islamic *umma*" (the community of Muslims), the Islamists placed themselves outside the classic trajectory of Algerian nationalism. Some FLN leaders declared: "We are nationalists, the ISF is not." Under such conditions, the influence of the Islamists, led by Abassi Madani and Ali Benhadj, could only have been momentary, short-lived. A year later, in 1991, it was necessary to face the facts: this movement was destined to last, its place within the Algerian political landscape was no longer in doubt. It was reaching a growing audience in Algeria, especially among the younger generations.

There is another analysis, which points to the inexorable, global rise of the "religious" in the public sphere. Why should contemporary Algeria be exempt from that pendulum swing? Emerging from a single-party system, that country (like Eastern Europe) was headed toward chaotic situations, in which the religious dimension acted to fill the political vacuum. It is true that religion may be the ideal vector for protest in already firmly Islamized Arab countries, where the population heeds any discourse that uses the traditional vocabulary of Islam, and where the ever-present mosque is less vulnerable than the parties or unions to attacks by the regime. In such cases, Islam is the only "place" possible for protest. And the Islamist movement is often the only one to allow the expression of opposition to the state, while the failure of other opposition structures (sometimes in exile, and always repressed) seems generally certain. It is the only one to be profoundly animated by a true search for identity, which allows young people to once more become aware of their culture by providing them with reference points that make it easier to set down roots (Etienne 1987).

That interpretation places the "ISF phenomenon" within a broader international framework (the reemergence of Catholic or Jewish fundamentalism, or of militant Hinduism). It too is inadequate if it does not take into account the internal "roots" of Algerian Islamism. Certain adversaries of the ISF have depicted it as a mere stand-in for the principal Arab power desiring the absolute victory of a religious society, namely, Saudi Arabia.

The economic context has also been analyzed as a factor in the development of the ISF. Beginning in 1988, Algeria began to emerge from a narrowly centralized, bureaucratized economy and to move, at a forced march, toward the market economy. The Islamists wanted to "aid" in this move, to act in such a way that the new economic actors would escape all possibility of control from above; thus, the economy would be removed from the political regime. In that spirit, during the month of Ramadan in 1991, the ISF inaugurated its first "Islamic souks." The marketplace represented a sphere where everyone, as buyer or seller, employer or worker, was in permanent competition with everyone else, forced to provide the maximum effort, seek the maximum yield, the maximum gain and profit. The market functioned as a sort of "nonsociety," a "free-for-all" which saw itself as unencumbered by any social, political, or ethical rules. Algerian society, already violated by a ruthless "modernization" decided from above, had a hard time adapting to that new crisis, a crisis that required the suppression of the ties of loyalty, the ban on unionist coalitions, and the abolition of any restriction on profit. The Islamists, even while actively favoring the shift to that market economy, proposed remedies to its consequences: a religious ethic of solidarity, heart-felt mutual aid, the counterweight of a reassuring kinship.

All these elements (the ideological disarray, the new function of the spiritual within the political, the role of Saudi Arabia, the bankruptcy of the single-party system, the shallow roots of the democratic parties, the shift to a market economy) combined to shore up the strength and originality of the Islamist movement. But another element is decisive in accounting for the process under way. The ISF did not just fall from the sky in a strange or accidental manner. On the contrary, it was the culmination of a history begun long before by Algerian nationalism.

The history of modern Algeria did not begin in 1962. The ISF did not emerge from a vacuum, but found the sources of its dynamism in a complex past that was still operating in the present. If we can grasp this history, we can rid ourselves of overly simplistic images (Stora 1991b).

The Islamist movement based its political action on the Muslim religion, understood first as the return to the traditions of a mythic nation destroyed by the arrival of the French. That initial postulate was decisive. It entailed the explanation that, for 132 years of colonization (1830–1962), two societies, two "nations" coexisted, without ever truly coming together. One nation, the French, had wanted to break, shatter the other, which, during that century and a half, had never stopped resisting through the instrumentalization of Islam. That Manichaean vision had two advantages. First, it allowed the demonization of any idea "exported" from France (secularity, republic, Marxism, or autonomization of the individual), while denying that there could be "several Frances" (one, the France of colonization, violently oppressive, the other a republican France, or the France of the workers' movement). Second, all those who wanted to appropriate or simply understand these "other Frances" were conveniently placed in the category of "traitors" and *harkis*. And this denied the dimension of the Algerian revolution that was indebted to the French notion of "insurrection," that is, the use of the universal principles of 1789 as a tool against colonial France. The approach of the Islamists of today recognizes only one aspect of the war of independence: the affirmation of an Algerian identity forged by Islam. It proceeds by denegation of any foreign contribution or debt within independent Algerian society. The French memory must not be assumed, but rather fiercely and continuously combatted. That repression of the past functions as a field of collective valorization.

The nationalist struggle thus continues via the rediscovery of the accents of populism, characteristic of the beginnings of Algerian nationalism. The Islamist militants have thus rediscovered the intonations of the Arab Islamists, introduced by the first Algerian organizations in the interwar period: the ulama of Abdelhamid Ben Badis, who said in 1930, "Islam is my religion, Algeria is my nation, and Arabic is my language"; and especially, the Parti du Peuple Algérien (PPA), a mass pro-independence organization. The PPA depended on the underprivileged in the slums, on peasants who had lost their class standing, and on small tradespeople or artisans, threatened at the time by European competition. The ideology of the PPA rested on the rejection of the destructuration caused by the decline of the Muslim city, and on Islamic values. The plebeian cadres of the PPA, relying on the growing mass of true social outcasts, destitute people living on the fringe, intended not to play into the French elite's strategy, and united the minor intellectual Muslim elites (Harbi 1993).

Even today, anti-intellectualism continues to be a strong force within the Islamist organization, which considers the (Gallicized) intellectuals "bourgeois" par excellence, a disdainful term for those who attempt to discover substitutes for the forward progress of the "people," and who ignore the realities of the common people because they are not in contact with them on a daily basis.

The strength of Islamism consists of proposing a new scission with the present state, of repeating the words, the vocabulary of the old fracture with the colonial state. These words reactivate a political memory in accordance with a process already set in place in colonial times: break off from a state considered impious or antireligious; break off from an official, institutional Islam (which, at the time, was accommodating itself to the French presence). In some sense, another "November 1" was necessary, new "sons" of nationalism would rise up. That triptych—nation/religious identity/people—seemed to be an expression, a ferment, and a consequence of such nascent neonationalism. It served to explain why the current structures had to disappear in the name of more profound, more ancient, and hence more legitimate realities. But, in the war of liberation, that conception had already been expressed via the Front de Libération Nationale (FLN), which saw the notion of "one people," established on a religious foundation, as an essential pillar of its ideology. That theme of "one people," the sole anonymous hero, was supposed to reduce the threats of foreign aggression (Gallicization, assimilation) and internal disintegration (regionalism, linguistic particularism). The latter aspect had to do essentially with the Berber question, which harbored a danger within an exclusively Arab Islamic vision of the nation.

Today, the ISF is turning to advantage the theme of "the unity of the nation," perceived as an indissociable, united, and unanimous figure. Already championed by the FLN (Addi 1990), that populism contributes to a simplification of politics, a radicalization of the opposition between friends and enemies in such a way that ordinary conflicts are discredited. Any opposition is perceived as a threat of civil war and as the sign of destructive conspiracies. The ISF is thus taking the populist logic conveyed by the FLN since its foundation and pushing it to the extreme by coloring it with religiosity. It intends to resolve the contradiction that the FLN was unable to apply its program (one people, united without social or cultural distinctions, applying shari'a, Islamic law), only because it was prevented by forces acting within it (Arabic, Nasserian, or Baasist Socialists, "democrats" under French intellectual influence). The ISF militants have thus posited themselves as the true heirs to an FLN stripped of all external ideology.

The Gulf War, a Revelation

Initially, the Gulf crisis, set off by Iraq's invasion of Kuwait on August 2, 1990, drew increasingly marked lines of separation within the Algerian political class. Although all the parties condemned the Western reaction—the massing of troops and weapons in Saudi Arabia—whose aim, according to some, was only to "preserve their interests," or even "seize control of hundreds of billions of Arab dollars and threaten the Islamic and Arab nation in its security," the position toward Saddam Hussein's regime was far from unanimous.

The ISF Islamists proved to be increasingly embarrassed. How ought one to "protect" Saudi Arabia's appeal for Western troops? Response: "Let us brandish the torch of Islam. Let us brandish the jihad. Down with the servants of colonialism! No to Iraqi intervention in Kuwait, no to the intervention of unbelievers in Saudi Arabia, no to the governments that have compromised with the West. Yes to the peace dialogue. My dear brothers, we reject all intervention in our affairs." The ISF preacher who gave this speech in Constantine ended it with the search for the inevitable scapegoat, "the Jews, who occupy all the holy places of Islam" (Sigau 1991).

The rejection of "the American war," which increased after the air offensive by the coalition against Iraq on January 17, 1991, did not signify adherence to the doctrine of Iraq's sole party, the Baas. From one end of the Maghreb to the other, the violence of the conflict provoked the return in force of the tradition of revolutionary populism, of a movement of unanimity without any possible differences in points of view. And yet, in the many pro-Iraqi demonstrations that occurred in Rabat, in Algiers, and in Tunis, a rift appeared.

On the one hand, there were those who demanded peace, an immediate cease-fire. They spoke of safeguarding the unity of the "Arab nation." They adopted the tone of the Third World movement of the 1960s, supported in the past by the Moroccan Mehdi Ben Barka and the West Indian writer Frantz Fanon: they denounced the oppression of the peoples of the "Arab nation" by a regime resolved to establish its hegemony over it. The rejection of US intervention against Iraq was accompanied by a denunciation of the petroleum monarchies in the Gulf. They were accused of placing their capital in Western financial institutions when, in the overwhelming majority of Arab countries, social progress remained very slow. But that effort at social clarification collided with the power of consensus based on identity, the sense of belonging to the same "Arab camp." And the "Palestinian cause" further united people. Some, however, particularly the heads of the human rights leagues, attempted to explain the necessary distinction between Saddam Hussein's totalitarian regime and the suffering of the Iraqi people.

On the other hand, in Morocco and Algeria the Islamist movement championed the jihad. The Western view of the Arab world, simplified to the point of caricature, encouraged this movement. Feeding the worship of a fixed past, the Islamist movement assimilated democracy (seen simply as a product of European history) to irreligion, that is, to one of the weapons in the vast conspiracy fomented by the enemies of the Prophet.

The West, out of habit or laziness, has relegated all the Arab countries to a global otherness—a homogeneous whole, sometimes invaded by abrupt fits of fever—without understanding that these peoples, in mobilizing against the war, aspired not to a return to military nationalism, but only to a greater degree of justice.

Public opinion brandished the democratic argument with the slogan "two weights, two measures." The Algerians emphasized the glaring inequality in the application of UN resolutions. But the majority of them did not embrace Saddam Hussein's regime. In Rabat and Tunis as well, there was a demand for more rights and not for the withdrawal of the international community.

The tragedy lay in the refusal by the "North" to take these considerations into account. It has then been easy for the Islamists to demonize the idea of democracy, understood as a product of the West and not as a universal principle.

January 11, 1992, the Boudiaf Assassination, a State of Emergency

The first pluralist legislative elections were scheduled for June 27, 1991. But the ISF, in a disagreement over the polling method and the planned division of the electoral constituencies, opted for clashes in the street. A dynamic was set in place with the call for a general strike launched by the ISF on June 15. The army, headed by General Khaled Nezzar, minister of defense, once more intervened. The elections were put off and the principal leaders of the ISF, Abassi Madani and Ali Benhadj, were arrested. A state of siege was decreed, and the prime minister, M. Hamrouche, who supported a political solution, resigned. He was replaced by Sid Ahmed Ghozali on June 5, 1991, who also declared himself a supporter of reinstating the electoral process.

The first round of legislative elections took place on December 26, 1991. Of all the parties on the ballot, only the "three fronts," the ISF, the FFS, and the FLN, came out ahead. The abstention rate was 42 percent. The Islamists took 188 seats in this first round, leaving the FFS (25 seats) and the FLN (18 seats) far behind. But the ISF lost more than a million votes when compared to the municipal elections of June 1990. Would there be a jump in the abstention rate in the second round of elections? Answering the call of the FFS, some 400,000 demonstrated in Algiers for "no police state, no fundamentalist republic."

But the second round of legislative elections did not take place. The army "fired" President Chadli, who was preparing to form a coalition with the ISF, on January 11, 1992. A "State High Commission," or SHC, was formed the next day. It instituted a state of emergency throughout Algerian territory and called upon Mohamed Boudiaf, one of the historic chiefs of the FLN, in exile for twenty-eight years in Morocco, where he was running a small brickworks. Mohamed Boudiaf, a man of integrity and a modernist, obtained a ban on the ISF on March 4, and then sought to attack the FLN. He wanted to build an "interdependent and just society" via a serious reform of the system. He would be the first head of state in the independent Maghreb to be assassinated, on June 29, in Annaba. He had jostled too many interests. Ali Kafi, another former nationalist in the war of independence against France, replaced him on July 2.

On July 8, 1992, after Sid Ahmed Ghozali's resignation, Belaïd Abdesselam, Boumédienne's all-powerful minister of industry, was given the responsibility of forming the new government. On July 15, the ISF leaders, Abassi Madani and Ali Benhadj, were sentenced by the military tribunal of Blida to twelve years in prison.

After Mohamed Boudiaf's assassination by a member of his close guard (twenty months later, it was still not officially known who had armed him), a new tragedy struck Algeria. On August 26, 1992, in the Algiers air terminal, a bomb attack, officially attributed to Islamists, cost ten people their lives and wounded dozens. For the first time since independence, indiscriminate terrorism had struck the civilian population. The country was in a state of shock.

Some among the "elite," academics or doctors, engineers or attorneys, considered leaving Algeria, especially since, in spite of the official press releases announcing "the last quarter hour of terrorism," a spiral of bloodshed had set in. The violence did not seem close to being checked. "A nameless war" began. Every day police officers, gendarmes, or soldiers were murdered, nearly four hundred between the promulgation of the state of emergency on February 9, 1992, and September 1, 1992.

Beginning on Saturday, December 5, and "for an indeterminate period of time," a curfew was set in place between ten o'clock p.m. and six o'clock a.m.

in Algiers and in the bordering *wilayas* of Blida, Tipaza, Boumerdes, Ain-Defla, and Bouira. The Algerian authorities intended in that way to shore up the struggle against the violence of the Islamists who, according to them, were in league with "the great wave of banditry." In particular, they accused Iran, via the Sudan, of financing a campaign of destabilization "from the Gulf to the Atlantic."

Nevertheless, despite the measures taken, deadly attacks continued to produce victims among officers of the law. In the early hours of the morning, on Monday, December 14, 1992, a police patrol was ambushed not far from the Apreval mosque in Kouba, a stronghold of fundamentalism. Five police officers were killed on the spot, a sixth gravely wounded. The all-terrain vehicle, with the six members of the police on board, had been blocked by a barrier of stones and tree trunks placed across the road, before being subjected to automatic weapons fire. It was the most deadly action to have taken place in 1992 against officers of the law.

17

Algeria at War

In the Maghreb, the years 1992–1995 remained largely dominated by the events in Algeria. The worsening of the situation in that country, marked by an escalation in the violence, led to a crisis of Maghrebian unity, plunged the population into anxiety, and impelled people to examine the nature of the Islamist movement. The latent civil war that took root in Algeria also had repercussions in France, where a large Maghrebian immigrant community was living. Paris, which participated in the restoration of the Algerian economy, found itself caught in the web of the conflict.

World stability was at stake not only in the East but also in the South. The large blocs that had installed themselves after the collapse of communism prefigured the world of the future. The countries of the Maghreb, which possessed raw materials but not technological initiative, found themselves suddenly confronted with the abrasive dynamics of democracy, the irruption of identity movements, and the market economy. But the Islamist fever in Algeria and the short-sighted calculations of the Maghrebian leaders distanced the prospect of building a coherent whole on the eastern side of the Mediterranean.

The Web of Violence

One year after the electoral process was interrupted, the Islamists attempted to lock the regime into the infernal logic of "total security measures." Ali

Kafi, president of the SHC, declared in January 1993 before the upper council of the magistrature: "It would be wrong to speak of the sovereignty of the law in a state that is facing destruction and whose stability is in danger." The democratic opposition parties demanded the reinstatement of the electoral process "to return hope to the population." Hocine Aït Ahmed's Front des Forces Socialistes (FFS), the main opposition force, felt that was the only way to "reconcile citizens with their institutions." In opposition, in its *Plate-forme pour l'Algérie républicaine* (Platform for Republican Algeria), published in January 1993, Saïd Sadi's Union for Culture and Democracy (UCD) declared that "today, it is more a matter of giving our country a credible regime than of giving it a regime legitimated by the voting booth." With the conception of the nation fractured, different visions of the society to be constructed appeared. The population, for its part, was weary of the exactions and the terrorism.

On February 13, 1993, seven months after Mohamed Boudiaf's assassination, Major-General Khaled Nezzar, minister of defense and strongman of the regime, barely escaped the first remote-control attack by booby-trapped car that independent Algeria had seen.

That spectacular attack illustrated the regime's powerlessness to check the violence. Despite the state of emergency proclaimed on February 9, 1992, passage of a far-sighted antiterrorist law of October 1992 outlining severe penalties for "crimes stemming from subversion," and the installation of a curfew in Algiers in December, not a day went by without an act of aggression.

In March 1993, the humanitarian organization Amnesty International accused the Algerian government of having used torture since the installation of the state of emergency. In its annual report of 1993, it indicated that whereas torture had "practically disappeared between 1989 and 1991," it was now again being used against the "extremists" and was "reported regularly in twenty detention centers, most located in the Algiers region, but also in other cities." Intelligence on this matter "had proliferated spectacularly" since October 1992. Amnesty International, harsh toward the government, also did not show any leniency toward the Islamists and the recourse to violence by some of their groups.

Between March and June 1993, the murders of several intellectuals caused great emotion: one by one, the sociologist Djilali Liabès (March 16), Doctor Laadi Flici (March 17), the writer Tahar Dajaout (May 26), and the psychiatrist M'hammed Boukhobza (June 22) were killed. The risk of an exodus by the intelligentsia was increasingly mentioned.

In late June in Chréa, above Blida, an army convey was ambushed "by a terrorist group": forty-nine soldiers were killed, and nineteen gravely wounded. In Berrouaghia, thirty kilometers southeast of Médéa, a barracks was deserted by its troops. After a few days of relative calm, in early July 1993 the summer clashes, ambushes, and murders resumed and were worse than ever. On July 7 in Tlemcen, seven Islamists were killed by law officers after a hostage-taking. The same day, in the region of Blida, five civilians, including an agricultural engineer and his wife, both former Communist militants, were murdered.

In Kabylia, and in the east of the country, huge fires of criminal origin destroyed 75,000 acres of forest. In that same summer of 1993, several fleets of municipal vehicles and several factories and schools went up in flames. Several journalists were murdered, including Rabah Zenati on August 3, or managed to escape attempts on their lives, among them Omar Belhouchet, editor-in-chief of *El Watan*.

On August 21, Redha Malek was named to succeed Belaïd Abdesselam at the head of the government. The new government team had to confront and accept formidable challenges, first, the "reestablishment of safety," but then also the question of restructuring Algeria's foreign debt within a domestic social context that was very difficult. In 1991 the number of unemployed was 1,226,000, for an active population estimated at 6 million; in early 1993, it had risen to more than 1.5 million, for an active population close to 6.5 million. For the newspaper *El Watan*, "all the forecasts hold that the unemployed population is destined to increase along with the deterioration of the national production apparatus, which can offer no more than about 70,000 jobs annually, even as new job seekers number more than 250,000. As a result, unemployment is becoming increasingly severe" (September 8, 1993).

1994: The War Takes Root

The attacks and murders attributed to the Islamist groups, and the actions of reprisal by the Algerian security forces, caused some thirty thousand deaths between the installation of the state of emergency in February 1992 and December 1994. The official toll announced in late 1994 listed ten thousand killed (the figure for the wounded was not known) but, according to reliable sources, the figure of thirty thousand victims was advanced by the Algerian authorities themselves. The number of persons killed every day in the country after May 1994 was estimated at between forty and sixty. Guerrilla groups existed throughout the country. Sixty-four foreign nationals, including nineteen French, had been victims of attacks since the first murders of foreigners on September 21, 1993 (two French surveyers were found with their throats slit near Sidi Bel Abbes).

The major figures of the Algerian cultural world, from the best known to the most modest, were the targets of Islamist groups. The list of writers, academics, attorneys, artists, and journalists killed or wounded for having tried to express themselves grew longer from one week to the next. On March 5, 1994, Ahmed Asselah, director of the Advanced School of Fine Arts in Algiers, was murdered along with his son. Salah Djebaïli, the rector of the University of Sciences and Technology in Bab Ezzouar, was killed on May 31. A journalist was murdered in the very center of Algiers on June 6, bringing to fourteen the number of journalists killed since May 1993. On June 18, Youcef Fathallah, president of the Algerian League for Human Rights, was murdered. Two bombs exploded on June 29 on the parade route for a march held by the Mouvement pour la République. Toll: sixty-four wounded and two dead. On August 6, the director of the Institute of Agronomy in Blida was murdered, the same day that the Armed Islamic Groups, or AIG, announced that they wanted "to ban all education in Algeria." In a "last warning," on August 17 the Islamic Salvation Army, the armed branch of the ISF, called on Algerian journalists "to no longer support the regime." On September 26, the singer Matoub Lounès, very popular in Kabylia, was abducted (he would be released on October 10). Three days later, on September 29, the rai singer Cheb Hasni was murdered in Oran. Certain Algerian intellectuals chose exile; others opted to continue their battle where they were.

On October 6, the minister of education announced that six hundred schools had been destroyed or burned down in Algeria and that about fifty teachers had been killed since 1993.

State violence also occurred on a vast scale: the use of torture, denounced by Amnesty International and the International League for Human Rights, detention without trial in camps in the south, special jurisdictions that pronounced death sentences, sweep operations, and summary executions. In the face of armed groups that were striking with terrible cruelty, law enforcement conducted an indiscriminate campaign of repression that extended far beyond Islamist ranks.

"Dialogue" or "Eradication"

In that climate of civil war, the political struggles redoubled in intensity, often in an abstruse manner. On the one hand, those who opposed the January 1992 interruption in the electoral process supported reintegrating the Islamists into the political game and championed the establishment of "dialogue"; on the other hand, those who embraced the Republic, but who had approved the army's intervention against an electoral victory by the Islamists, knew that they ran the risk of being the major losers in any eventual bargain struck between the army and the Islamists. They said they wanted to "eradicate" the Islamist presence in Algeria.

The army and the Islamists sized each other up via indirect contacts, then clashed, plunging the country into internal war. Redha Malek, prime minister at the time, asserted that to counter terrorism the state "had not yet used all its means" and that it might decide to do so "in the near future"; at the same time, the (dissolved) ISF called for the continuation of the armed struggle against the "junta" in power. Things became less tense in early 1994. On January 30, 1994, the High Security Council, or HSC, entrusted the "presidency of the state" to General Liamine Zéroual. A few days later, the new head of state presented himself in his first speech as a supporter of a "serious dialogue." He evoked the need to "find, before the end of the year, a consensual solution to the crisis" and conceded that "the security solution is not adequate in itself." Contacts, called "promising" and "encouraging," were made with representatives of the ISF to attempt to bring them into a "national conference," but to no avail. However, certain Islamist leaders did not prove insensitive to the overtures of the government. In early February, Anouar Haddam, having sought refuge in the United States, made a "declaration against violence" for the first time. Two weeks later, the release of two ISF leaders was announced: Ali Djeddi and Abdelkader Boukhamkham, cellmates of Abassi Madani and Ali Benhadj.

The two camps blew hot and cold. The Ministry of the Interior called for the mobilization of all citizens who had completed their national service and the promulgation of a law on "civil defense." He explained that the dialogue would concern only the parties who "respected the constitutional order and national values." Nevertheless, the execution of death sentences was suspended (three special courts had pronounced nearly five hundred death sentences since February 1992), and relations were not broken off in spite of the strong opposition of the "eradication" camp. In February 1994, General Mohamed Lamari, considered one of the proponents of the "hard line," was authorized to sign on Liamine Zéroual's behalf, thus limiting the latter's power and installing de facto a dual system of government undermined by two opposing agendas. On March 27, Saïd Sadi, head of the Union for Culture and Democracy (UCD), launched a spectacular appeal for "armed resistance" against the Islamists.

From his prison cell on April 7, Ali Benhadj made a proposal for dialogue with the government to resolve the crisis, but without condemning the outbreak of violence. On April 10, President Zéroual, who had secretly met with the Islamist leaders in November 1993, dismissed Prime Minister

Redha Malek and Minister of the Interior Selim Sadi, who had more or less been classified in the camp of "eradicators," supporters of repression and opponents of dialogue. In so doing, Zéroual gave himself a wider margin for maneuvering. Mokdad Sifi, the new prime minister, appealed to the opposition forces, especially the Islamists, to join his government's efforts to put an end to the conflict.

In mid-summer, things began to move more quickly. On July 15 the United States urged Algiers "to widen its political base," following the meeting of the G-7 nations in Naples, which called for the resumption of dialogue in Algeria. Algeria was put under external political—and especially, economic—pressures.

On June 1, 1994, Algeria obtained a restructuring of its foreign debt, estimated at $26 billion, from the Club de Paris. That readjustment, negotiated with the representatives of seventeen creditor countries, would allow Algeria to reduce by $5 billion the reimbursement payments it had to make between May 1994 and 1995. The payment of these $5 billion would be spread out until 2009. None of Algeria's debt was written off. For its part, the IMF made its accord conditional on an economic adjustment program. On April 10, the Algerian dinar was devalued by 40.17 percent. In fact, Algeria's principal creditors, which, in descending order, were France, the United States, Italy, Germany, and Japan, made economic aid dependent on the opening of a political dialogue in the country.

In August, declarations, correspondence, and various contacts multiplied between the ISF leaders and the army. Confronted with the existing realities, the head of state promised a return to the electoral process "as soon as possible"; at the same time, on September 3, Abassi Madani proposed a military truce in exchange for his freedom and that of his companions. He asked that the "armed branch" of the Islamist movement be brought into the dialogue. That proposal underscored the limits of his authority in the face of the mujahideen (fighters), who were much less disposed to compromise with the "junta," and who were increasingly attracted to the radicalism of the AIG. The AIG provided itself with a "countergovernment" on August 26, which was quickly disavowed by the ISF leadership.

On August 21 the political dialogue in Algeria officially resumed. Five opposition parties, including the FLN, formerly the only existing party, agreed to participate; the Islamists refused, as did the Front des Forces Socialistes (FFS), Hocine Aït Ahmed's organization deeply rooted in Kabylia. The "eradicators'" camps violently denounced that dialogue, judging it was a capitulation to Islamist demands.

On September 13, Abassi Madani and Ali Benhadj were freed from their prison in Blida and placed under house arrest. The Islamists felt the gesture was inadequate. Negotiations were broken off and the violence resumed. On October 8, five booby-trapped cars exploded simultaneously in the Algerian capital.

For their part, the supporters of democracy knew that they ran the risk of being the losers in future negotiations. At the appeal of the Berber Cultural Movement (BCM), a general strike, accompanied by huge demonstrations for the recognition of Berber culture, paralyzed all of Kabylia.

In Algeria, however, the official watchword was still dialogue. Yet the authorities gave the impression that they had chosen indecision and the continuation of the repression to mask their differences regarding the goals of negotiation. As for the ISF leaders, they demanded new concessions (such as the release of all political prisoners) before agreeing to new negotiations. They thus avoided having anyone test their representativeness, their influence on the proponents of terrorism.

France Caught in the Web

On August 3, 1994, the murder of three gendarmes and two French consular agents in Algiers abruptly placed the Algerian tragedy on the French internal political scene. On August 5, Minister of the Interior Charles Pasqua placed seventeen alleged Islamist Algerians under house arrest in Folembray (they would be expelled to Burkina Faso on August 31). He invited the Western countries "to repress the activity of Islamist militants" and to take spectacular measures of police deployment in the locations in France where Algerians lived.

To leave or to stay? France had a position as a privileged commercial partner with Algeria, as two statistics will illustrate: in 1989, 27 percent of Algerian imports came from the Hexagon; and, by 1993, that share had reached 33 percent. The withdrawal strategy was not so simple, therefore. In addition, France, as a result of its past as a former colonial power, maintained a tumultuous and passionate relationship with Algeria.

Should France support the Algerian regime? Beginning in August 1994, that policy seemed far from receiving unanimous support within the French state apparatus. Paris attempted to relativize its support by insisting that it "was extended to the Algerian people and not to a government," and by evoking the "discreet steps" taken with the leaders to "incite [them] to a rational use" of the financial aid and to urge them to do everything to "broaden their base."

Should all the French of Algeria be repatriated? On October 8, 1994, Jean-Pierre Manière, age 59, a French engineer living in Algeria for many years, was found with his throat slit, not far from the Islamist bastion of Meftah southeast of Algiers. In a communiqué, the Islamists of the AIG accused France of supporting the Algerian regime. According to them, the aid granted by Paris allowed the "impious" regime to continue. On October 11, Alain Juppé, minister of foreign affairs, pointed out to the National Assembly that, since November 1, 1993, more than six thousand French nationals had arrived in France, more than eleven hundred with the aid of the consulates and the Comité d'Entraide aux Français Rapatriés (Mutual Aid Committee for Repatriated French). But there were still fifteen hundred French expatriates in Algeria, not counting the binationals, often the offspring of mixed couples, whose numbers were difficult to estimate.

Should all the Algerian refugees be admitted to France? On August 24, Alain Juppé announced that visas would no longer be issued from Algeria, but rather in France by a centralized service established in Nantes. For many Algerians, France had decided to close its Mediterranean border. The Algerians, held hostage between the incessant Islamist attacks and the widespread repression that resulted from it, felt increasingly isolated, with travel abroad now so difficult. After the French border closed, the Moroccan border followed in late summer 1994, subsequent to a terrorist attack in Marrakech.

The Maghreb in Disorder

The fall of the Eastern bloc, the Gulf War, and the instability in Africa imposed new power relations. The scope and complexity of the challenges, both economic and cultural, made formidable the threats that weighed on every nation-state, and, as a result, on the Maghreb as a whole. The countries of that region, in spite of the official discourse on the Union of Arabic Maghreb, faced alone the problems that transcended their borders. Hence, with 60 million consumers, Maghrebian commercial trade barely exceeded 5 percent in 1994.

In the face of an upsurge in Islamism, all parties believed they possessed the miracle recipe, from the most radical in Tunisia, which, in appearance, had eliminated fundamentalist protest, to the "softest" in Morocco, where Hassan II capitalized on his title as commander of believers, and including the violent recipe in Algeria, where the regime, still in search of legitimacy, was engaged in armed confrontation. The Maghrebian states, born of decolonization, operated in parallel worlds, even though there existed a profound aspiration for unity on the part of the peoples of the Maghreb. The response to the terrible tragedy that was shaking Algeria and determining the future of the region depended on taking into account the desires expressed throughout the Maghreb: to establish Arab, Berber, and Muslim identity; to advance toward greater citizenship; and to recover political legitimacy.

Algeria became accustomed to living in anxiety and expectation, with most adults feeling very strongly that the nation was collapsing. The young, for their part, became locked in resentment and amnesia. The attacks continued, targeting politicians, journalists, and academics. Islamist militants were sentenced to death and shot. The murder of foreign nationals plunged the country into doubt and confusion.

Between the installation of the state of emergency in February 1992 and the end of 1994, the death toll rose by about thirty thousand, and more than twelve thousand were interned in camps or prisons.

1995, 1996, Continuation of a "Nameless War"

In the Maghreb, 1995 will be remembered above all for the escalation and continuation of the violence in Algeria; the (aborted) attempt at a political accord between the Algerian opposition (the FLN and the FFS), the Islamists (the ISF), and the regime via the Rome accords; and, the election of Liamine Zéroual to the presidency of the Algerian Republic.

In Morocco, the transition of which King Hassan II had been speaking for several years may well have come about. But a government of technocrats, not expecting the opposition to associate with it (as would be the case in 1998, with Youssouffi as prime minister), led the country after June 7, 1994. In Tunisia, where, as in the neighboring countries, human rights were terribly restricted, President Zine El Abibine Ben Ali, who had led the country since November 7, 1987, put down all protest or criticism of the regime.

As for France, thirty-one of its nationals had been murdered in Algeria since the beginning of the most recent Algerian conflicts in the 1990s, and its policy toward that country has never been clear: it became the hostage of that Algerian war. The war had existed on French soil since July 25, 1995, marked by the constant threats of the mysterious "Armed Islamic Groups," attacks or attempted attacks that caused several deaths and dozens of wounded.

Violence and Politics

The beginning of 1995 in Algeria set the tone for a sequence of events that continued the terrible conflict. It was Monday, January 30, 3:20 p.m., in the very center of Algiers, near the central police station. The residents of Algiers were hurrying into banks and stores in this very busy neighborhood. A booby-trapped car exploded, plunging the street into hell. The toll was 42 dead and 256 wounded. On the morning of Wednesday, February 22, the Algerian security forces mounted an assault to break apart an uprising of Islamist militants in Serkadji Prison. The toll was 99 Islamists killed and 4 guards with their throats cut. Lembarek Boumaarafi, President Boudiaf's alleged assassin, was gravely wounded. These two events within less than a month in the single city of Algiers (140 dead) illustrate the state of high tension reigning in Algeria.

The hijacking of an Air France jetliner on December 24, 1994, by an AIG commando showed that the war (in the form of publicity-seeking terrorism) could erupt on French soil. But "when the war appears purely warlike, it is at its maximum political intensity" (Clausewitz). That was the case in Algeria with the bargaining conducted between the army and various political organizations, and, above all, the establishment of an Algerian opposition in the "Rome meetings" of January 1995.

The signs of social atomization in Algeria (the constitution of militias that live on war; smuggling/*trabendo;* the crisis in familial ties; the exile of a portion of the Francophone elites; drug trafficking; property transfers; and so on), and the legitimate preoccupations to which they lead, do not, however, authorize us to neglect the political factors. Algerian society was "adrift" because it no longer had *political representations.* The phenomenon of violence, the transition to war, the constitution of guerrilla forces or militias often relying on delinquency and terrorism, could now be eliminated only by a *return* to the political stage of traditional organizations.

Beginning from that point, and given the impossibility of pursuing a "total security" policy, the Algerian army, which remained the sole power in the political realm, was confronted with the problem of renovating the political realm to put an end to violence.

In fact, with the approach of the presidential election in Algeria, whose first round was scheduled for November 16, 1995, violent acts multiplied in that country. The number of murders and attacks by booby-trapped cars could no longer be counted. On August 17, two booby-trapped cars exploded at Club des Pins, one of the best protected official residences in Algeria. Toll: two dead and seven wounded. On August 31, the headquarters of the General Office of National Security, or GONS, located in the "hot" neighborhood of Bab-el-Oued, was targeted. Nine people were killed, about a hundred wounded. And, on September 28, Aboubakr Belkaïd, former minister of labor, higher education, and communication, who was considered a high dignitary of the regime, was assassinated while driving to a meeting of the veterans of the FLN's Fédération de France. A few weeks before his assassination, Aboubakr Belkaïd had repeatedly made contact with leaders of the central and western regions, in view of an alliance between these two areas, with the aim of counterbalancing the weight of a regime that had always originated in the eastern regions of Algeria.

Nearly four years after the interruption of the electoral process by the army in January 1992 (when the victory of the ISF had seemed certain), what could be expected in Algeria from the presidential elections? For a long time, the essential question in Algeria was the legitimation of the successive governments. "By weapons, not the ballot box": that was how the question was raised in the aftermath of the war waged against France. The presidential elections held by a regime that sought political legitimacy were carefully set up: 32,000 voting bureaus were planned in 8,000 centers, and 14 million voters were expected, supervised by 37,000 agents. The signers of the Platform of Rome, the Front de Libération Nationale (FLN), the Front des Forces Socialistes (FFS), and the Islamic Salvation Front (ISF), refused to participate in that electoral vote. They maintained that a political negotiation (for example, on the lifting of the state of emergency that had been in force for three years) had to precede the elections. Yet the activities of the armed Islamic groups continued to escalate by building on that political refusal, even while trying to "extend beyond" the political field of the "three fronts." The question was whether the rejection of these elections would allow a "political front of refusal" to be constituted, or, on the contrary, whether it would be translated into a crisis, an implosion, of the "three fronts"; whether it would reinforce the Islamist movement or lead to its disintegration. The Algerian problem remained that of a real political alternation, lacking which there was a great risk that the space would be left exclusively to the supporters of extreme violence, via the destruction of the traditional political field—including the ISF—in favor of the armed groups alone (even if they were losing ground). The four candidates for the presidential election, those who had collected at minimum the 75,000 signatures required, were General Liamine Zéroual; Mahfoud Nahnah of the Islamist movement Hamas, considered a "moderate"; Saïd Sadi, secretary general of the Union for Culture and Democracy (UCD); and Nourredine Boukrouh, head of the Party of Algerian Renewal (PAR). Could these elections end the violence? Some thought at the time that it might be necessary to bring the participants in the "Meeting of Rome" accords into a new dialogue process, which would include a condemnation of violence. Whatever the result of the presidential elections, that would have made it possible to associate all the components of Algerian political life with the holding of new legislative elections, to bring about a (difficult) return to civil peace.

In was therefore in a climate of war, and against the will of the principal opposition parties, that the Algerians, threatened by the armed Islamic groups, went to the polls. The Algerian regime was counting a great deal on the votes of the emigrant community. In France, nearly 2 million voters were expected at the consulates between November 11 and 16.

On November 16, 1995, General Liamine Zéroual, acting president since January 1994—he had been named by the army—was elected president of the Algerian Republic in the first round of elections, with 61 percent of the vote. That election was unanimously called the "election of hope." The new president had taken the first steps toward a dialogue with the democratic opposition and the Islamists. The Islamists seemed to confirm the desire to stop the violence, expressed by the number of Algerians participating in the electoral process (the official participation rate was 75 percent, but, according to other estimates, the reality was closer to 50 percent, which is still significant). The FLN and the FFS (headed by H. Aït Ahmed), which had called for a boycott of that election day, were now on the defensive.

Political dialogue was not set in place, however, and the terrorist attacks resumed. State violence did not fall off either. Over the months of 1996, the news arriving from Algeria was frightening. Hence, in the single month of August of that year, the Saudi newspaper *Al Hayat* reported that sixty-three civilians, including women, children, and elderly people had had their throats slit in the Aurès. On August 19, the authorities denied that massacre. But, the same day, the Algerian daily *El Watan* reported that seventeen men traveling aboard a bus had been savagely killed by an armed group. In addition to the crimes officially announced by the press were those that were never made public. Hence, in May 1996, in the region of Jijel, a fundamentalist stronghold in the eastern part of the country, a family of "patriots" was decimated by armed Islamic groups. The "patriots," as the self-defense groups armed by the Algerian regime called themselves, then carried out reprisals on the families suspected of being close to the "terrorists." Death toll: more than one hundred.

The Islamists, sure that they had the "support of God," ruthlessly massacred the "patriots," and the patriots, when they got their hands on "terrorists," countered with terrible savagery. Over the years, other factors were added to the political violence: tribal hatred, rackets, antagonism between villages, factional or personal revenge sometimes going back to the "first Algerian War." During this time, the Algiers authorities labored to convince their foreign economic partners that terrorism was in its "last gasps," that it was "residual." On May 11, the government submitted a memorandum to the different parties (with the exception of the ISF) calling for the "resumption of a national dialogue." The bill setting forth a radical revision of the constitution adopted in 1989 was opposed by the principal political organizations (the FFS, the UCD, and Hamas), but approved by the FLN, which had moved closer to the regime. That reluctance was not enough to discourage the head of state. The regime, playing on the hesitations and divisions in the opposition (even within the Islamist movement, where the AIG was confronting the ISF militarily), intended to complete its plan to "normalize" the Algerian political scene, set out in the presidential election of November 16, 1995. President Zéroual proposed to hold legislative and communal elections, in the first and second half of 1997, respectively, after a referendum on a revision of the constitution. The "conference on national harmony," on September 14 and 15, 1996 (boycotted by several opposition organizations), carved out a legislative bill that would replace the majority vote in two rounds by a proportional representation system.

Against the background of a search for political solutions, violence in Algeria continued. Hence, in early September, a booby-trapped car completely destroyed the Hôtel d'Angleterre in Algiers; a bomb in a restaurant in Staoueli (a seaside resort near the capital) caused twenty deaths. And, in 1996, the Catholic Church in Algeria suffered cruel blows. "We have cut the throats of seven monks": It was with these words that a communiqué, bearing the seal of the AIG and dated May 21, announced the murder of seven French clergymen abducted on March 27, 1996, from their monastery of Tibehrine near Médéa, in southwest Algiers. That massacre, the largest committed against the French in Algeria since the beginning of the violence in 1992, was denounced by all the Algerian political parties, including the ISF. In France emotion ran high. The totality of French political organizations called for a demonstration of "solidarity and national protest." On Sunday, May 26, the death knell sounded in all the churches of France.

A new appeal was launched by Paris to the last French people residing in Algeria. But could the alternative be reduced so easily to leaving or staying? Staying meant risking one's life, and even other people's. Leaving meant playing into the hands of those who intended to draw a final line through any trace of the French presence in Algeria. In July 1994, Monsignor Pierre Claverie, archbishop of Oran, expressed the matter of conscience this presented for foreigners: "Must one remain at any price?" And he immediately responded by quoting his own Muslim friends: "Do not listen to the 'last call' siren. Stay, we need you." Two years later, on August 1, 1996, the archbishop of Oran was murdered in a bomb explosion near his home. Pierre Claverie's death brought to nineteen the number of Christian clergy killed in Algeria between 1993 and 1998. That murder brought to a tragic end the visit of M. Hervé de Charette, French minister of foreign affairs, who had come to Algeria on August 1 and 2, 1996, "to give a new start" to relations between the two countries. These events showed that neither the Algerian government nor the armed groups had renounced making France one of the stakes of their struggle.

France in the Algerian Snare

The situation in the Maghreb, characterized primarily by violence in Algeria, obviously cannot leave France indifferent, especially since the "Algerian War" overflowed into its own territory as of July 11, 1995, the date of the murder of Imam Sahraoui (founding member of the ISF) in his mosque in Paris.

Whether France wishes it or not, its responsibility, born of the ties built by a long history, is significant in the tragedy buffeting the country. Algeria remains one of the largest Francophone countries in the world; its vast Mediterranean façade (1,200 kilometers) is a wide "border" with Europe. Its human potential (28 million inhabitants), its demographic dynamism (65 percent of its inhabitants are under thirty), its energy resources (oil, and especially, natural gas), its central position in the western Mediterranean, the size of the Algerian community in France (officially, 1 million people) all join together to make the Algerian problem a passionate and decisive one. In addition, at the dawn of the twenty-first century, France remains Algeria's foremost commercial partner.

Moreover, the accords on Algerian natural gas, with the construction of the trans-Mediterranean gas pipelines (to Italy via Tunisia, and to Spain and Morocco), have henceforth established long-term economic and social interdependence (whatever the political future of Algeria) between Algeria and southern Europe. The problem for France in Algeria is not to "stay" or to "break off," but rather to lay the foundations for a lasting policy.

This is especially true in that an abrupt, radical change (in favor of the Islamists, or a political coalition including them) in Algeria would completely reshuffle the cards in the region. In the Maghreb, which is in transition toward a market economy, Algeria represents an important test case. In that situation, France seems locked in a dilemma: either maintain an increasingly fragile status quo ("neutrality") in the terrible war being waged in Algeria, and hence be perceived as supporting the regime in place; or make an effort to favor a process of dialogue among all the Algerian political organizations.

It seems difficult for France not to take into account the interest elicited in the rest of Europe by the "platform" adopted by the "three fronts" (the ISF, the FLN, and the FFS) in Rome in January 1995, proposing to negotiate "a process of democratic transition and national pacification." In reality, the Algerian problem has put France on the spot: either choose the political "recomposition" desired by the current Algerian regime, on behalf of presidential elections (the emergence of new leaders and the effacement of the "three fronts"); or let an internal economic logic of the market play itself out, which, in the end, would make it possible to "resolve" the political chaos (even though the war may last several years in Algeria).

But that last, short-sighted view does not address the possible solutions to enormous problems: the social exclusion and powerful migratory pressure toward the North, the relation between democracy and political Islamism, even the future of the Muslim world as a whole and its relations with the West.

Since 1992, France's Algerian policy has been not to get involved in the "Algerian War." But since the latter has been unfolding on French territory since the terrorist attacks of summer 1995, Jacques Chirac has wanted to depart from that policy of noninterference. On October 22, 1995, during a celebration of the UN's fiftieth anniversary, he agreed to meet with Algerian president Liamine Zéroual, but Zéroual went back on his decision to meet the French president. In refusing to meet the president of the French Republic, Candidate Liamine Zéroual, who had every chance of winning the presidential election, adopted the tone of an easily offended Algerian nationalism, and set the stage for a new era in the wake of November 16, 1995 (the reestablishment of ties with the traditional French partner). But things had not come about quite so simply. Jacques Chirac, president of the French Republic, during an official visit to Tunis in October 1995, had announced that financial aid to Tunisia was to be nearly doubled, from 594 million to 1 billion francs. In early 1996, Paris also wiped out a billion francs of Moroccan debt. In contrast, France decided to reduce noticeably its aid to Algeria.

That decision was announced on June 25, 1996. The abduction and tragic deaths of the seven monks of Tibehrine could have done nothing to improve the relations of France with the Algerian military authorities, who were accused by Paris of having attempted to preserve their own interests above all, rather than seek to safeguard the lives of the hostages. Nevertheless, France cannot fail to take an interest in Algeria at the economic level. Although that country receives only 1 percent of French exports (it is barely France's twenty-sixth most important supplier), the surplus realized by Paris in Algeria in 1995 reached 6.7 billion francs, that is, the sixth-best bilateral positive balance. In particular, France is the exporter of automobile and pharmaceutical products, and Paris remains by far the foremost supplier of Algiers. It is thus difficult for France to disengage itself from Algeria, especially since, in addition to the terrorist threat and the unrest of the identity movements racking that country, there is also the social turbulence to come.

On Sunday, July 7, 1996, Algerian Prime Minister Ahmed Ouyahia indicated that the country had 2 million unemployed for a population of 28 million; 80 percent of that population was under thirty. He maintained that Algeria "[was] currently experiencing a critical phase" on the economic level. According to a study of the National Office of Statistics (NOS) published in September 1996, unemployment had affected nearly 30 percent of the active population.

A Way Out of War?

In 1997, one thing became obvious, and several years of war have proved it: the Islamists could never take power *alone* in Algeria. The population, despite the terror and intimidation, did not massively move to adopt Islamist views (the shari'a). The ISF lost ground on both sides: the population was growing increasingly weary of the exactions by the armed groups, and a radical fringe of young people (in the urban centers) was joining these groups. Contrary to appearances, time was working against the ISF as a homogeneous political force. That is why it condemned "the murder of innocents" (communiqué of January 5, 1995), met with the leadership of the FLN, and sought negotiations. Could the army encourage an FLN/ISF accord to reintroduce the political ISF into the game? That scenario never saw the light of day, and the army turned the military and political situation to its advantage.

In 1997, the Algerian army launched major "cleansing" operations against the Islamist guerrilla forces. For the undertaking, it relied on tens of thousands of armed civilians ("patriots" and village self-defense groups) and benefited from very sophisticated armaments provided by the Western powers. On the political level, all the Algerian political organizations (with the exception of the dissolved ISF) agreed to "reinstate" the political game by participating in the legislative elections of June 1997. The "Rome accords" fell apart, since the FLN and the FFS were now seated in the Algerian National Assembly, and the latter had only very reduced powers. President Zéroual's party, the National Democratic Union, or NDU, won an absolute majority of seats in the assembly. All the Algerian organizations—in particular, the Islamist movement Hamas—violently protested what they called "ballot box-stuffing." The Islamic Salvation Front, politically isolated by the defection of its allies in Rome—the FLN, the FFS, and Louisa Hannoune's small Trotskyist organization, the PT—called upon its men, organized into the guerrilla forces of the Islamic Salvation Army, or ISA, to put down their weapons. The truce, actually a disguised military surrender, was proclaimed by the ISA on October 1, 1997.

It was during this phase of negotiation and surrender between the ISF and the army, in late summer 1997, that the appalling massacres of the "second Algerian war" took place. In August, September, and October 1997, entire villages—Bentallha, Rhaïs, and Benni Messous—were decimated. Hundreds of women, children, and elderly people had their throats cut, were burned alive, or hacked to pieces. Barbarism reached the "height" of horror and deeply moved international public opinion. Many wondered: Why did the army not intervene to prevent the carnage? Some called for the creation of an international investigation commission to find the perpetrators of these dreadful massacres. In 1998, two "missions," one by European members of Parliament in February, the other by the UN in July, went to the site. They confined themselves to asking for the "continuing reinforcement of the process in Algeria." The Algerian regime, so decried by humanitarian organizations such as Amnesty International and the League for Human Rights, did not emerge weakened by these terrible massacres.

In fact, it was from within that regime that the strongest jolts came. Against the background of terrorist violence, the struggles of factions became more acute at the summit of the state. In summer 1998, a press campaign at the initiative of a group of newspapers was launched against Mohamed Betchine, personal adviser to Liamine Zéroual, president of the Republic. On September 11, 1998, Liamine Zéroual announced in a televised speech that he was cutting short his term—which was to expire in the year 2000—and would not run again for the presidency of the Republic. All the Algerian political organizations were surprised. Presidential elections were thus scheduled for 1999.

Conclusion
The Uncertain Paths of the Future

When so many contradictory factors that have borne hope or desolation have blurred the uncertain paths of the country's future, it appears necessary to return to those of a very immediate past, the first forty years of Algerian independence. We must rediscover the past through the present, not let the events grow stale, not wait any longer for the traditional sources in order to understand. This book "of immediate history" seeks to respond to the growing needs of those who are not content with description and who seek explanation.

Ever since the violent riots of October 1988, which led to the collapse of the system established in 1962, the themes of "modernity" and "crisis" have been at the core of contemporary debates concerning Algeria. To know whether Algeria has entered into a lasting crisis provoked by the rise in power of political Islamism or, on the contrary, into a political modernity coming about by fits and starts is no small matter. The effect of the discourse of crisis is to instill fatalism, to justify opposition to progress, to discredit in advance many cultural or social initiatives. Moreover, the discourse of modernity, marked by too much optimism, prevents us from looking lucidly at what remains of the system, with the army and the formidable military security at its center. And no one can reasonably say whether, for example, the massive assertion of the religious sphere has constituted rear guard actions or signs portending a redefinition of the question of the nation. The installation of a lasting crisis and the difficult entry into economic and

231

political modernity are part of the long term and can be demonstrated only a posteriori. The historical transformations are slower, more complex, more sinuous than the discourses of forecasters. The difficulties in apprehending the present, however, do not justify taking no interest in the present. It is one thing to practice the critical distance dear to historians, but one must also explain the delays, the successes, and the breakdowns that modern-day Algeria is encountering. To evaluate the capacity that country has to become a homogeneous nation, remaining faithful to its Arab Muslim traditions, even while progressing toward democracy; or, on the contrary, to assess the risk it runs of "stalling," of becoming mired in a war that might destroy even its national unity—in either case, the implication is that simple and reliable historical data and a pertinent representation of the sources of difficulties are available. In particular, this raises the problem of the relation to the war of independence, and the succession of political generations following that period.

Emerging from a Culture of War

Beginning in Algeria in July 1993 there were forests burning once again in the Aurès, Algiers was still living under a curfew, terrorist attacks attributed to Islamists were striking police officers and intellectuals, and hundreds of "suspects" remained in detention, sometimes without trial. The Algerian press had begun to mention the "sweep operations," and the French press added reports from "the underground." "Terrorism" and "torture" made their reappearance in the vocabulary of all the triumphant communiqués, announcing, on the one hand, the "eradication" of the "last armed groups," and, on the other, "the imminent victory of the Muslim people." A strange sensation has developed that this is a remake of the war of independence: an impression of *déjà vu* or "déja entendu."

Forty years later, the vocabulary is unifying, consolidating the two eras, making them look alike. Has the country, then, entered a second—and identical—Algerian war?

Nothing is less certain. In the first place, in history, formal analogies have but little pertinence if they confine themselves to highlighting the similarity between certain forms, in this case the resurgence of terrible forms of violence. And, in the second place, the Algeria of the 1990s has only a very distant relation to that of 1962.

The country today is highly urbanized; the rural areas no longer play the same role; more than 60 percent of the population is under thirty; and the rate of schooling is very high. The differences could be multiplied, with, at the center, the end of the colonial system, the massive departure of *pieds noirs*, and the political operation of an independent state. It may therefore seem absurd to assert that the same scenario is being repeated. Yet the protagonists in the confrontation—the followers of the ISF, the "democrats," the army—have intentionally adopted the terms inherited from the past of the Algerian War. And that is what is truly of interest—Islamists speaking of "the valorous mujahideen," wanting to hunt down "the new *pieds noirs*" who have appropriated the revolution; "democrats" calling the ISF militants *"harkis"* who want to crush the Algerian nation. Some circles within the regime have launched campaigns against the "secular assimilationists," as during the time of the colonial system, when a lost identity had to be reestablished. And all the camps mention a shadowy "party of France" (*Hizb França*) supposedly destabilizing Algeria.

This mimicry is striking. The memory of the war of independence operates as a factor in the assignment of the roles to be played. The contemporary actors dress in theoretical garments borrowed from the past. But, if they do not realize the novelty of the present, and if they subjectively replay the old situation, it is because they remain under the automatist influence of a memory fabricated forty years ago.

That memory is transmitted especially by Algerian schools and school manuals, which have made the Arab Islamism propounded by the leader of the ulama (the clergy) Abdelhamid Ben Badis (who died in 1940) the only protagonist in constituting Algerian nationalism. That memory has hidden away the values championed by Ahmed Messali Hadj and Ferhat Abbas, pioneers of Algerian nationalism in the interwar period: the values of republican, plebeian socialism, the secularization of the religious. That official memory has evacuated the pluralism that was at work in nationalism, even during the war, with the debates and confrontations between "Messalists," "Frontists," and Communists. It has obscured the figures of the founding fathers of the FLN in Algeria: who knew Mohammed Boudiaf before his return in January 1992? It has repressed the Berber question, even though it was debated in pro-independence ranks in the 1940s and 1950s. And finally, it has excessively privileged the principle of the armed struggle in the war of independence, at the expense of the political factor.

This tragic past, a true culture of forgetting maintained by the FLN after 1962, produces formidable automatisms, especially in the young. A good number of the protagonists of the 1990s have mentally replayed a ready-made scenario that official memory has bequeathed to them: Arab Islamism, armed struggle, communitarian nationalism. And the Algerian tragedy feeds in part on the myths forged during the war of independence. This overflowing, falsified memory stands as an obstacle to a true reappropriation of the past, the construction of a nationalism based on the republican spirit and a tolerant Islam. It also prevents any approach to the future. The rekindling of identity continues to be contrasted to the modernization of the nation.

Will Algeria, in order to confront the challenges of modernity on the horizon of the twenty-first century, finally be able to emerge from the constantly replayed scenario of a certain version of the Algerian War?

Nested Wars within the "Second Algerian War"

In the "first" Algerian War, behind the very visible clashes between colonial France and nationalist Algerians, other fracture lines gradually appeared: the bloody conflicts among Algerians for hegemony in the political struggle, and the Franco-French battles between adversaries and supporters of Algerian independence.

The conflict that really began with the assassination of President Mohamed Boudiaf in June 1992 also allowed successive truths to be unveiled via the tragic series of events: behind social projects, whether religious or secular, a power struggle was evident between men and factions; behind the power struggles there were economic issues and the will of the large oil and natural gas companies; behind a cruel and incomprehensible violence, there stood the long history of a tradition of force at work in a long-colonized society, as well as in the building of the Algerian nation apart from France.

In six long years, within the recesses of a war between the military and the Islamists, other wars, both decisive and indistinct, were hidden. Wars nested within other wars, plots within plots, full of dark passages, of caches equipped with false bottoms, of false doors and booby-traps.

The Mythologies of Secrecy

Reality and irrationality appear together when the "second Algerian war" is mentioned. Hence, in late 1997 and early 1998, the "scientific" analysis faced head on the specters of the terrible carnage emerging from the shadows of a conflict already six years old: seventy thousand deaths and the exodus of the villagers of the Mitidja; the fear of residents in the neighborhoods of Algiers; the confusion of all Algerians in the face of a savage and destructive violence. How can one find reason within the disorder of interests and the desire for vengeance? Within the dynamic of the conflict, the outbursts have become uncontrollable, and disruptive passions seem to be destroying political calculations.

The succession of tragic situations has continually altered the initial motivations behind that war (the panic of Islamism and the repression of that movement beginning in 1992). The motives of the actors supposedly confronting each other vanish behind each new abominable crime. The killers who come forward, smoking gun or blood-soaked knife in hand, within a country plunged into fire and violence, look like demoniacal phantoms emerging from a dark night of madness, specters held in the grip of darkness. The sharp, well-defined lines that divided the two principal protagonists (the regime and the Islamists) and the clear circles within which the acts of war took place have decomposed over the years into dark corridors, into inextricable twists of mazes.

What do the Islamists truly want, and who are they? What do those in power and the movement headed by M. Nahnah have in common? What is shared between those who were forced underground (the former ISF) and want to negotiate their return to the traditional political game, and those who have joined the guerrilla forces, who would not hear of anything but extreme violence to achieve a hypothetical Islamic republic? And who are the real protagonists of a regime that has made opacity an essential weapon of government? Former members of the FLN? An elite *nomenklatura* disguised as "democrats"? Apparatchiks with new careers in "business"? Soldiers engaged in the field who do not want to see their military victory slip away? Other officers, occupied in the factional struggle to hold on to their power? Supporters of dialogue with the radical Islamists? Or proponents of the total "eradication" of Islamism? The men and women of the democratic "third way" are also divided on the question of "dialogue" and "eradication."

From all these assemblages, incoherent, obscure, and apparently incomprehensible lines have formed constantly. The battle landscape has been further obscured by the fact that the Islamists, like the regime, do not *communicate* their designs, plans, strength, or ambitions to the world. That intentional opacity does not facilitate the struggle for understanding, or for possible marks of solidarity outside the country.

The war and the bargaining have unfolded behind closed doors, or in the shadows. *The culture of secrecy* is the mode of operation of Algerian political society. And the supposed usefulness of secrecy rests on a *technician's idea* of politics, and, in particular, of the art of governing.

In Algeria secrecy is conceived as a political "trade secret," incompatible with the principle of the "res publica." Secrecy came into being in the political underground, against the colonial system; it was legitimated by the anticolonial war, and perpetuated in the highest echelons of the government, in the great single-party tradition. In six years, the current war has not brought much change: the regime's existence is still invisible and distant. Its adversaries move about in shadow. The "nameless war" has been replaced by the faceless war.

The culture of secrecy is nothing new. It originated in the war of independence but also in the conduct of a regime where a group of men hide behind a thick curtain to control the country. For the last few years of this terrible conflict, it has been very difficult to discern who is who in this role-playing where everyone comes forward masked. The regime's refusal to let the international press come and do its job suggests it has something to hide. In any case, that creates a climate of suspicion.

However, the Islamists do not communicate very much, either. When they deny everything at random and in toto, while at the same time claiming responsibility in the streets of Algiers for the murder of one intellectual or another, it can simply be said that a culture of conspiracy exists on their side as well. The same model, the same rejection of transparency, is found in both camps.

But the culture of secrecy is collapsing in the erosion of nationalist populism and the call for a state of law by the popular will.

French Representations of the "Second Algerian War"

"The second Algerian war": that expression has been much used in France since 1992. More than the historical principle of "repetition" (of the first conflict against the French presence), it is the notion of *recidivism* that is invoked: Algeria is a land destined for war, struck by a curse, embarked on a perpetually tragic destiny. The violence may have calmed for a time after 1962; then it resumed, unleashed with even more energy. It is erupting today, incandescent, unpredictable, with infinite cruel variations. Under the French "spectators'" gaze, everything lies in the words, the accounts; the images are almost impossible to look at.

In the almost conceptual and abstract installation of brute force, in the confusion of the senses, and in the dizziness born of horror, a paralysis and a wait-and-see attitude have set in. The paralysis was engendered by fear, of course; but the wait-and-see attitude is also a vengeful response: "You fought against us, now do without us." According to a poll taken for *L'Evénement du Jeudi*, one week after the massacres of Raïs and Beni Messous on the outskirts of Algiers in early September 1997 (four hundred casualties), *a majority of French people said they were opposed to any intervention by France in the Algerian conflict,* even though they acknowledged that it constituted a major threat (74 percent of those questioned). And 50 percent of them said they were against a diplomatic intervention by France (45 percent in favor).

Are we to remain resolutely separated (and hence enemies)? That feigned indifference, an ambivalence pushed to the extreme, has the look of a perverse desire. So it seems we can go on living off that hatred from the "first" Algerian War? Yet, at the same time, the two countries are absolutely attached to each other (if only by virtue of the presence of more than 1 million Algerians on French soil), and the mutual historical, social, and cultural links (once colonial, now of immigration) continue to cause tormenting problems. Can we accept the de facto "closing" of the French borders to the Algerians? In fact, since 1994, the French consulates have been closed in Algeria, which makes obtaining a visa very difficult, and Air France no longer offers flights to that country. The Algerians, many of whom have family in France, have a difficult time dealing with the situation, and experience it as a sort of inflicted punishment. The Franco-Algerian "mental" landscape, necessarily unstable, once more raises the question of what is to be done in the face of a barbarism far removed from the constant escalation created by pictures on television.

In fact, when one fails to make Algerian suffering a television spectacle, one makes demonstrations of emotion or consensus more difficult. The first photograph of Algerian suffering "splattered" across the front page of newspapers throughout the world was not published until September 24, 1997, six years after the beginning of the conflict (a woman is shown in a state of collapse after the massacre of Bentallha; she has lost her eight children. The woman trying to support her has lost her parents). Those in the media find it very difficult to appear compassionate toward the Algerian tragedy. The questions are abrupt and directly political. Should one support the ("modern") state against ("obscurantist") Islamism? The line between "good" and "evil" seems to have become more uncertain as the Algerian conflict has expanded.

But the dominant tendency in French public opinion is still fundamentally anti-Islam. On the Algerian question, the mixture of antireligious republicanism and anti-Islamic religiosity operates at full capacity. If the situation in that country is perceived as a "threat," it is not so much because of the possibility that terrorism will move from one bank of the Mediterranean to the other, as because of a fantastical apprehension of Islam, revived by the memory of the war lost in 1962. The feigned neutrality of the French gaze reveals itself in that logic of continuous, deep-seated prejudice.

The paralysis and the wait-and-see attitude are also the result of misunderstanding. After independence in 1962, Algeria disappeared long ago from the field of scientific knowledge in France. The near total absence of

French researchers on that country before the 1990s (when radical Islamism irrupted) was part of an unformulated obligation not to remember the "first" Algerian War. It is simply *unavowed conflictual feelings* that sustain the paradoxical sense that France and Algeria have something in common.

On the eastern side of the Mediterranean, in contradistinction to that forgetting of resentment, there has arisen an extreme valorization of the tradition of the war, won by violence against the old colonial power. That culture of war will be transmitted, and it may allow us to understand in part the incredible violence being perpetuated within Algerian society.

The New Allegiances in the Algerian Nation

In the 1980s Algeria found itself once more confronting the question of the nation and its representation that had surfaced in colonial times. The colorful plurality of local entities, the Berber cultural protests, the resurgence of religious feeling at the foundation of populism (Islamism), and the relics of unassumed French memory have undermined the central authority. Within the very history of the Algerian nation, the notion of the Islamist movement challenging the state in the name of religion is part of a tradition whereby religion is used against the colonial state. To counter a powerful, arbitrary, authoritarian state, there is a tradition of seeking refuge in a private space (to be called the religious), which allows one to resist a state considered impious and antireligious. That memory extends from Abdelkader's resistance against French colonial penetration all the way down to the Algerian War. The relation of defiance toward the state through the instrumentalization of religion will continue to be transmitted. That relation is deeply rooted in Algerian society, especially since, after independence, the Algerian state has operated on the single-party principle, banning plural, contradictory expressions.

Similarly in 1962 the Algerian state installed Islam as the state religion. In that situation, the mosques were able to become a space of protest against the central Algerian power. Then the possibility of contesting the state and its leaders, in some sense on Islamic foundations, presented itself. The "regenerated" and harmonious society promised by the "revolutionary freedoms" of pro-independence nationalism collided with the continuing strength of ancient practices. The disenchantment with collective utopias, and especially, with Third World Socialism, did not lead to a slippage toward other millenarian beliefs capable of transcending the nation-state. The ideology of the *umma islamiya*, the transnational community of Muslim believers, which spread throughout the Islamic world after the Iranian theocratic revolution and the war in Afghanistan, has not really found mass support.

In the development of the current tragedy, it is possible to see that the allegiance to the Algerian nation does not come about solely through the intermediary of collective political ideologies, but in a more personal, private manner, where familial memories play a significant role. Nationalism emerges more from a way of belonging to the world, to one's country, to one's land, than from political ideology imposed from above. The terrible crisis has changed many fundamental conceptions (assistance provided by providence in the form of the state); has toppled the old peasant communities (via displacements due to the war); and divided loyalties and families (one son may be a police officer, another a member of the Islamist rebel forces). Other effects accumulate.

The massive migration of Francophone cadres and intellectuals as a result of the crisis is profoundly changing—and will continue to change—the structure of the Algerian state, by means of the larger place granted to Arabophones. In addition, that new migration is different from that of the years 1950–1960, which primarily supplied the industrial metropolises of the "North" with labor. Today's exile can give a new impetus to the conception of the nation, which remains "alive" outside its borders via intellectual "agitators" or entrepreneurs ready to invest funds.

The rapid urbanization in these last years of conflict, through the upheaval of the peasantry, has also changed the social composition of the traditional army. The large battalions of that army came from the rural world, and national service acted as a training ground for the Algerian citizen in a regional and social mix. The war has placed a professional army in the foreground. The divorce between the strengthening of the military ideological system (a tradition of collectivity and strength) and the dominant values of Algerian society, increasingly founded on individualism, are part of a new perception of the nation-state in Algeria. The conception of the "people's army," a legacy of the Algerian War, is coming to an end: the society is "separating" itself from the army, asking it simply to carry out the tasks of keeping the citizenry safe, *protecting* the nation, but not ensuring its cohesion.

The war is also uprooting people in one essential dimension, that of time. The haunting inquiry into the origins of such a virulent Islamism in Algeria, into the multiple causes of the war, and into the outbreak of extreme violence have led to the nation's genealogical quest. That genealogy has revealed a heterogeneous past, where the scattered pieces of colonial republicanism, orthodox Islam, and ancestral, Maraboutic, and peasant practices converge. Religion does not have the monopoly on representing the nation.

Practically speaking, secularization, the notorious separation of Islam and state, is being constructed as a result.

In 1998, Algerian society, emerging from a difficult war, was becoming autonomous in relation to the political sphere. Algerian citizens are not demanding: "Down with the state!" More modestly, they are asking that the state fulfill its obligations to protect, to hold regular trials, to assume fully its constitutional duties. The demand for a state of law includes a separation of the political and the religious, of the political and the military.

The Construction Zones of Unachieved Liberation

Seventy thousand dead in six years—that statistic suffices to express the terrible conflict that has severely shaken the Algerian nation since 1992. National feeling, however, has not vanished over the course of that long tragedy. The clashes between the state and the armed Islamist groups have not dismantled the national framework. The fracture lines still run along the borders of the territorial and administrative structures installed by the colonial system, rather than those of "rival ethnic communities" (Kabylia versus the eastern part of the country, for example). The prophecies of a shattering, a "Lebanonization" of the country, have not come true. That is one of the major revelations of that war, especially since the clashes have intensified the perception of the question of the nation in Algeria.

Above all, the current conflict has awakened the memories and reflexes of the anti-French war (1955–1962), and has reactivated the political positions of the time: attitudes toward Western culture, toward the Arab Muslim world, the retreat into tradition and family. Many other factors of that memorable period are surfacing once more: the shift to different behaviors by virtue of the entry into politics, the new view of religion as a refuge or a place of defiance vis-à-vis the state, acquaintance with different Algerian populations via displacements due to the war, and women's citizenship role.

All that "work of nationhood," to which the place of Berber identity could be added, was not really carried out after 1962. When the weapons fell silent after independence, that did not signify the end of the legacies of colonial history, or of the conflict between France and Algeria itself. There was not merely a residual transference of colonial history to the current tragedy, a "residual conflict" via strata of wounded memories. Construction zones of unachieved liberation remained in Algeria, leading deeper into the problem of national, religious, cultural, and linguistic identity—into the question of the distinction between a state belonging to a minority and a state belonging to society as a whole.

In addition to the histories of acculturation and dispossession, self-identity and self-hatred, and the relation to others, there are the contemporary histories of the conflict that began in 1992. That new history is now producing its own political divisions, ruminations on memory, personal hatred, unsatisfied revenge, splits within families. A new history is being grafted onto the old colonial history of scissions. How are we to emerge from it without an amnesty of the heart and mind, as a reflection of the overabundance of French amnesties?

Chronology (1830–1994)

1830

June 14 — A French army of 37,000 disembarks in the bay of Sidi-Ferruch.

July 5 — The dey of Algiers sets his seal on the agreement handing Algiers over to the French

1831

January 4 — Taking of Oran.

March 27 — Taking of Bône by Yusuf.

1832

November 22 — Abd-el-Kader is presented by his father to the Hachem Beni-Amer tribes. He is twenty-four. He proclaims the first jihad against the infidels.

1833

September 29 — Taking of Bougie by General Trezel.

1834

February 26 — Signing of two treaties between Abd-el-Kader and General Desmichels, which recognize the sovereignty of the "emir of believers."

July 22 — Order ratifies the definitive character of the French conquest. A governor-general is named to administrate "the French possessions in northern Africa."

1835

June 28   Abd-el-Kader inflicts a defeat on General Trezel at LaMacta.

1836

January 13   Taking of Tlemcen.

September   General Clauzel leases colonization plots in the Mitidja.

1837

May 30   The Tafna treaty, signed by Bugeaud, recognizes Abd-el-Kader as the sovereign of two-thirds of Algeria.

October 13   Taking of Constantine.

1839

November 18   Abd-el-Kader declares war. The order is given to evacuate the Mitidja. End of the early colonization period.

1841

February 22   Bugeaud is named governor-general of Algeria. End of "limited occupation"; total war.

1843

March 24   The lands of the *habbous* are turned over to the State.

May 14   Taking of Abd-el-Kader's *Smala* by the duke of Aumale. Massacre of the surrounding populations. Abd-el-Kader takes refuge in Morocco.

1844

August 14   Battle of Isly near Oujda.

1845   Uprising, at the call of Bou Maza, in Kabylia, the Dahra, the Chéliff Valley, and the Ouarsenis.

1847

April 13   Bou Maza surrenders to Saint-Arnaud.

December 23   Surrender of Abd-el-Kader.

1848

November 12   Algeria proclaimed an integral part of France by the constitution.

1850   Insurrection in the Aurès and the Zibans at the call of Bou Ziane. The entire Zaatcha tribe (between Biskra and Ouarbla) is massacred.

1851   Insurrection in Kabylia under the leadership of Bou Baghla. Thirty villages destroyed in reprisals.

1852   Revolt of Laghouat against the caliphates named by the French.

1860

September 17–19   Napoleon III travels to Algiers. He will raise the possibility of an "Arab kingdom."

1863

April 22   Senatus consultum on the collective property of the tribes. Creation of mixed communities.

1864

March 11   Insurrection of the Flittas in the Relizane region, and of the Ouled Si-Cheikh, championed by Si-Lalla.

1865

June 3   250,000 acres go to the Société Générale Algérienne, headed by Paulin Talabot.

July 14   Right to naturalization on demand is granted to Jewish and Muslim natives.

1867

November   Terrible famines until June 1868.

1870

October 24   The Crémieux decrees grant French nationality to the Jews of Algeria.

1871

March 14   Beginning of the insurrection headed by the *bachaga* Mokrani and his brothers to protest plans to confiscate the lands. It affects primarily Kabylia.

April 8   Holy war is proclaimed by El Haddad, sheikh of the Khouan Rahntaniya. Admiral de Gueydon, the new governor-general, arrives in Algiers.

May 5   Mokrani is killed by French troops.

September 13   Surrender of the Zouara. Kabylia is conquered. 1,500,000 acres of the best lands are confiscated in Kabylia in December.

1872

July 2   Consecration of the basilica Notre-Dame d'Afrique.

1873

July 26   Warnier Act on jointly held lands.

1878

September 30   Decree on colonization, inspired by certain of Bugeaud's ideas.

1881　　　　　　　　　　For the program of reattachments, Algeria is directly
integrated into France. The civilian territories
(104,830 square kilometers) are divided between 196
communes de plein exercice and 7 *communes mixtes.*
Under the leadership of Bou Amama, the Ouled
Si-Cheikh revolt once more. Installation of the Native
Code, which sets a series of exorbitant common law
penalties for Muslim Algerians.

1886
September 10　　　　　　A decree strips qadis of all jurisdiction over real estate
throughout Algeria.

1889
June 26　　　　　　　　A law imposes French citizenship on all the children of
foreigners who do not refuse it. That automatic
naturalization does not affect Muslim Algerians.

1898
January 20–25　　　　　Anti-Jewish riots in Algiers for the abrogation of the
Crémieux decree.

August 25　　　　　　　Algeria receives the promise of financial autonomy and
the immediate creation of an elected colonial
assembly, the *financial delegations.*

1900
December 29　　　　　　A law confers a civil identity and a special budget on
Algeria.

1901
April 26　　　　　　　Margueritte, a village of colonization, is attacked by
about a hundred Muslim Algerian insurgents.

1903
September 5　　　　　　Sheikh Abdou, mufti of Cairo and principal leader of the
Nahda reformist movement, comes to Algeria. He
declares he is struck by the religious conservatism and
strictness there.

1908　　　　　　　　Publication of a plan for extending obligatory
conscription to the Muslim Algerians.

1911
January 31–February 3　Publication of the decrees instituting obligatory military
service for Muslim Algerians. "Exodus of Tlemcen":
Five hundred Muslim families leave Algeria to escape
the conscription program.

1914–1918　　　　　For the war, indigenous recruitment supplies 173,000
soldiers, including 87,500 volunteers; 25,000 Muslim

soldiers and 22,000 French of Algeria die in combat. In addition, 119,000 workers go to work in the metropolis.

1919

February 4   Promulgation of laws and decrees granting elected representation to a greater number of Muslims in all the Algerian assemblies (100,000 for the general councils and financial delegations; 400,000 for the *douar* councils).

March   Founding of *Ikdam* (resolution, daring) by Emir Khaled, a descendant of Emir Abd-el-Kader.

May   Khaled's petition to President Wilson.

November   Overwhelming victory of a list of candidates headed by Khaled in the Algerian municipal elections (elections voided in 1920).

1920

October   Great famine in Algeria.

1921

September   Steeg named governor-general of Algeria.

1922

April   Publication of the first issue of *Paria*, created at the initiative of the Communists for the independence of the colonies.

October   Victory of Emir Khaled in the departmental by-elections in Algiers.

1924

July   Emir Khaled has meetings in Paris.

December   The Congress of North African Workers is held in Paris by the PCF.

1925

May   Maurice Viollette named governor-general of Algeria.

July   Publication of the first issue of *Al Moutaquid* (The Critique), a newspaper founded by A. Ben Badis, expressing the ideas of the reformist Muslim current.

1926

June 20   Founding in Paris of Etoile Nord-Africaine, which demands "the independence of North Africa."

1927

September   Creation of the Fédération des Elus Indigènes d'Algérie (Federation of Native Elected Officials of Algeria) with, at its head, Doctor Ben Djelloul, one of the representatives of the Jeunes-Algériens movement.

1928

April 4   The governor-general of Algeria takes measures to check
                                      emigration to France.

1929

November 20   Dissolution of Etoile Nord-Africaine.

1930

May   Major celebrations of the centennial of the French
                                      conquest in Algeria.

1931

May 5   Abdelhamid Ben Badis founds the Association des
                                      Oulémas Réformistes d'Algérie (Association of
                                      Reformist Ulama of Algeria). Its slogan: "Arabic is my
                                      language, Algeria is my country, Islam is my religion."

                                      Ferhat Abbas publishes *Le jeune Algérien.*

1933

May 28   Reconstitution of Etoile Nord-Africaine with Messali
                                      Hadj at its head.

1934

May 18   The abbé Lambert is elected mayor of Oran, defeating
                                      the Socialist M. Dubois.

August 5   Bloody clashes between the Muslim and Jewish
                                      populations of Constantine.

1935

March 30   Promulgation of the Régnier decree repressing the
                                      "anti-French demonstrations."

June   Huge parade of 150,000 of Colonel de La Rocque's
                                      Croix-de-Feu in Oued Smar.

1936

June 7   The Fédération des Elus, the ulama, and the
                                      Communists found the Congrès Musulman Algérien
                                      within the framework of the Front Populaire.

November   Discussion of the Blum-Viollette plan (full citizenship
                                      for 21,000 Muslim French). Rejection of the plan in
                                      "ultra" European circles and among the pro-
                                      independence forces of Etoile Nord-Africaine.

1937

January 26   Dissolution of the ENA by the Front Populaire
                                      government.

March 11   The Algerian nationalists proclaim the Parti du Peuple
                                      Algérien (PPA).

1939

February 11   M. Thorez characterizes Algeria as "a nation in formation."

September 26   Dissolution of the democratic organizations in Algeria. Arrest of the principal Algerian nationalist leaders.

1940

October 7   Minister of the Interior Peyrouton abolishes the Crémieux decree naturalizing the Jews of Algeria.

1942

November 8   Anglo-American landing in Algiers.

1943

May 26   Presentation of the "Algerian Manifesto."

May 30   General de Gaulle arrives in Algiers.

December 12   In a speech in Constantine, General de Gaulle announces reforms for Algeria.

1944

March 7   De Gaulle signs an order abolishing all special measures applicable to the Muslims. The former Muslim electoral college is opened to all Algerians age 21 or older.

1945

April 2   First congress of the Amis du Manifeste et de la Liberté (Friends of the Manifesto and of Freedom).

May 8   Start of the violent repressions in Constantinois, Sétif, and Guelma. A total of 103 dead among the Europeans, several thousand Algerian Muslim dead.

August 17   An order grants the Muslims in the second electoral college the possibility of sending to Parliament a number of representatives equal to that of the French in the first college.

1946

March 17   The Constituent Assembly passes an amnesty law regarding Algeria.

April   Founding of the Union Démocratique du Manifeste Algérien (UDMA) by F. Abbas.

October 15   "Industrialization plan" for Algeria.

October 20   Founding of Messali Hadj's Mouvement pour le Triomphe des Libertés Démocratiques (MTLD).

November 10   Legislative elections. Five MTLD deputies are elected.

1947

February 15   The MTLD congress decides to create a clandestine organization for armed struggle in Algeria (the Organisation Spéciale, or OS).

August 27	Adoption of the "Statute on Algeria" by the Council of Ministers.
September 20	Adoption of the "Statute on Algeria" by the National Assembly. All the Muslim deputies object.
October 19–26	Municipal elections. In the second college, the MTLD seizes the totality of seats in the large Algerian cities.

1949

April	"Berberist" crisis in the MTLD's Fédération de France.

1950   The police proceed to break up the OS in Algeria.

1952

February 2	Creation in Paris of a Front d'Unité et d'Action (Unity and Action Front) among the nationalist parties of North Africa.
December 3–8	Uprising in Morocco against the assassination in Tunisia of the trade unionist Ferhat Hached.

1953

April 20	Congress of the MTLD. The supporters of Messali Hadj are dismissed from the central committee. Crisis between "centralists" and "Messalists."
August 20	The sultan of Morocco is deposed. Beginning of urban terrorism in that country.

1954

March–April	Creation of the Comité Révolutionnaire pour l'Unité et l'Action (CRUA), which intends to pave the way for insurrection in Algeria.
July 13–15	The congress of Messali's supporters in Hornu, Belgium, marks the definitive splintering of the MTLD.
November 1	The CRUA transforms itself into the Front de Libération Nationale (FLN). FLN commandos set to work throughout Algeria. The war begins.
November 5	The MTLD is dissolved by the French authorities.
December 3	Messali Hadj proclaims the creation of the Mouvement National Algérian (MNA).
December 10	Debate in the assembly on French policy in North Africa. Military reinforcements are sent to Algeria.

1955

January 5	F. Mitterrand, minister of the interior, champions the use of force and presents a program of reforms for Algeria.
January 20	First major operations of the French army in the Aurès.
February 1	Jacques Soustelle is named governor-general by the Mendès-France government, replacing R. Léonard.

February 15	J. Soustelle settles in Algiers: "A choice has been made in France: integration."
February 23	Investiture of the Edgar Faure government.
March 20	Mairey report to Edgar Faure on the behavior of the police.
April 1	A state of emergency in Algeria is passed in the legislature for a period of six months.
April 18–24	Afro-Asian conference in Bandung.
April 23	Establishment of peremptory censorship in Algiers.
May 13	General Cherrière, commander in chief in Algeria, defines the principle of collective responsibility.
June 16	General Lorrillot replaces General Cherrière.
August 20	Major ALN offensive in North Constantinois. Seventy European victims. Forceful repression: 1,273 is the official death toll.
August 30	The 1954 military class is kept in service.
September 12	The Parti Communiste Algérien is banned. Publication of *Alger-Républicain* suspended.
September 15	The journalist Robert Barrat publishes an interview with "rebel chiefs" in *France-Observateur.* He is arrested.
September 26	Sixty-one Muslim deputies make a motion rejecting integration.
October.	Movement of soldiers for peace in Algeria.
November 29	Edgar Faure is overthrown.
December 2	Dissolution of the National Assembly.
December 10	The elections in Algeria are postponed indefinitely.
December 23	The UDMA elected officials resign and call for the creation of an Algerian republic.

1956

January 2	Victory of the Front Républicain in the elections.
February 1	Investiture of the Guy Mollet government.
February 2	Jacques Soustelle leaves Algiers, cheered by the European population.
February 6	Guy Mollet booed in Algiers.
February 9	Robert Lacoste is named minister resident.
March 12	The National Assembly passes the "special powers."
April 22	Ferhat Abbas officially joins the FLN.
May 18	Massacre of French soldiers in Palestro.
May 27–28	First sweep operations in the Casbah.

June 20–22	Wave of individual attacks in Algiers.
June 26	Oil gushes in Hassi-Messaoud.
July 5	Strike called to mark the anniversary of the taking of Algiers on July 5, 1830.
August 10	"Counterterrorist" bomb on rue de Thèbes, dozens of Muslim casualties.
August 20	FLN congress in the Soummam Valley: creation of the Conseil National de la Révolution Algérienne (CNRA).
September 30	First FLN bomb attacks in Algiers.
Summer 1956	Clashes between the MNA and FLN guerrilla forces, which turn to the advantage of the FLN.
October 22	Hijacking over Algiers of the airplane carrying Ben Bella and his companions, who are arrested.
November 1	Beginning of the Suez expedition.
November 13	General Raoul Salan is named commander in chief in Algeria.
December 24	Discovery of General J. Faure's plot.
December 27	Assassination of Amédée Froger. Arabs beaten at his funeral.

1957

January 7	An order of the superprefect of Algiers grants General Massu and the Tenth Paratroopers' Division policing powers over greater Algiers.
January 16	Bazooka attack on General Salan.
January 28	Start of an eight-day strike on the FLN's orders.
February 10	Bombings of stadiums in Algiers.
February 18	After taking a position against torture, General Jacques Paris de Bollardière is relieved of his command.
February 25	Arrest of Larbi Ben M'hidi.
March 4	Creation of the plan of action for urban protection.
March 5	"Suicide" of Ben M'hidi.
March 23	"Suicide" of Ali Boumendjel.
March 24	First letter of resignation from Paul Teitgen.
April 5	Establishment of the Commission de Sauvegarde des Droits et Libertés Individuels (Commission for the Safeguarding of Individual Rights and Liberties).
May 21	Fall of the Guy Mollet government.
May 29	Massacres of Mélouza.
June 11	Arabs are beaten at the funerals of the victims of the

	bombings at the Casino de la Corniche. Arrest of Maurice Audin.
June 17	Investiture of the Bourgès-Maunoury government.
July 7	In a speech in Algiers, R. Lacoste denounces the "exhibitionists of heart and mind."
September 12	Resignation of Paul Teitgen.
September 24	Arrest of Yacef Saadi, head of the FLN's autonomous zone of Algiers (ZAA).
September 30	Fall of the government over the outline law.
October	Capture of Ben Hamida. Complete dismantling of the autonomous zone of Algiers. End of the battle of Algiers.
October 8	Death of Ali La Pointe, assistant to Y. Saadi.
November 22	The king of Morocco and Habib Bourguiba propose a goodwill mission to settle the Algerian question.
November 29	The outline law on Algeria and the Algerian electoral law are passed.
December 11	Publication of the comprehensive report of the Commission de Sauvegarde.
December 26	Abbane Ramdane is murdered by other FLN leaders.

1958

January 28	Dissolution in Paris of the Union Générale des Etudiants Musulmans d'Algérie.
February 8	The French air force bombs the Tunisian village of Sakiet.
February 14	Meeting of the CCE in Cairo.
February 25	Robert Murphy, an American diplomatic adviser, arrives in Paris for his "goodwill" mission.
April 15	Fall of the Félix Gaillard government.
May 13	In Algeria, demonstrators seize control of the general government. Formation of a committee of public safety headed by General Massu.
May 14	Investiture of the Pierre Pflimlin government. Massu's appeal to General de Gaulle. Declaration by General Salan: "I am temporarily taking the fate of French Algeria in hand."
May 15	General de Gaulle declares he is ready "to assume the powers of the Republic."
May 16	Franco-Muslim "fraternization" on the Forum of Algiers.
May 17	Jacques Soustelle arrives in Algiers.
May 19	Press conference by General de Gaulle.

May 26	Committees of public safety in Corsica.
May 29	General de Gaulle agrees to form the government.
June 1	Investiture of the de Gaulle government.
June 2	Censorship is lifted.
June 4	General de Gaulle in Algiers: "I have understood you!"
June 7	General Salan is named delegate general of the government and commander in chief in Algeria.
July 2	General de Gaulle again travels to Algeria.
September 7	Reestablishment of the Commission de Sauvegarde.
September 19	Constitution of the provisional government of the Algerian republic (GPRA), headed by Ferhat Abbas.
September 28	Referendum on the constitution.
October 3	In a speech, General de Gaulle announces the Constantine plan.
October 23	At a press conference, General de Gaulle offers "the peace of the brave."
October 25	The GPRA rejects the offer of "the peace of the brave."
November 23–30	Legislative elections. Success of the Union pour la Nouvelle République.
December 4	General de Gaulle again goes to Algeria.
December 13	By a vote of 35 to 18, with 28 abstentions, the UN General Assembly rejects a resolution recognizing Algeria's right to independence.
December 19	General Salan is replaced by Delegate General Paul Delouvrier and General Challe.
December 21	General de Gaulle is elected president of the Republic.
1959	
January	Algerian prisoners are pardoned, Messali Hadj goes free.
March 7	Ben Bella and his companions in captivity are transferred to the island of Aix.
March 28	The commanders of *wilayas* III and VI are killed in battle.
April 29	General de Gaulle to Deputy Pierre Laffont: "The old Algeria is dead."
July 21	Beginning of the "Jumelles" operation in Kabylia.
Early August	First of General de Gaulle's "tours of the canteens."
September 16	General de Gaulle announces the principle of self-determination via referendum for the Algerians.
September 19	Georges Bidault forms the Rassemblement pour l'Algérie Française.

September 28	Evasive response by the GPRA to General de Gaulle's September 16 speech.
December 16	Beginning of the CNRA's meeting in Tripoli.

1960

January 13	Resignation of Antoine Pinay, minister of finances and economic affairs.
January 18	General Massu is replaced by General Crépin at the head of the Algiers army corps.
January 24	Beginning of "barricades week."
January 28	Paul Delouvrier and General Challe leave Algiers.
February 1	The entrenched camp of the Faculties, headed by P. Lagaillarde, surrenders. End of the "barricades."
February 2	The National Assembly passes special powers for one year.
February 5	Jacques Soustelle leaves the government.
February 10	The government creates a Comité des Affaires Algériennes (Committee of Algerian Affairs). The army's psychological action services are eliminated.
February 24	Discovery of the Jeanson network lending support to the FLN.
March 3–5	Second "tour of the canteens." De Gaulle speaks of "Algerian Algeria."
March 30	General Challe is replaced by General Crépin.
June 10	Si Salah, head of *wilaya* IV, is received at the Elysée Palace.
June 14	In a declaration, de Gaulle offers to negotiate with the leaders of the insurrection.
June 25–29	The Melun talks, which fail.
September 5	The Jeanson network trial. Publication of the *Manifeste des 121* on the right to insubordination.
November 3	Beginning of the barricades trial.
November 4	In a speech, General de Gaulle alludes to an "Algerian Republic, which will exist some day."
November 22	Louis Joxe is named minister of Algerian affairs.
November 24	Jean Morin is named delegate general in Algeria, replacing Paul Delouvrier.
December 9–13	General de Gaulle travels to Algeria. Violent European demonstrations. First mass demonstration held by the FLN in Algiers.
December 19	The UN General Assembly recognizes Algeria's right to independence.

1961

January 8	Referendum on General de Gaulle's Algerian policy. Broad success of the yes vote.
January 25	Popie's murder by a commando of the Front de l'Algérie Française.
February	Constitution of the Organisation Armée Secrète (OAS).
February 20–22	Ahmed Boumendjel meets with Georges Pompidou in Lucerne and Neuchâtel.
March 17	Announcement of talks between France and the GPRA.
March 31	The mayor of Evian is murdered by the OAS.
April 11	In a press conference, General de Gaulle alludes to a "sovereign Algerian state."
April 22	Generals Challe, Jouhaud, and Zeller, soon joined by General Salan, seize power in Algiers.
April 23	Oran is in the hands of the putschists, but the coup fails in Constantine. The government decrees a state of emergency and recourse to article 16 of the constitution.
April 25	Failure of the putsch. General Challe surrenders. Salan, Jouhaud, and Zeller go underground.
May 5	First secret meeting of the OAS in Algiers, under the leadership of Colonel Godard; the organization is established.
May 20	Opening of the Evian negotiations.
May 31	The OAS murders Commissioner Gavoury. General Challe is sentenced to fifteen years in prison.
June 7	General Ailleret is named commander in chief in Algeria.
June 13	The Evian negotiations are suspended.
July 5	Repression of the FLN demonstrations in Algiers: at least seventy dead.
July 19	Opening of the Lugrin conversations, suspended on July 28.
August 5	First pirate radio broadcast by the OAS.
August 26	Ben Khedda succeeds Ferhat Abbas at the head of the GPRA.
September 8	Failed assassination attempt of General de Gaulle at Pont-sur-Seine.
October 17	Violent repressions of the demonstrations by Algerians in Paris. Dozens of victims.
November 4	Arrest of Abderrahmane Farès.
December 16	In Oran, Colonel Rançon is murdered by the OAS.

1962

February 5	Press conference by General de Gaulle: he announces that the outcome in Algeria is imminent.
February 8	Anti-OAS demonstration in Paris. Brutal intervention by the police in the Charonne metro: eight dead.
February 10	Opening of conversations between the GPRA and the French government at Les Rousses.
February 19	Protocol of accord between the two parties.
February 26	Unprecedented wave of attacks against the Muslims in Algiers.
March 7	Opening of the second Evian conference.
March 18	Signing of the Evian accords. A cease-fire goes into effect in Algeria the next day.
March 21	Christian Fouchet is named high commissioner in Algeria.
March 26	Fusillade on rue d'Isly in Algiers. The army fires on the European demonstrators: forty-six dead.
March 29	Establishment of the provisional executive body, headed by Abderrahmane Farès.
April 8	Referendum very favorable to the government's Algerian policy.
April 14	Georges Pompidou is named prime minister to replace Michel Debré. General Jouhaud sentenced to death.
April 18	General Fourquet replaces General Ailleret.
May 3	In Algiers, explosion of a booby-trapped car: sixty-two Muslims die.
May 24	General Salan is sentenced to life imprisonment.
June 7	The CNRA adopts the "Tripoli program."
June 15	Conversations between the OAS and the FLN for a cessation of attacks.
July 1	Self-determination referendum in Algeria passes, 5,975,581 to 16,534.
July 3	France officially recognizes the independence of Algeria. Independence is proclaimed in Algeria. The GPRA arrives in Algiers.
July 4–5	Abductions and executions of *pieds noirs* in Oran.
July 22	Internecine struggles in independent Algeria. In Tlemcen, Ahmed Ben Bella and his friends announce the formation of a "political bureau" against the GPRA.
July 25	Occupation of Constantine by the "Tlemcen group" and Mohamed Boudiaf's declarations "against the coup d'état."

August 22	General de Gaulle escapes an attack at the Petit-Clamart, organized by an OAS commando.
End of August	Bloody incidents between rival *wilayas* in Algeria. Beginning of exactions against the *harkis*.
September 9	The Armée Nationale Populaire (ANP), under the command of Colonel Houari Boumédienne, enters Algiers.
September 20	Election of an Algerian constituent assembly.
September 27	Mohamed Boudiaf, "one of the historic chiefs of the FLN," creates the Parti de la Révolution Socialiste (PRS).
November 29	The Parti Communiste Algérien is banned.
December	Massacre of *harkis*.

1963

January 17	Opening of the first UGTA congress.
March 29	A. Ben Bella presents the decree regarding the organization and management of businesses and vacant agricultural operations (decrees on "self-management").
April 16	Mohamed Khider resigns his post as general secretary of the FLN. A. Ben Bella succeeds him.
August 14	Ferhat Abbas resigns the presidency of the Algerian Assembly.
September 8	The Algerian constitution is approved by referendum. Installation of the single-party regime.
September 29	In Kabylia, Hocine Aït Ahmed and Mohand Ou el Hadj join the resistance against Ben Bella. Hocine Aït Ahmed creates the Front des Forces Socialistes (FFS).
November 5	Cease-fire and end of "the sands war" with Morocco (it had begun on October 8).

1964

April 16	The meeting of the first congress of the FLN adopts the "Algiers Charter."
June 15	Retreat of French troops from Algeria; troops remain only in Mers-el-Kebir and in the Sahara.
August	Mohammed Khider officially announces his opposition to Ben Bella, and keeps "the FLN's secret funds."
October 17	Hocine Aït Ahmed, leader of the FFS, is arrested in Kabylia.

1965

June 19	A council of the revolution, headed by Houari

Boumédienne, removes Ahmed Ben Bella from office and declares it is assuming all powers.

1966

February 5 — Municipal elections to the communal popular assemblies (APC).

June. — Gillo Pontecorvo's film *La battaglia di Algeri* wins the Golden Lion at La Mostra in Venice. The film is banned in France.

1967

January 4 — Mohammed Khider murdered in Madrid.

December 15 — President Houari Boumédienne discharges Colonel Tahar Zbiri, the chief of the general staff who has gone over to the opposition, and takes over the command of the Armée Nationale Populaire.

1968

January — The Mers-el-Kebir base, use of which the French army had obtained until 1977, is evacuated for financial reasons.

May 20 — Nationalization of the sectors of mechanical construction, fertilizer, and metallurgy.

June 21 — Nationalization of the sectors of chemicals, machinery, cement, and food.

December 27 — The French and Algerian governments sign an accord bringing the annual contingent of Algerians workers, candidates for employment in France, to 35,000 for a period of three years.

1969

January 15 — Treaty of Ifrane, which establishes neighborly relations among Algeria, Morocco, and Mauritania.

March 23 — Adoption of the *wilaya* charter.

1970

October 20 — Krim Belkacem, one of the "historic chiefs" of the FLN, is discovered strangled in a Frankfurt hotel.

November 2 — Promulgation of the statute on agricultural cooperatives.

1971

January 15 — Dissolution of the Union Nationale des Etudiants Algériens (UNEA).

February 24 — Nationalization of the pipelines, of natural gas, and of 51 percent of the worth of French petroleum companies (ELF and CFP).

November 8 — Promulgation of the order on the agrarian revolution and the charter of the agrarian revolution.

November 16	Promulgation of the order on the charter of the Gestion Socialiste des Entreprises (GSE).

1973

September 4	The murder of the *pied noir* poet Jean Senac, who had lived in Algeria since independence, is announced.
September 9	The fourth summit of the nonaligned countries meets in Algiers. Algeria establishes a "list of grievances" from the Third World against the attitude of the Northern countries.
September 19	The Algerian government decides to unilaterally suspend emigration to France.
October	Arab-Israeli War. Algeria is co-organizer of the embargo leading to the first "oil crisis." Sharp increase in petroleum receipts.

1974

April	At the UN, Boumédienne champions a "new international economic order."
June 3	Death of the nationalist leader Messali Hadj. On June 7, more than twenty thousand people attend his funeral in Tlemcen.
August 14	Launching of the "Green Dam" project, designed to prevent the advance of the Saharan desert.

1975

April 10	For the first time, a French head of state, Valéry Giscard d'Estaing, visits independent Algeria.
May	Mohamed Lakhdar-Hamina's film, *Chronique des années de braise*, wins the Palme d'Or at the Cannes Festival.

1976

February 27	The Polisario Front proclaims the "Sahrawi Arab Democratic Republic," with the support of Algeria. On March 7, relations with Rabat are broken off.
March 9	Four former FLN leaders during the war, Ferhat Abbas, Ben Youssef Ben Khedda, Cheikh Kheirredine, and Hocine Lahouel, launch a public appeal in Algeria against Boumédienne's policy.
June 27	Referendum on the National Charter.
November 19	The Algerian constitution is approved by referendum (99 percent of the vote).
December 10	Houari Boumédienne is elected president of the Republic.

1977

February 23   Election of the National Popular Assembly.

1978

December 27   Death of Houari Boumédienne after six weeks in a coma. Rabah Bitat becomes acting head of the state.

1979

February 7   Colonel Chadli Bendjedid is named president of the Republic.

1980

January 2   The FLN's central committee encourages families to acquire private property.

April 20   In Tizi-Ouzou, three days of rioting follow the expulsion of instructors and students from the university, which was occupied on April 7 (after a lecture by the writer Mouloud Mammeri was banned). The insurgents demand recognition of Berber culture in Algeria.

October 10   An earthquake destroys the city of El Asnam. Several thousand casualties.

October 30   Lifting of the "special measures" taken against former president Ahmed Ben Bella and Colonel Tahar Zbiri.

December 24   Fourth session of the central committee. The "cadres of mass organizations" and members of the assemblies are required to join the FLN.

1981

April 8   First congress of the Union des Juristes Algériens (Union of Algerian Jurists): Algerianization of legislative texts; the Arabic language is to be used within the administration.

November 30   François Mitterrand, on a visit to Algiers, proposes that Franco-Algerian relations be "a symbol of the new relations between the North and the South."

1982

February 3   The signing of the Franco-Algerian natural gas accord inaugurates a "new type of cooperation" between the two countries (Algeria and France).

November 2   Violent incidents at the university housing complex of Ben Aknoun between "progressives" and "Islamists."

1983

February 26   Meeting between Chadli and Hassan II, and reopening of the Algerian-Moroccan border.

August 6   Decree on the organization of studies at the National School of Meftah for the training of religious cadres.

October–December	Thousands of people are evicted from the slums of Algiers and sent to the interior of the country.

1984

January 12	President Chadli Bendjedid is reelected with 95.3 percent of the vote. Meeting of the central committee, which endorses the list of candidates for the new political bureau. The office of the FLN's central committee is headed by Mohamed Chérif Messaadia.
April 16	Major Islamist demonstration in Kouba during the funeral of Sheikh Soltani.
May 29	Ahmed Ben Bella's Mouvement pour la Démocratie en Algérie (MDA) is formed in Chantilly.
June 9	A "code on the family" is adopted by the National Popular Assembly, which limits the rights of women.
October 24	In Algiers, formal reburial of Krim Belkacem and eight former FLN leaders, who have been rehabilitated by the regime.
November	Reorganization of the army. Promotion of Generals Belhouchet, Benloucif, and Nezzar.

1985

April	Trial of 135 Muslim fundamentalists accused of belonging to an underground organization, the Islamic Movement of Algeria. Violent demonstrations in the Casbah of Algiers to demand improvement of housing conditions.
June 30	Creation of a League for Human Rights headed by Ali Yahia. It is recognized by the International League for Human Rights, and does not obtain government authorization.
December 24	Death of Ferhat Abbas, first president of the GPRA.

1986

January 16	Adoption of the new National Charter by referendum (98.37 percent of the vote). It insists on the progressive character of Islam, introduces a reference to the Berber people, and encourages the private sector.
November 8–12	Violent demonstrations of high school and college students occur in Constantine and Sétif.

1987

April 7	Ali Mecili, attorney of the Paris bar and founder of the newspaper *Libre Algérie*, directed by the FFS, is murdered in front of his home.
June 24	Two hundred and two Islamist defendants appear before

the State Security Court of Médéa. It is one of the largest trials in Algerian history.

1988

May 16 — Normalization of diplomatic relations between Algeria and Morocco, twelve years after being broken off.

October 4 — Beginning of riots in Algiers. The commercial center of Algiers is ransacked.

October 10 — An unofficial toll for the six days of riots lists six hundred dead. A collective of seventy journalists demands freedom of the press. President Chadli Bendjedid appears on television and promises political reforms.

November 3 — Referendum on the modification of the constitution, which makes the government responsible before Parliament (92.27 percent of the vote, with a participation rate of 80.3 percent).

November 5 — Kasdi Merbah is named prime minister to replace Abdelhamid Brahimi.

November 27–28 — The sixth congress of the FLN provides for the separation of the party and the state, and designates Chadli Bendjedid as sole candidate for the presidential election.

December 22 — Reelection of Chadli Bendjedid to the presidency of the Algerian Republic.

1989

February 5 — The Algerian press publishes the text of the new constitution, which no longer refers to socialism or to the FLN. The fundamental legislation opens the way for a multi-party system (article 40).

February 15–17 — Summit of Marrakech between the heads of state of Morocco, Mauritania, Algeria, Tunisia, and Libya, who proclaim the formation of a Arab Maghreb Union.

September 10 — Mouloud Hamrouche replaces Kasdi Merbah at the head of the government.

September 14 — The government legalizes the Islamic Salvation Front (ISF), created a few months earlier.

October 28 — Death of Kateb Yacine, the great Algerian writer. On November 1 in Algiers, his funeral is the occasion for incidents with Islamists.

December 15 — Hocine Aït Ahmed returns to Algeria. His party, the FFS, had obtained official recognition on November 20.

December 21 — Several tens of thousands of women in *hidjeb* (Islamic headscarfs) converge on the National Assembly, demanding the application of the shari'a (Koranic law).

1990

April 20   One hundred thousand supporters of the ISF demonstrate in Algiers, demanding, among other things, the abandonment of bilingualism and the application of the shari'a in Algeria.

May 17   Several tens of thousands of FLN militants demonstrate in Algiers.

May 31   One hundred thousand supporters of Hocine Aït Ahmed parade in Algiers at the call of the FFS.

June 12   Victory of the Islamic Salvation Front (ISF) at the municipal elections.

September 27   Ahmed Ben Bella returns to Algeria after ten years in exile.

December 26   By an overwhelming majority (173 votes to 8), the Algerian deputies adopt legislation generalizing the use of the Arabic language.

December 27   Four hundred thousand people parade in Algiers for democracy, and against the generalized use of the Arabic language.

1991

January 17   Beginning of the Gulf War following Iraq's invasion of Kuwait on August 2 of the previous year.

March 12–13   General strike launched by the UGTA, observed by 90 percent of government employees.

June 5   Deadly clash between Islamists and law enforcement. A state of siege exists. Sid Ahmed Ghozali is named prime minister to replace Mouloud Hamrouche.

June 15   The ISF calls for a general strike.

June 30   The two leaders of the ISF, Abassi Madani and Ali Benhadj, are arrested and imprisoned.

December 26   In the first round of legislative elections, the ISF wins 188 seats.

1992

January 2   Some 300,000 people demonstrate in Algiers, at the call of the Front des Forces Socialistes (FFS), for the "safeguarding of democracy."

January 5   Creation of a National Committee for Safeguarding Algeria.

January 11   Armored vehicles are deployed in the principal cities. President Chadli Bendjedid, suspected of wanting to "cohabitate" with the Islamists, is forced by the army to resign. The National Assembly is dissolved. The next day the elections are voided.

January 14	A High State Committee (HCS), headed by Mohamed Boudiaf, takes power.
June 29	President Boudiaf is murdered in Annaba.
July 2	Ali Kafi is co-opted to head the HCS.
July 8	After the resignation of Sid Ahmed Ghozali, Belaïd Abdesselam is charged with forming the new government.
July 15	The military tribunal of Blida sentences Abassi Madani and Ali Benhadj to twelve years in prison.
August 26	An attack at the Algiers airport causes nine deaths and 128 injuries.
September 30	Law decreed on "the struggle against terrorism and subversion," which sets the age for penal responsibility for crimes of terrorism at sixteen instead of eighteen. The identity of the magistrates cannot be divulged under penalty of imprisonment for two to five years.
December 1–9	Dissolution of 123 local councils and more than 200 municipal councils controlled by the ISF.

1993

February 13	General Khaled Nezzar escapes an attack in Algiers.
February 23	Establishment of special jurisdiction courts in Constantine, Oran, and Algiers.
March	The annual report of Amnesty International (1993) denounces the use of torture in Algeria.
March 16–17	Djilali Liabès, former minister of higher education, and Ladi Flici, member of the national advisory council, are murdered.
May 26	The writer Tahar Djaout is murdered.
June 15	Murder of Mahfoud Boucebci, internationally renowned psychiatrist.
July 10	General Khaled Nezzar is replaced by General Liamine Zéroual at the head of the Ministry of Defense.
August 21	Redha Malek is called to succeed M. Abdesselam at the head of the government. Kasdi Merbah, the former head of military security (1962–1979), is murdered on the same day.
August 31	Execution of seven Islamists. The number of death sentences pronounced since the beginning of the year rises to 278.
October 10	Murder of Djilali Belkhenchir, professor of pediatrics.
October 24	Three French consular agents are abducted in Algiers and released a few days later.

December 25	The HCS decides to extend its mandate until January 31, 1994.

1994

January 23	The "national conference" opens in Algiers; it is boycotted by the principal opposition parties.
January 30	The High Security Council (HSC) entrusts "the presidency of the state" to General Liamine Zéroual.
February 24	Anticipated release of two high officials of the ISF, Djeddi and Boukhamkhan, who were serving four-year sentences for attack on state security.
March 5	Ahmed Asselah, director of the Advanced School of Fine Arts in Algiers, is murdered.
March 19	The Islamists decree Blida "a dead city." The commandos of the army occupy the city; several dozen casualties.
March 27	The head of the UCD, Saïd Sadi, launches an appeal for "resistance."
April 7	From his prison, Ali Benhadj proposes dialogue with the regime to resolve the crisis, but without condemning the violence.
April 10	The Algerian dinar is devalued by 40.17 percent.
May 8	Two French clergymen are killed in the Casbah of Algiers; a few thousand supporters of "dialogue" march in Algiers.
May 18	The FLN criticizes the repression of the Islamists.
May 31	Murder of Salah Djebaïli, rector of the University of Science and Technology at Bab Ezzouar, on the outskirts of Algiers.
June 1	Algeria obtains a restructuring of its foreign debt, estimated at 26 billion dollars. A local leader of the AIG, Abdelkader Hattab, his wife, and nine men are murdered by a rival group.
June 6	Murder of a journalist in the very center of Algiers. Since May 1993, fourteen Algerian journalists have been killed.
June 7	The minister of the interior increases state censorship of the media.
June 15	The former head of the AIG, Abdelkader Layada, extradited from Morocco, is sentenced to death by the special court of Algiers.
June 18	Murder of Youcef Fathallah, president of the Algerian League for Human Rights.
June 29	Two bombs explode on the parade route of a march held

	by the MPR and the RCD, to demand the truth about the murder of Mohamed Boudiaf. Toll: two dead, sixty-four wounded.
July 5	Liamine Zéroual gives a speech promoting dialogue "with respect for the constitution and the laws, and with the rejection of violence."
July 7	Seven Italian sailors have their throats slit in the port of Djendjen, 360 kilometers east of Algiers.
July 12	The ISF accuses the G-7 countries of "catering to the Algerian regime."
July 15	The United States urges the Algerian regime to "broaden its political base."
August 2	In a communiqué made public, the executive authority of the ISF abroad announces a scission within its ranks.
August 3	Three gendarmes and two French consular agents are murdered during a botched attack by booby-trapped car in Algiers.
August 5	Seventeen alleged Algerian Islamists are placed under house arrest in Folembray, France.
August 6	The AIG announces that it wants to ban all education in Algeria. The director of the Institute of Agronomy in Blida is murdered.
August 7	France's minister of the interior invites the Western countries to repress the activities of Islamist militants.
August 11	Eleven dead near Tlemcen in an attack on a barracks by the armed Islamist groups.
August 17	In a "last warning," the Islamic Salvation Army calls on Algerian journalists to "no longer support the regime."
August 21	Resumption of political dialogue in Algeria, in the absence of the ISF, the FFS, and the UCD.
August 24	In no longer issuing its visas in Algeria, France closes its borders to the majority of Algerians.
August 25–27	Three meetings take place between the leaders of the ISF, held in the military prison of Blida, and emissaries of Liamine Zéroual.
August 26	The AIG gives itself a countergovernment, which is disavowed by the ISF.
August 28	Morocco reestablishes visas for Algerian nationals.
August 29	Algiers decides on the "complete closure" of its border with Morocco.
September 2	The ISF envisions the possibility of a "truce" with the regime.

September 3	Algerian soldiers announce they have killed forty-one Islamists in a single day, September 1.
September 6	A letter from five ISF leaders demands that "the armed branch" be brought into consultations with the regime.
September 13	The Algerian presidency announces that Ali Benhadj and Abassi Madani have been placed under guard at their homes.
September 21	General strike in Kabylia for the recognition of Berber culture.
September 29	Murder of the rai singer Cheb Hasni in Oran.
October 2	Major demonstration for Berber culture in Kabylia.
October 6	The Ministry of Education announces that six hundred schools have been destroyed or burned in Algeria and that approximately fifty instructors have been killed.
October 8	An eighteenth Frenchman is murdered in Algeria.
October 10	Release of the singer Matoub Lounès, who was abducted on September 26.
October 31	In a "message to the nation," President Zéroual pronounces the failure of "dialogue" and recommends an escalation in the war against the Islamists.
November 21–22	The representatives of the FLN, the ISF, and the FFS meet in Rome to draft an opposition platform.
December 26	In Marseilles, an Air France jetliner, hijacked in Algiers by an AIG commando, is stormed.

1995

January 13	"Pact of Rome" signed by Algerian opposition groups (IFS, FSF, FLN).
February 22	Uprising at the Serkadji prison in Algiers. One hundred prisoners killed.
April	Establishment of fossil fuel exclusion zones in the southern part of the country to conserve fossil fuel resources.
November 16	General Liamine Zéroual elected president of the Algerian Republic with 61.01 percent of the vote.

1996

November 13	Passage of new constitution, which increases the powers of the presidency and bans religious and regionalist parties. New constitution approved by 85.81 percent of the voters.

1997

June 5

Legislative elections. President Zéroual's Rassemblement National Démocratique wins the election with its ally, the FLN. The RND receives 155 of the 380 seats, the FLN, 64. The opposition denounces electoral fraud.

August–September

Large-scale massacres in villages surrounding the capital city, notably at Bentalha and Raïs.

1998

September 11

Liamine Zéroual steps down and announces that new presidential elections will be held.

1999

April 27

The new president of Algeria, Abdelaziz Bouteflika, takes the oath of office.

June 6

The military wing of the dissolved Islamic Salvation Front (ISF), the Islamic Salvation Army, inactive since 1997, announces that it will disarm and accept the authority of the state, and calls for an end to violence.

July 8

By a substantial majority, Algerian legislators pass a law on civil peace (*concorde civile*), which stipulates partial amnesty for armed Islamists. The law will be promulgated on July 13.

July 12

The Algerian president proclaims to his fellow African leaders that his country is "in good health." He claims that holding the thirty-fifth summit of the Organization of African Unity in Algiers will provide both moral and political support for his efforts at national reconciliation.

September 16

Algerians vote overwhelmingly in favor of the referendum on the law on civil peace (98.63 percent of the vote).

November 22

Abdelkader Hachani, the "number 3" man in the Islamic Salvation Front, is assassinated during a meeting in Algiers.

December 23

Senator Ahmed Benbitour, former minister of finance, is named head of the Algerian government; he replaces the resigning Smaïl Hamdani.

2000

February 24

Algerian president and minister of defense Abdelaziz Bouteflika institutes organizational reforms in the military.

April 11

Announcement of President Bouteflika's state visit to France, planned for June 14–16.

Bibliography

Abdi, N., C. Blin, R. Redjala, and B. Stora. 1992. *200 hommes de pouvoir en Algérie*. Paris: Indigo.

Achour, C. 1985. *Abécédaires en devenir. Idéologie coloniale et langue française*. Algiers: ENAP.

Addi, L. 1990. *L'Impasse du populisme: L'Algérie, collectivité politique et État en construction*. Algiers: ENAL.

Ageron, C. R. 1991. *La Décolonisation française*. Paris: A. Colin.

Ageron, C. R., and C. A. Julien. 1979. *Histoire de l'Algérie contemporaine*. 2 vols. Paris: PUF.

Aït, A. 1989. *L'Affaire Mecili*. Paris: La Découverte.

Alleg, H., ed. 1981. *La Guerre d'Algérie*. 3 vols. Paris: Temps actuels.

Ammour, K., C. Leucate, and J. J. Moulin. 1974. *La Voie algérienne: Les contradictions d'un développement national*. Paris: Maspero.

Assidon, E. 1978. *Sahara occidental, un enjeu pour le Nord-Ouest africain*. Paris: Maspero.

Balta, P., and M. Duteil. 1981. *L'Algérie des Algériens vingt ans après*. Paris: Éd. Ouvrières.

Balta, P., and C. Rulleau. 1978. *La Stratégie de Boumediene*. Paris: Sinbad.

Barbier, M. 1982. *Le Conflit du Sahara occidental*. Paris: L'Harmattan.

Bedrani, S. 1981. *L'Agriculture algérienne depuis 1967*. Paris: Economica.

Benamrane, D. 1980. *Agriculture et développement en Algérie*. Algiers: NPDC.

———. 1980. *La Crise de l'habitat*. Algiers: NPDC-CREA.

Benhouria, T. 1980. *L'Économie de l'Algérie*. Paris: Maspero.

Benissad, M. E. 1979. *Économie du développement de l'Algérie, 1962–1978*. Algiers: OUP.

Blin, L. 1990. *L'Algérie, du Sahara au Sahel*. Paris: L'Harmattan.

Boudjedra, R. 1971. *Naissance du cinéma algérien*. Paris: Maspero.

Bourdieu, P. [1964] 1977. *Le Déracinement. La crise de l'agriculture traditionnelle en Algérie*. Paris: Minuit.

———. 1963. *Sociologie de l'Algérie*. Paris: PUF.

271

Bourges, H. 1967. *L'Algérie à l'épreuve du pouvoir*. Paris: Grasset.

Brahimi, B. 1990. *Le Pouvoir, la presse et les intellectuels en Algérie*. Paris: L'Harmattan.

Burgat, F. 1988. "L'islamisme au Maghreb." *Les Temps Modernes* 501 (March).

Burgat, F., and M. Nancy. 1984. *Les Villages socialistes de la réforme agraire algérienne*. Paris: CNRS.

Chikh, S. 1981. *L'Algérie en armes ou le temps des certitudes*. Paris and Algiers: Economica/OUP.

————. 1989. "L'ouvrier, la vie et le prince." In *L'Algérie et la Modernité*. Dakar: Codesria.

Cote, M. 1983. *L'Espace algérien. Les prémices d'un aménagement*. Algiers: OUP.

Cubertafond, B. 1979. *La République algérienne démocratique et populaire*. Paris: PUF.

Deheuvels, L. W. 1992. *Islam et pensée contemporaine en Algérie*. Paris: CNRS.

Dejeux, J. 1982. *Situation de la littérature maghrébine de langue française*. Algiers: OUP.

————. 1993. *Maghreb, littérature de langue française*. Paris: Arcantère.

Destanne de Bernis, G. 1969. "Industries industrialisantes et les options algériennes." *Revue Tiers-Monde* (July–September).

Djeghloul, A. 1989. "Algérie." In *Encyclopaedia universalis*. Paris.

Duprat, G. 1973. *Révolution et autogestion rurale en Algérie*. Paris: A. Colin.

Durand, J. P., and H. Tengour. 1982. *L'Algérie et ses populations*. Brussels: Complexe.

Ecrement, M. 1986. *Indépendance politique et libération économique: un quart de siècle du développement de l'Algérie, 1962 à 1985*. Grenoble and Algiers: PUG/OUP.

Einaudi, J. 1991. *La Bataille de Paris, 17 octobre 1961*. Paris: Le Seuil.

Encyclopédie coloniale. Algérie-Sahara. 1948. Paris: Encyclopédie de l'Empire français.

Étienne, B. 1977. *Les problèmes agraires au Maghreb*. Aix-en-Provence/Paris: CRESM/CNRS.

————. 1987. *L'Islamisme radical*. Paris: Hachette.

Francos, A., and J. P. Serini. 1976. *Un Algérien nommé Boumediene*. Paris: Stock.

Gadant, M. 1988. *Islam et nationalisme à travers "El Moudjahid" 1956–1962*. Paris: L'Harmattan.

Grimaud, N. 1984. *La Politique extérieure de l'Algérie*. Paris: Karthala.

Haddad, M., and T. Khenniche. 1981. *L'École en milieu rural*. Algiers: CNRS-CREA.

Hamon, H., and P. Rotman. 1979. *Les Porteurs de valises. La résistance française à la guerre d'Algérie*. Paris: Le Seuil.

Hamoumou, M. 1993. *Et ils sont devenus harkis*. Paris: Fayard.

Harbi, M. 1975. *Aux origines du FLN: Le populisme révolutionnaire en Algérie*. Paris: Bourgois.

————. 1980. *Le FLN: mirage et réalité*. Paris: Jeune Afrique.

————. 1993. *L'Algérie et son destin: Croyants ou citoyens*. Paris: Arcantère.

Kaufer, R. 1986. *L'OAS, histoire d'une organisation secrète*. Paris: Fayard.

Khodja, S. 1985. *Les Algériennes du quotidien*. Algiers: ENAL.

Koroghli, A. 1989. *Institutions politiques et développement en Algérie*. Paris: L'Harmattan.

Koultchizki, S. 1974. *L'Autogestion, l'homme et l'État. L'expérience algérienne*. Paris: Mouton.

Lacheraf, M. 1965. *Algérie, nation et société*. Paris: Maspero.

Lacouture, J. 1985. *1962, Algérie: La guerre est finie*. Brussels: Complexe.

————. 1986. *De Gaulle, le souverain*. Paris: Le Seuil.

Laks, M. 1970. *Autogestion ouvrière et pouvoir politique en Algérie (1962–1965)*. Paris: EDI.

Lamchichi, A. 1991. *Islam et contestation au Maghreb*. Paris: L'Harmattan.

Launay, M. 1963. *Paysans algériens*. Paris: Seuil.

Leca, J., and J. C. Vatin. 1975. *L'Algérie politique. Institutions et régime*. Paris: FNSP.

————. 1977. "Le système politique algérien: idéologie, institutions et changement social." In *Annuaire de l'Afrique du Nord*. Paris and Aix-la-Chapelle: CRESM/CNRS.

Le Mire, H. 1982. *Histoire militaire de la guerre d'Algérie*. Paris: Albin Michel.

Leveau, R. 1993. *Le Sabre et le turban. L'avenir du Maghreb*. Paris: F. Bourin.

Levine, M. 1986. *Les ratonnades d'octobre*. Paris: Ramsay.

Maherzi, L. 1979. *Le Cinéma algérien*. Algiers: NPDC.

Marseille, J. 1989. *Empire colonial et capitalisme français: Histoire d'un divorce*. Paris: Seuil.

Maschino, M., and F. M'Rabet. 1972. *L'Algérie des illusions, la révolution confisquée*. Paris: Laffont.

M'Rabet, F. 1979. *La Femme algérienne and Les Algériennes*. Paris: Maspero.

Nair-Sami, K. 1982. "Algérie, 1954–1982, forces sociales et blocs au pouvoir." *Les Temps modernes* 432/433 (July–August).

Naudy, M. 1993. *Un crime d'État, l'affaire Mecili*. Paris: Albin Michel.

Paillat, C. 1972. *La Liquidation*. Paris: Laffont.

Perville, G. 1984. *Les Étudiants algériens de l'Université française*. Paris: CNRS.

————. 1991. *De l'Empire français à la décolonisation*. Paris: Hachette.

Raffinot, M., and P. Jacquemot. 1977. *Le Capitalisme d'État algérien*. Paris: Maspero.

Rafot, M. 1982. "Un développement à marche forcée." *Le Monde diplomatique* (November).

Redjala, R. 1988. *L'Opposition en Algérie depuis 1962*. Paris: L'Harmattan.

Rioux, J. P., ed. 1990. *La Guerre d'Algérie et les Français*. Paris: Fayard.

Roux, M. 1991. *Les Harkis, les oubliés de l'histoire*. Paris: La Découverte.

Saadi, N. 1982. "Syndicat et relations du travail dans les entreprises socialistes en Algérie." In *Annuaire de l'Afrique du Nord*.

Sanson, H. 1983. *La Laïcité islamique en Algérie*. Paris: CRESM/CNRS.

Sigaud, D. 1991. *La Fracture algérienne*. Paris: Calmann-Lévy.

Sirinelli. "Les intellectuels français dans la bataille." In *France en Guerre d'Algérie*, edited by L. Gervereau, J. P Roux, and B. Stora.

Stora, B. 1985. *Dictionnaire biographique de militants nationalistes algériens*. Paris: L'Harmattan.

————. 1991a. *Histoire de l'Algérie coloniale, 1830–1954*. Repères. Paris: La Découverte.

————. 1991b. *La Gangrène et l'oubli*. Paris: La Découverte.

————. 1992. *Aide-mémoire de l'immigration algérienne, 1922–1962*. Paris: L'Harmattan.

————. 1992. *Ils venaient d'Algérie. L'immigration algérienne en France*. Paris: Fayard.

Taleb-Ibrahimi, A. 1973. *De la décolonisation à la révolution naturelle*. Algiers: NPDC.

Teguia, M.1982. *L'Algérie en guerre*. Algiers: OUP.

Teillac, J. 1965. *Autogestion en Algérie*. Paris: Peyronnet.

Thiery, S. P. 1982. *La Crise du système productif algérien*. Grenoble: IREP.

Touati, H. 1982. "La rue, le prolétaire et l'atelier en Algérie." In *Annuaire de l'Afrique du Nord*.

Vandevelde, H. 1980. *Femmes algériennes à travers la condition féminine dans le Constantinois depuis l'indépendance*. Algiers: OUP.

Vidal-Naquet, P. 1975. *La Torture dans la République*. Paris: La Découverte/Maspero.

Villers, G. de. 1987. *L'État démiurge. Le cas algérien*. Paris: L'Harmattan.

Weiss, F. 1970. *Doctrine et action syndicales en Algérie*. Paris: Éd. Cujas.

Winock, M. 1985. *La République se meurt, 1956–1958*. Paris: Gallimard.

Index

Abbas, Ferhat: appeal of Boumédienne's policy by, 260; death of, 262; departure of, 139; during World War II, 21; founding of newspaper by, 248; and the GPRA, 83, 122, 254; Jacques Soustelle's meeting with, 40; and the Jeune Algérien movement, 17; joining of Algerian nationalist camp by, 48; joining of FLN by, 251; and memory, 233; and negotiations with France, 79; as president of the assembly, 129; and "reformism," 174; replacement of, 84; resignation of, 133, 258; support of "Tlemcen group" by, 126; and the UDMA, 45, 249; and the Union Algérienne, 26; and the writing of history, 173
Abd-al-Kader, 4–5
Abdelkader, 238, 243–44
Abdessalam, Belaïd, 145, 183, 200, 210, 215, 265
Agrarian reform, 131, 133–35
Agrarian revolution, 125, 146, 156–57, 185, 259
Aït Ahmed, Hocine: arrest of, 258; banning of memory of, 190; boycott of 1995 elections by, 224; call for democracy of, 214; creation of the FFS by, 139; demonstration by supporters of, 264; exile of, 144; indictment of Ben Bella by, 133; and negotiations with SFIO, 47; and the November 1 insurrection, 36–37; refusal of dialogue by, 218; resignation of, 126; resistance

against Ben Bella of, 258; return of, 198, 203, 263
Al Qiyam, 172, 192
Algerianization, 131, 165, 169, 261
Algiers Charter, 138, 258
Algiers, battle of, 49–50
Algiers: bombing of air terminal at, 210, 265; riots of, 263
Alleg, Henri, 51, 88–90
Amirouche, 61, 75, 84, 191
Amis du Manifeste et de la Liberté, 21, 249
Ammar, Ali, 170, 196
Amnesia, 114–15, 193, 221, 233–34, 238, 241
Amnesty International, 214, 216, 229, 265
Amnesty, 112–14, 241, 249
Anglo-American landing, 20, 249
Anti-intellectualism, 206–7
Anti-Semitism, 10–11, 20, 246
Arab conquest, 2–3
Arab Maghreb Union, 263
Arab-Israeli War, 114, 160, 260
Arabization, 169–70, 238, 264
Armed Islamic Groups, 218, 220–22, 225, 267
Armée de Libération Nationale, 43, 54, 58, 102–3
Armée Nationale Populaire, 139, 144, 258
Army, Algerian: "cleansing" operations of, 228; and Boumédienne, 140, 143–45; role of, 118, 133, 221, 231
Assembly, Algerian, 25–26, 247

275